BLAIN VILLAGE
and the Fort Ancient Tradition in Ohio

CONTRIBUTORS

Dr. Olaf H. Prufer, Kent State University

Dr. Orrin C. Shane, III, Kent State University

Mr. C. Owen Lovejoy, Kent State University

Dr. Kingsbury G. Heiple, The Medical School of Case Western Reserve University

Dr. Paul W. Parmalee, Illinois State Museum

Mr. James L. Murphy, Case Western Reserve University

Dr. Walton C. Galinat, University of Massachusetts

Dr. Lawrence Kaplan, University of Massachusetts

BLAIN VILLAGE
and the Fort Ancient Tradition in Ohio

BY

Olaf H. Prufer and Orrin C. Shane, III
Kent State University

The Kent State University Press

Kent Studies in Anthropology and Archaeology, I

Olaf H. Prufer and Orrin C. Shane, III
General Editors

One of the most important problems of future Fort Ancient studies will be to provide as accurate a temporal framework as possible in order to ascertain the ceramic and other changes which took place over the approximately six hundred years of the existence of Fort Ancient. These changes need to be recorded in the several sub-areas so that minor environmental variations can be observed. There is a great need for a drastic revision of our thinking about Fort Ancient.

James B. Griffin (1967)

Contents

I

Introduction

Blain Village was excavated during the summer field seasons of 1966 and 1968 as part of a long-range project investigating the interrelationship between Woodland and Mississippian cultures in Ohio. This work was sponsored by grants GS–838 and GS–1700 from the National Science Foundation. The 1966 excavations were directed by Prufer, while those conducted in 1968 were under the leadership of Shane. As far as the present report is concerned, we have each analyzed the results of our respective field seasons. The final conclusions have been arrived at jointly.

The field crews consisted of students from Case Institute of Technology, Oberlin College, and Kent State University. To all crew members we wish to express our gratitude and appreciation for their efforts to make the two seasons an outstanding success.

On a professional level we are beholden to Dr. James B. Griffin, of the University of Michigan, for his continuing interest in our labors, and for his advice pertaining to the Fort Ancient problem. Our gratitude is also due to the Radiocarbon Laboratories of the University of Michigan and Ohio Wesleyan University for dating the Blain C–14 samples.

On a local level we wish to thank Mr. Clarence Blain, of Chillicothe, Ohio, for granting us permission to excavate on his land; Mr. Alva McGraw, of Chillicothe, for his help in maintaining local relations and for sharing with us his very substantial knowledge of the archaeology and ecology of Ross County, Ohio; Mr. Kenneth Goodman of AVC Inc., Columbus, Ohio, for generously supplying us with

1

the prototype of his Archaeometer; and Mr. Robert Harness, of Chillicothe, for spending many an hour on the site with his bulldozer, stripping the overburden of the Blain Mound.

Finally, we wish to extend our gratitude to our many good friends in Ross County, who over the years have always made us feel welcome in the area, and who have supplied us with valuable data on the distribution of archaeological sites and finds in the Scioto Valley.

Olaf H. Prufer
Orrin C. Shane

Kent, Ohio
April 30, 1969

II

The Site

Blain Village is located on the west bank of the Scioto River, approximately two miles southeast of Chillicothe, near Renick Junction, in Scioto Township, Ross County, Ohio. Range and Section cannot be given, because, being part of the old Virginia Military District, the area in question has not been so subdivided. The map coordinates are 39° 18′ 49″ North latitude, and 82° 56′ 16″ West longitude. The site is situated on the Clarence Blain Farm within the confines of the 600 foot contour line which also constitutes the southeastern boundary of the ancient settlement. The highest point of the site is at 605 feet. Based on surface indications, the village appears to have covered an area of about eight acres. As far as local topographic context is concerned, Blain Village is located within a roughly rectangular area, oriented northwest-southeast, and approximately two–by–four miles in extent. It is bounded on three sides by the Scioto River and the Paint Creek, whose confluence forms the southernmost corner of this stretch of land. Access to the rectangle is from the west–northwest corner which is presently occupied by the town of Chillicothe. At this time, the nearest point on the Scioto is at a distance of about 2,500 feet northeast of the site; the nearest point on the Paint Creek lies approximately 3,000 feet to the southwest. These measurements may not be of great significance, because the contemporary configuration of the Scioto–Paint Creek confluence is, as will be shown below, of recent vintage. Still, it seems clear that even in prehistoric times the site was sandwiched between the two streams. The elevation of both rivers in this area is, on the average at, or just below, the 590 foot contour line.

Presently the site is traversed at its northern boundary by (old) Routes 35/50. To the South it barely missed being disturbed by the Baltimore & Ohio Railroad track. The modern highway follows the course of an earlier historic road, known as the Richmondale Pike, which was already in existence when Squier and Davis (1848) surveyed the area. In all probability this road goes back to contact times, and may even have been an Indian trail. The site of the earliest historic settlement in the area, Station Prairie, is situated just northeast of Blain Village, and appears to relate to the position of the Richmondale Pike. The significance of this historic settlement, recently located beyond a doubt by Mr. Alva McGraw of Chillicothe, will be discussed below. At this time it should merely be noted that near the northern boundary of Blain Village there are traces of an early historic structure which may have been related to Station Prairie (Plate I). The area here is strewn with historic materials such as pottery, nails, etc., and, most importantly, it was here that the owner of the land, Mr. Clarence Blain, found the brass barrel of a pistol which should date from the second half of the eighteenth century. The evidence for this assignation rests upon a datable stamp on the barrel. The stamp also identifies the weapon as being of English manufacture.

During both seasons, excavation procedures were the same. Following a brief survey of the site in the spring of 1966, the summer of that year was devoted to the excavation of the mound and selected areas of the village. In the ccurse of 1967 it became apparent that the locality was threatened with imminent destruction by a major realignment of the local highway system (Eastern Avenue). For this reason, and because the field operations of the previous year had by no means solved all the problems of the site, it was decided to devote a second season to Blain Village. Thus, after some additional testing in the spring, the summer of 1968 saw another major excavation campaign at the locality.

The field strategy in the village area involved the layout of seven excavation units (I-VII) at various points of the site (Figure 1). The choice of unit location was determined on the basis of surface evidence

Plate I.   Aerial view north of Scioto Valley near Blain Village

The following labels appear on the photograph: Chillicothe, McGraw, Station Prairie, Blain, Scioto, Highbanks Earthworks

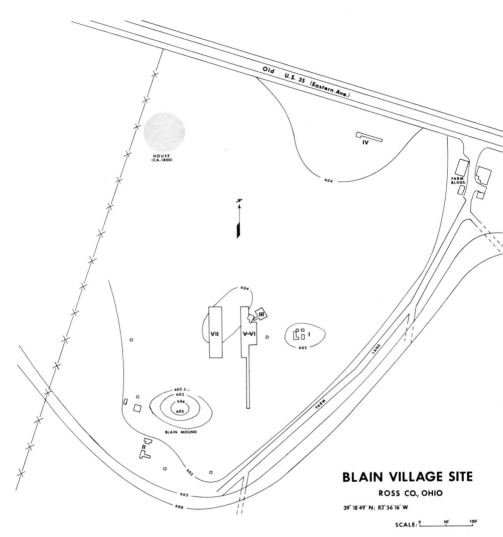

BLAIN VILLAGE SITE

ROSS CO., OHIO

39° 18′ 49″ N; 82° 56′ 16″ W

SCALE: 0   50′   100′

Figure 1.   Plan of Blain Village.

and in 1968 with the help of the Goodman Archaeometer. This instrument is an earth-resistivity measuring device developed by Mr. Kenneth Goodman of AVC Inc. in Columbus, Ohio. It utilizes five conducting probes placed in a line at intervals of four feet. Current flow through the soil between the probes completes a circuit, and earth resistance can be determined in the usual fashion ($I = E/R$). Anomalies in the soil such as refuse pits, hearths, soil formations, etc., appear as anomalies in earth resistivity (Goodman and Shane, n.d.). The results of this survey were excellent. Eight of the refuse pits found in Unit–V were detected prior to excavation by the Archaeometer. Furthermore, the 1966 excavations in this area also appeared as resistivity anomalies. For these features, detection was one hundred percent accurate. Shallow midden areas, discovered during excavation, did not appear as anomalies during the survey.

The excavation units were staked out in five–foot squares. Vertical control was maintained by means of four–inch arbitrary levels. Wherever it was indicated, the content of features was flotated to insure maximum recovery of organic remains.

In addition to the seven units, a number of isolated squares were excavated in various sections of the site. This was done on the basis of surface indications. In this manner, an extensive area of the locality was sampled. In order to determine the nature of the presumed plaza (Feature 45), a long trench was dug from Unit–V toward the mound.

During the 1968 season, mechanical equipment was used in certain areas of the village site in order to strip off the extremely compacted overburden of the plowzone. Due to the spring flood of that year and the following extremely hot and dry weather, the top soil, even though plowed, had acquired a near cement–like consistency which made it almost impossible to remove this overburden by manual excavation. The procedures used to excavate the mound are described in Chapter 12.

III

Environmental Setting

This chapter deals with three topics pertaining to the environmental setting of Blain Village: the evidence for flooding, the vegetation in the general area under investigation, and the faunal resources in aboriginal times.

Although the site is located on somewhat higher ground than the lowest bottom lands, it is nonetheless subject to periodic flooding. This has demonstrably altered the land surface in recent times, and presumably in the prehistoric past as well. Within recent memory, at least three major floods have scoured portions, if not all, of the site. The most dramatic flood in the entire Ohio Valley which occurred in 1913, literally ripped away or, depending on local conditions, added to the low–lying areas of the Scioto Valley. Undoubtedly the Blain Site was affected by this major disaster, although our information, based upon hearsay, does not reveal the exact nature of the damage. The much less extensive floods of 1959 and 1968 demonstrably affected the site. As far as the earlier of these inundations is concerned, Prufer saw evidence of its ravages in 1966. Even at that late date, there still were traces of shallow channels, cutting into the southern edge of the locality, right up to the area of the mound. These channels were strewn with plow–damaged, recently deposited, freshwater gastropods. The channel cutting was so extensive that Mr. Clarence Blain was obliged to fill in the damaged gullies, in order to prevent further erosion. The effects of the 1968 spring flood were observed by Shane, who saw the area submerged, and who was thus in a position to determine the extent of the destruction since the 1966 excavations. He found that the flood waters differentially altered the surface of the site, cutting away in some areas, and adding to the land in others.

The effect of flooding has also been noted in connection with the immediately adjacent McGraw Site (Prufer, 1965). In a general sense, our information, obtained in the course of extensive archaeological fieldwork in the lower Scioto Valley, indicates that the river and its tributaries are active indeed. Local informants repeatedly pointed out the results of flooding on low-lying archaeological sites. After such inundations some buried sites may suddenly be exposed, others, long-known for their productivity, disappear under alluvial deposits, while others again, are actually washed away. Our own observations have confirmed these accounts. Thus, in the summer of 1966 Prufer surveyed in the Scioto bottom lands, approximately five miles downstream from Blain Village, an area he had previously examined in 1963. The sites, which at that time had been entirely exposed, were now covered with a 2-3 inch deposit of alluvial mud. Similarly, the edge of the Morrison Village locality, excavated by Prufer in 1965 (Prufer and Andors, 1967), proved to have been substantially scoured by the spring flood of 1968. Finally, there is evidence, at least for the recent past, that the river is shifting its bed. At the Salt Creek confluence, the most recent floods have substantially cut into the right bank of the Scioto River, while at the same time adding several acres of land to the left bank. Aerial photographs indicate that in the vicinity of the Blain Site, the confluence of the Paint Creek and the position of the adjacent (upstream) Scioto meanders have, in the past, repeatedly shifted. There are clear indications of ancient meanders. It is not possible to determine when these shifts took place. Comparison between the modern topographic sheet (Chillicothe East Quadrangle, 1963) of this area and an early map by Squier and Davis (1848: Plate II) shows clearly that even in the last one hundred and twenty years the streams have shifted their position to a considerable extent.

All of these data on fluvial activity do, of course, pertain only to the historic period which demonstrably witnessed many modifications of the landscape that may have severely affected the behavior of the river and its tributaries. In order to determine the prehistoric position of the Blain Site in relation to the Scioto River and Paint Creek, it is necessary to determine to what extent river activity in prehistoric times differed from the modern situation.

One observation which can be verified empirically is that flooding could not have been as serious in the past as it has been since the colonization of the area, simply because, if it had been, many of the still existing localities on low ground undoubtedly would have been destroyed. This, however, is patently not the case. Thus, the present extensive damage done to such archaeological localities must be largely of recent vintage. From this we conclude that destructive river activity must have increased in recent decades, not only quantitatively, but also in severity. Apparently this can be correlated with deforestation after 1840. According to Diller and Lannan (1944:87), the forest cover of Ohio was reduced from 70 percent in 1840 to 14 percent in 1900. Since that time the decrease has been minimal, although the trend has not been reversed except locally. In this connection a pertinent observation has been made by Sears:

> Forest removal has decreased the absorptive capacity of the soil and increased the evaporative power of the atmosphere, making rainfall less efficient and more destructive. Also, the system of sectional highways has imposed a new, powerful and wholly artificial pattern of drainage over the entire State . . . Floods appear to be more frequent and are certainly more destructive than before. For example the thirty–eight foot flood stage at Marietta averaged once in 7 years from 1810 to 1898 . . . From 1898 to 1927 it appeared on the average of once in 1.8 years. (1942:229).

Thus, the correlation between flooding and deforestation is quite apparent. Furthermore, data computed from Cross (1946) indicate that flooding near Chillicothe has remained quite constant in severity since 1920, apparently as a function of the arrested deforestation. We conclude from these data that the recent regimen of the river is of historic origin, and cannot readily be used for interpreting the prehistoric situation.

The prehistoric behavior of the river can only be inferred. As a general statement we would venture the guess that flooding was very much less severe, simply because much of the crucial land in the upper Scioto drainage basin was probably under heavy forest cover. We doubt whether at the time of the Blain occupation such formative agricultural settlements as existed in the upstream areas could have sufficiently affected the forest stand to cause major fluctuations in the presumably moderate flooding pattern of the southern drainage area.

Still, there is internal evidence for some flooding and other fluvial activity in the vicinity of Blain Village. The most direct data derive from the excavations. Although it is clear that much of the original land surface of the settlement has been damaged by recent agricultural activity and flooding, there are some indications that flood deposition took place in prehistoric times as well. It should be noted that the presumed houses, Features 5 and 6, were found to contain substantial charred logs, interpreted as remnants of structural members. These logs or collapsed posts were lying on what must have been the original floor level of the houses. They could not possibly have survived if they had remained exposed for any length of time. Yet they did survive and, moreover, they were covered by a sufficiently thick soil deposit, relatively sterile in cultural content, to have escaped destruction by modern plowing. Demonstrably, most other features of the site were ripped into by farm machinery. From this we conclude that localized areas of the site, presumably in line with minor topographic elevation differentials, were buried under alluvium shortly after they had been abandoned by the Blain people. As noted earlier, such highly localized deposition and erosion can still be observed today.

Evidence pertaining to prehistoric shifts of the Paint Creek is more direct. It derives from careful study of aerial photographs. They indicate that in the past, but apparently not recently, a meander of the Paint passed within a few hundred feet south of the site. Although we cannot prove that this was the position of the stream when Blain Village was occupied, we suggest it as a clear possibility, because it would directly relate the village to the river system on which the inhabitants so heavily relied in their economic activities.

As far as the vegetational picture is concerned, the location of the Blain Site is of considerable interest. This situation cannot be discussed without some reference to the general setting of the Scioto Valley in the vicinity of Chillicothe. The town is located at the narrow gap where the Scioto River enters the dissected and hilly Appalachian uplands of southern Ohio. The boundary between the glaciated plateau to the north and the hills to the south is quite abrupt. As soon as the river enters the Appalachian highlands, it forms a broad, well-defined, very fertile valley, flanked by densely forested hills which rise to elevations of 1,100 feet and above.

This general area was marked, at contact time, by three forest zones which have been reconstructed from the study of some of the original timber stands and from the records of early pioneers (Chapman, 1944). The northern section, stretching from the area of Chillicothe into the glaciated plateau and till plains of central and east-central Ohio, were covered by Oak–Hickory stands with prairie openings. Blain Village was located at the extreme southern boundary of this forest zone. There is historic evidence that the extensive rectangular area, outlined by the Scioto–Paint Creek confluence, was a typical prairie opening of this zone. It was here, less than 2,000 feet north of the Blain Site (and immediately adjacent to the McGraw Site) that Nathaniel Massie, in April 1796, established the first settlement of Chillicothe, known as Station Prairie. As the name indicates, the land at that time was open. It was immediately brought under cultivation by Massie's settlers, who, that very year, turned three hundred acres into cornfields, presumably encompassing the Blain locality or parts of it. It is of interest to note that the land proved extremely fertile. John McDonald, one of Massie's companions, noted that "That season was attended by great prosperity to the settlers. Although they suffered, at one time, greatly for the want of some of the necessaries of life, yet in this they were soon relieved by the luxuriant crops of their plantations." (cited in Massie, 1896:62).

Immediately south of the Blain locality, i.e. south of the Scioto–Paint Creek confluence and in the hills east of the river, the forest cover consisted of a narrow band of Beech–Maple stand, forming a transition between the northern Oak–Hickory zone and the characteristic mixed Oak–Hickory–Chestnut forests of the hilly, unglaciated tracts of southern Ohio. This type of forest had its northern boundary a few miles south of Blain Village.

This is as far as the evidence goes. We can conclude from the data that in aboriginal times Blain Village was located at the boundary of two major physiographic areas, and three forest types. The evidence further indicates that the confluence of the two streams may have been open prairie which did not require major clearance for purposes of agriculture.

On the assumption that climatic conditions have not substantially changed since the occupation of the site, the following contemporary data are taken to be reasonably valid for early Fort Ancient times as well. In the Chillicothe area the mean maximum temperature in July is 88° F; mean minimum temperature in January is 26° F. The mean annual temperature amounts to 54.5° F. As far as frost is concerned, the mean date for the final spring frost is April 25 and for the first fall frost, October 15. Thus, on the average, Ross County has 173 frost-free days. Annual precipitation in Chillicothe averages 39.3 inches. Most of this falls between March and August. There is no definite dry season (Pierce, 1959).

As far as faunal conditions in the area are concerned, contemporary data are only of limited validity, because of the substantial changes in the environment and animal population which have taken place since contact times. On the other hand, the abundant faunal remains, discussed in detail in Chapter 13, permit a very precise reconstruction of the faunal resources available and utilized by the Blain people. It is clear that all aspects of the environment were exploited. As far as published information goes, no Fort Ancient site on record has shown evidence of such a wide range of faunal use as Blain. Since this matter will be discussed extensively later in this volume, suffice it here to indicate very briefly the range and diversity of the fauna represented in the assemblage:

Fishes	12 species
Amphibians	3 species
Reptiles	9 species
Birds	16 species
Mammals	26 species
Pelecypods	26 species
	92 species

Excluded from this list are twenty-nine species of gastropods which are obviously incidental to the occupation. On the other hand, their presence at the site should not be ignored, because they were part of the total environment. This list can also be viewed in terms of habitat types; the following specific habitat zones could be associated with the Blain fauna:

> Aquatic–Riverine
> Riverine–Edge
> Grassland–Prairie
> Deciduous Forest Edge
> Mature Deciduous Forest
> Second Growth Deciduous Forest
> (Migratory)
> (Domestic)

All in all, the evidence indicates that Blain Village was located in a highly favorable and diversified environment. Thus, it is not surprising that the immediate vicinity of the site is virtually dotted with other prehistoric settlements. Over the past six years, we have located, and in part excavated, more than a dozen previously unknown sites within the rectangle delineated by the Scioto River and Paint Creek. In addition, there are numerous other localities in this limited area (see for instance Squier and Davis, 1848). Ranging beyond this territory into the Scioto and Paint Creek valleys, prehistoric sites are literally legion (Prufer, 1967b). In fact, it can fairly be said that Blain Village is located in the very center of that classic prehistoric area which saw the climactic developments of the Adena, Hopewell, and Fort Ancient cultures.

IV

Features

The excavations revealed a total of forty-seven features. Some of these were part of the major excavation Units I–VII, others were isolated features encountered either on the basis of surface evidence or during test excavations in widely separated areas of the site. We would judge that the vast unexcavated areas of the village conceal a multitude of additional features, probably similar in distribution density to those encountered in the regular excavation units. The only area to be excluded from this estimate is the ground surrounding the mound (Feature 44) which, upon extensive testing, proved to be largely sterile below the plowzone. We believe that the startling negative evidence in the vicinity of the mound can be interpreted as a feature in its own right—a formal plaza in the classic Mississippian sense.

Before discussing some of the more significant features in detail, a brief feature classification is in order. The following list identifies the nature of all features encountered during the excavations:

1.	Cylindrical refuse pits	14
2.	Bell-shaped refuse pits	7
3.	Shallow, basin–shaped refuse pits	3
4.	Irregular refuse pits	2
5.	Special purpose pits	1
6.	Unexcavated or partially excavated pits	2
7.	Shallow midden deposits	9
8.	Isolated charred logs (posts?)	3
9.	Postmold patterns, presumed houses	3
10.	Hearths	1
11.	Burial mounds	1
12.	Plazas	1
		47

In order to keep this report within reasonable limits, we have decided to discuss in detail only those features which, on the face of the evidence, appear to have been of archaeological importance. However, in the following paragraphs a general description is given for all feature categories.

Cylindrical Refuse Pits (Features 2, 3, 8, 9, 10, 11, 14, 16, 17, 21, 29, 33, 34, 36). These features, with the exception of two elliptical pits, were circular in plan and straight–walled in shape. The circular pits range in diameter from 30 to 65 inches, and in depth from 26 to 49 inches as measured from the base of the plowzone. The elliptical pits have major radii ranging from 38 to 50 inches; both proved to be 48 inches in depth below the plowzone. In the total series six pits were stratified. The nature of stratification varied from single primary deposits covered by fill to pits containing up to five individual loads of refuse, each separated from the succeeding load by fill. The unstratified pits were filled with refuse to the truncated top. There are some indications that at least some of the pits were filled in a very short period of time. The evidence for this derives from the curious distribution of scavenging terrestrial gastropods which, when encountered in quantity, invariably occur in thick clusters near the top of the features. This implies that the pits were filled rapidly, thus not permitting the accumulation of scavengers until the pits were loaded to capacity. At this time, apparently, they were left open for a sufficiently long period of time for snails to crawl onto the exposed refuse in fairly large numbers. In the light of the fact that all pits were truncated by recent plowing, this further implies that they must ultimately have been filled with a deposit of "clean" fill. Had this not been the case, the gastropod cappings would have been destroyed by recent disturbances.

The artifact distribution in these pits is uneven. The refuse layers themselves are characterized by black greasy soil which contained whatever artifacts and other refuse material was present. It was noted that most pits contained very considerable quantities of archaeological remains. However, a series of adjacent pits in Unit II (Features 8, 9, 10, 11) proved to be almost sterile, although the soil content was highly organic. Evidently these features were fille exclusively with completely perishable remains. Inasmuch as such faunal and mollusc remains as were found were in excellent condition, it follows that the overall scarcity of recoverable material cannot be attributed to destructive chemical agents in the soil. Finally, it should here be noted that Feature 17 yielded the partial remains of a human infant (see page 37).

Bell-shaped Refuse Pits (Features 4a, 15, 18, 19a, 23, 27, 37). In all respects other than those discussed below, these features are similar to the cylindrical pits. As the designation implies, bell-shaped pits are relatively narrow at the top. For some distance down they are cylindrical, and they markedly flare in the basal section. Such pits are typical of Fort Ancient. Diameters at the truncated top range from 26 to 51 inches, and at the base from 40 to 60 inches. In depth they range from 36 to 59 inches. All but two pits proved to be stratified, and all were rich in cultural remains.

Shallow Basin-shaped Pits (Features 13, 19b, 31). These features are almost casual in construction. They are basin-shaped, with sloping sides, and shallow relative to the top diameter. All are circular in plan. Top diameters range from 30 to 58 inches, and depth from 16 to 36 inches. None were stratified, and none proved rich in cultural remains. However, the black soil content indicates heavy organic refuse.

Irregular Refuse Pits (Features 1, 35). Two features fall within this category. One of these (Feature 1) will be discussed below. These pits are characterized by their amorphous shape. They do not exceed 120 inches in diameter, and 40 inches in depth. Both were stratified and rich in cultural refuse.

Special Purpose Pits (Feature 4b). The only feature in this category will be discussed below.

Unexcavated or Partially Excavated Pits (Features 38, 39). Because of time limitations these two circular pits could only be cursorily examined. Both proved to have top diameters of 36 inches.

Shallow Midden Deposits (Features 7, 12, 20, 24, 25, 26, 28, 32, 43).
All of these features were truncated by recent disturbances. We sus-
pect that all are remnants of larger midden deposits. Presumably the
preserved remains were located in shallow depressions and thus escaped destruction. These features consist of sheet deposits of culturally rather unproductive midden. They all rest on sterile alluvium.
None proved to be stratified. All occur in the vicinity of house structures or pit clusters. The largest lateral dimension does not exceed
120 inches, and the greatest extant thickness is 8 inches. Most of the
middens are considerably smaller than this.

Isolated Charred Logs (Posts?) (Features 22, 40, 41). These features
appear to be remnants of collapsed and burnt structures. They are
located in the vicinity of what we interpret as houses, but sufficiently
removed from the latter to warrant their classification as independent
features. None can definitely be associated with a house pattern.
The charred logs are horizontally distributed; there is no evidence of
postmolds in their immediate vicinity. They are 2—4 inches in diameter, and the largest section is 48 inches in length. They rest on
sterile alluvium. Just as in the case of the charred house remains to
be discussed below, the fact that these burnt logs remained intact beneath the plowzone suggests that after their deposition they were
covered by soil possibly laid down by flooding.

Postmold Patterns, Presumably Houses (Features 5, 6, 42). There is
some evidence for three independent structures at Blain. Two of
these are inferred from overlapping postmold patterns in Units III
and V. A third such structure was identified from an isolated set of
postmolds with associated burnt logs; the ends of some of these
posts terminated at the postmolds (Feature 6). These structures will
be discussed below.

Hearths (Feature 30). A single hearth was found in Unit VII. It was in
the vicinity of a number of refuse pits. The feature consisted of a
roughly circular array of river cobbles, 45 inches in diameter, con-

taining quantities of charred wood, some artifacts (none burnt!) and charred box turtle bones representing at least three individuals. The top of the hearth was disturbed by plowing.

Burial Mounds (Feature 44). The Blain Mound will be discussed in a separate section of this study. At this time, suffice it to say that the mound is obviously an integral part of the *Baum Phase* occupation of the site. The content of the burials, the materials found at the base of the mound, and the scattered remains from the mound fill leave no room for other conclusions.

Plazas (Feature 45). This feature is the open space surrounding the mound. Its outer limits are determined by the dense cultural refuse of the actual settlement. On the basis of test trenching, this plaza is estimated to have been roughly three hundred feet in maximum extent. Its shape could not be determined.

Before embarking upon a detailed description of the more noteworthy features, a few general observations are in order. First it should be noted that in contrast to the pits from such sites as Baum and Gartner, lined storage pits containing massive deposits of vegetable remains were not encountered at Blain. The only possible exception, Feature 4b, would appear to have been in a different category; its peculiar content suggests a ceremonial function. Similarly, no refuse pits such as those at Baum (Mills, 1906:62), which contained basal deposits of bone refuse, were found at Blain. In this respect the Blain pits are very similar to those reported from Graham Village (McKenzie, 1967:67).

Second, there is some evidence for time depth, no matter how great, in the nature of some of the features. Features 4a and 4b, and Features 19a and 19b constitute clusters of two intersecting pits, i.e. one pit in each group must of needs post-date the other. Inasmuch as the cultural remains from these interlocking pits proved to be indistinguishable from each other, the time depth involved cannot have been of any great magnitude.

Finally, there is clear–cut evidence for the actual complete contemporaneity of certain pits. Two groups of such features, one consisting of two, the other of three pits (Features 29, 34, and Features
21, 27, 30) yielded bone elements of the same individual animals
whose remains were disposed of in different features. The bones involved consist of two matching mandibular fragments of bear from
Features 29 and 34, and matching skull elements of the same grey fox
from Features 21, 27, and 30. This evidence conclusively proves that
the pits in each group must have been in use at the same precise
period in time. The pits in question did not yield any matching artifacts.

The following features deserve more detailed treatment, because
of their unusual nature and content:

Feature 1 (Figure 2). This is an irregularly shaped, stratified pit in
Unit II. The top part was truncated by recent agricultural activity. Its
outline became clear directly beneath the plowzone. The maximum
dimensions were 10-by-8 feet. Maximum depth was 36 inches. The
walls of the pit sloped irregularly toward the center. The stratigraphic
records indicate that the top level, to a depth of 10 inches below
plowzone, consisted of ashy deposits intermingled with what appear to
have been individual loads of refuse. A small and shallow irregular
pit, culturally contemporary with the remainder of the feature, in-
trudes into this deposit. Being "minimal" in size and content this intrusive depression was not given a separate feature number. Beneath
the top level was a well–defined deposit of densely packed mollusc
shells, on the average four inches in thickness. On one side of the
pit this layer slopes upward and appears to have reached the surface. Beneath the shell deposit, to a depth of 36 inches from the surface, there was a rich refuse layer characterized by black greasy soil
interspersed with sandy brown lenses which apparently were individual loads of relatively sterile soil. At the very base, further
small deposits of mollusc shells, ashes, and midden were encountered.

The content of Feature 1 proved to be of more than passing interest. Clearly, of all features, this pit produced the largest amount

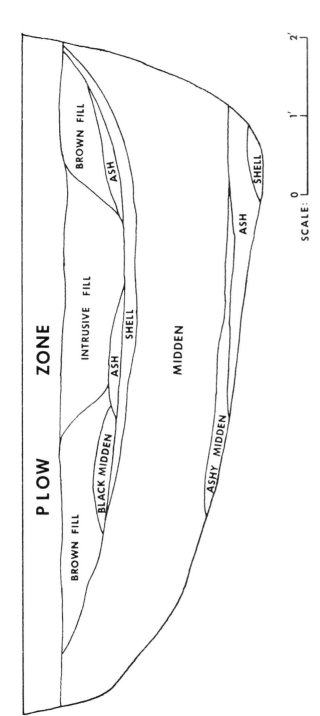

Figure 2. Profile of Feature 1.

of cultural material in all of the major classes of artifacts. These archaeological materials were found throughout all layers of the pit. Since they were homogeneously consistent with the typical *Baum Phase* assemblage, there is no need to enumerate them in detail. However, one artifact deserves special consideration, because it provides a very significant link with the Blain Mound. This object is a medium–sized, circular shell gorget made on a pelecypod. It has a large central hole, and two small perforations near the margin. A similar, although much larger gorget made on a marine shell was found with Mound Burial 5. The occurrence of two such specimens, one in the mound, the other in the village refuse, provides clear evidence for the contemporaneity of the entire site complex. Finally, the mollusc shells from Feature 1 and Feature 15 are of special interest, because they afford an insight into the food gathering habits of the Blain people. It was noted that, in addition to adult bivalves, there were large numbers of immature specimens. Significantly, the mature shells are represented primarily by disjointed valves. On the other hand, the immature specimens are overwhelmingly represented by intact bivalves, most of which do not appear to have been opened. This implies that the immature specimens were never used; they appear to have been discarded intact. The best explanation for this situation would seem to be that the Blain people harvested molluscs by some technique that did not discriminate between mature and immature shells. After harvesting, the catch was sorted selectively in favor of adult shells; the immature individuals were thrown away. This would imply that these molluscs were not individually gathered from their beds, but that they were collected *en masse*. Such a technique of collection must have involved a seine or rake, and may well have involved collective efforts.

Feature 2. This is an unstratified, cylindrical pit, 37 inches in diameter and 39 inches in depth below the plowzone. Structurally it does not differ from other cylindrical pits at the site; its significance is a function of the unusual content. At the outset, let it be stated that there can be no question that Feature 2 was an integral part of the site. The majority of the artifacts recovered is clearly attributable to the *Baum*

Phase. In addition, however, there are certain elements which are clearly Woodland in character. Before discussing their significance, the following list briefly presents the artifactual inventory recovered:

1.	Sherds of *Baum Cordmarked Incised, Var. Blain*	76
2.	Sherds of *Baum Shell–tempered, Var. Blain*	1
3.	Limestone–tempered sherds	1
4.	Sherds of *Peters Cordmarked*	1
5.	Sherds of *Peters Plain*	1
6.	Partial vessel of *McGraw Cordmarked* (14 sherds)	1
7.	Flint drills	1
8.	Retouched flakes	1
9.	Flint debitage	164
10.	Celts	1
11.	Slate gorgets	1
12.	Bone and antler tools (including one beamer)	5
13.	Lumps of yellow and red ochre	3
		257

The feature also yielded some charred vegetable remains, including kernels of corn, and quantities of bone refuse and mollusc shells.

The aberrant material here is represented primarily by the fragmentary *McGraw Cordmarked* vessel which has specific parallels at the late Hopewellian Ginther Mound in Ross County, Ohio, and at the Rutherford Mound in Illinois (for details see page 72). The fourteen sherds of this vessel were found at various depths. Their condition makes it abundantly clear that the vessel was broken before it became deposited in the feature. In the absence of any other Middle Woodland ceramics (let alone features) at the site, it would be difficult to argue that these sherds were accidentally introduced into the feature. We are thus convinced that the pot in question, regardless of typology, was part of the original assemblage disposed of in Feature 2. Furthermore, the presence of two indisputable Late Woodland sherds representing two distinct pottery types in this same feature, adds to its unusual nature. Although *Peters Cordmarked* sherds occasionally occurred in other parts of the site as well, nowhere has the presence of three extraneous ceramic types been noted elsewhere in a single feature. Finally, it should be noted that Feature 2 yielded the earliest date from the site: A.D. 915, normalized to A.D. 970. All things considered, we believe that the clustering of all these elements is significant, and may be indicative of the earliest occupation of Blain Village.

Features 4a and 4b (Figure 3,a). These are two interlocking pits in the vicinity of Unit III. Clearly, Feature 4a predates 4b, although this piece of internal chronological evidence is of no great significance. Typologically the content of the two pits is indistinguishable and, therefore, presumably on the same general time horizon. Before embarking upon a detailed discussion of the two features, a comment on their identification as two separate entities is in order. They did not appear as two distinct pits immediately beneath the plowzone. The first eight inches below the plowzone revealed a horizontal plan of irregular shape, suggesting an irregular refuse pit. Only beneath that level did it become apparent that two circular, interlocking pits were present. We assume that the aboriginal disturbance of the earlier feature (4a) by the later one (4b) caused a generally disturbed, diffused soil horizon which did not permit segregation of the two features in the top levels. Inasmuch as the double nature of these features was not recognizable until the two pits became distinct in outline, the content of the upper levels was lumped into single level bags during the field operations. They are thus included in Feature 4a. (Originally, when it was thought that only one feature was present, the designation was Feature 4, which is the designation that appears on the relevant level bags). Since nothing of great significance was found in the top levels, the matter is actually of no significance. The mixed assemblage involves 96 sherds of *Baum Cordmarked Incised*, *Var. Blain*, 2 sherds of *Baum Shell–tempered*, *Var. Blain*, 1 limestone-tempered sherd, and 76 chips.

As has been indicated, Feature 4a predates Feature 4b. Originally it was a bell–shaped pit, 48 inches in top diameter, 60 inches in basal diameter, and forty-nine inches in depth below the plowzone. No stratification was noted. As usual in refuse pits, the soil content proved to be black, interspersed with charcoal and cultural refuse. Faunal remains and mollusc shells occurred in abundance. In addition, there were some charred vegetable remains, including corn. The artifactual content of the pit (inclusive of the mixed top layers)

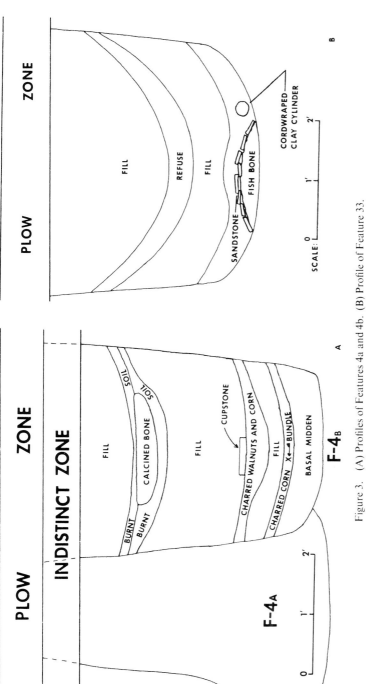

Figure 3. (A) Profiles of Features 4a and 4b. (B) Profile of Feature 33.

is typical of the site. It is listed here only because of the special nature of the intersecting pit, Feature 4b.

1.	Sherds of *Baum Cordmarked Incised, Var. Blain*	287
2.	Sherds of *Baum Shell-tempered, Var. Blain*	5
3.	Limestone–tempered sherds	3
4.	Sherds of a miniature vessel	1
5.	Projectile points, including 3 triangular specimens	4
6.	Flint drills	1
7.	Other flint tools	9
8.	Flint debitage	207
9.	Celts	1
10.	Ground sandstone palettes	1
11.	Abrading stones	1
12.	Bone and antler tools	1
13.	Lumps of yellow ochre	1
		522

There is nothing distinctive about this feature; in all respects it is characteristic of the majority of the Blain pits.

As noted, Feature 4b did not become recognizable as a distinct circular pit until the 8 inch level below the plowzone was reached. Upon excavation it turned out to be a cylindrical pit, 40 inches in diameter and 49 inches in depth below the plowzone. It was stratified.

Directly beneath the indistinct 8 inches, the soil consisted of a moderately black fill, 10 inches in thickness. Below this level there were two layers, altogether 7 inches in thickness, consisting of brick–red, deeply burnt clay, into which was embedded a dense mass of completely calcined, totally fragmented bones. Most of these appeared to be bird bones. This mass was roughly circular in outline, 24 inches in diameter, and 3 inches in thickness. Beneath this complex capping deposit, there was a moderately burnt soil fill, 15 inches in thickness. As far as cultural remains and general refuse are concerned, these layers, with the exception of the calcined bone deposit, were not particularly productive; artifacts of any kind were certainly uncommon. The boundary between the lowermost of these deposits and the next level was sharply defined. At this boundary, in the center of the pit, there was found, lying upside–down, a so–called cup stone. It rested upon a deep black deposit, 4 inches in thickness, primarily characterized by completely charred, unshelled black walnuts, interspersed with corn kernels and other vegetable remains. Bone and shell refuse, as well as all kinds of artifacts were found in abundance in this deposit which was separated from the next lower level by a sharply defined boundary. This earlier layer, 4 inches in thickness, consisted of a moderately burnt and not particularly productive soil horizon. Just as before, this level was sharply separated from the preceding one, which consisted of a 3 inch deposit of densely packed charred corn kernels and unshelled ears of corn, intermingled with faunal and cultural refuse. Roughly in the center of this mass of charred remains, there was a deposit of sherds and other artifacts. The latter are of special interest. They included a bi–pitted stone, a complex beamer worked secondarily into three tools, a small serrated slate pendant or gorget, two curious pear-shaped and fabric-impressed bituminous objects, three bone "tinklers" made on deer bone phalanges, and three box turtle carapace dishes or cups. Finally, the lowermost level of Feature 4b consisted of a moderately distinct and moderately productive soil deposit, 6 inches in thickness.

Before discussing the implications of this feature, it might be useful to present the following list of artifacts found in this pit:

1.	Sherds of *Baum Cordmarked Incised, Var. Blain*	497
2.	Sherds of *Baum Shell–tempered, Var. Blain*	2
3.	Sherds of *Peters Cordmarked*	1
4.	Plain grit–tempered sherds	13
5.	Sherds of an unbaked miniature vessel	11
6.	Projectile points including 9 triangular specimens	12
7.	Flint drills	3
8.	Other flint artifacts	13
9.	Flint debitage	664
10.	Bi–pitted stones	1
11.	Cup stones	2
12.	Mortars or metates	2
13.	Utilized pebbles	1
14.	Slate pendants or gorgets	1
15.	Bone tools incl. 1 specialized beamer, 2 beads, 3 tinklers	15
16.	Turtle shell dishes or cups	4
17.	Cut shell fragments	2
18.	Pear–shaped, fabric–impressed, bituminous objects	2
		1246

It is obvious on the evidence that Feature 4b was no ordinary pit. It certainly cannot be explained either as a refuse or storage pit. All indications point to the conclusion that it served very special functions.

Before proceding to an interpretation of this feature, two further points should be noted: (1) Among the vegetable remains, a few beans, pumpkin, pawpaw, and, most significantly, large quantities of sumac were recovered. (2) The pit was located in the general vicinity of the house structures designated Features 5 and 42; in other words the pit was not an isolated feature.

The stratification did not suggest casual disposal of refuse, nor is the evidence of the totally charred vegetable remains consonant with interpreting it as a storage pit. The deposits suggest deliberate and careful placement. The nature and significance of the calcined bone deposit embedded in layers of markedly burnt soil cannot be fathomed. Just as in the case of the charred vegetable remains, this deposit was probably burnt *in situ.*

As noted, the upper layer of charred organic matter consisted primarily of charred walnuts, overlain by a cup stone which had been placed upside–down on the vegetable remains. The important point about these walnuts is that they had been burnt intact, i.e. unshelled. Thus, in a conventional sense, this deposit cannot constitute food refuse. Kaplan (in this volume, page 231) suggests that these walnuts were used for fuel, since their flesh, being saturated with highly combustible oil, would have burnt with great intensity. The second organic layer consisted of charred corn kernels and unshelled ears of corn. Roughly in the center of this mass of material rested the cluster of artifacts, suggesting by composition and nature of disposition, that it might have been a bundle, conceivably a medicine bundle. Both charred organic layers contained large amounts of sumac.

Whatever the meaning of this complex may have been must, of course, remain a matter of speculation. However, it should be pointed out that sumac is ethnohistorically known to have been used by Woodland tribes for the preparation of a (mildly intoxicating) tea; among some Indians it served medicinal purposes (Yarnell, 1964:153). As far as the charred corn is concerned, it may be worth mentioning that in the past as well as today, certain tribes such as the Creek and Natchez burn ears of corn ceremonially as part of the Busk or Green Corn Festival (Howard, 1968). Although today this involves no more than the burning of a few ears, there is historic evidence, supplied by DuPratz, that the Natchez, in one phase of the lengthy Busk, burnt piles of corn, corn stalks, and weeds up to two feet in thickness (Howard, 1968:83–84). Furthermore, during the Busk ceremony various sacred paraphernalia play a considerable role.

Although it is obviously not possible to determine the significance of Feature 4b with any certainty, we believe that a tentative case could be made here to the effect that it affords prehistoric evidence for Green Corn ceremonialism. The "bundle" of artifacts, the charred unshelled corn, the charred sumac seeds which may be indicative of something akin to the "Black Drink", all permit this conclusion. Inasmuch as in late prehistoric and early historic times Green Corn Ceremonialism is well documented—cf. the engraved shells from Spiro suggesting the Busk—and since the societies involved were, at least in part, of Mississippian cultural affiliation, the interpretation here suggested is enticing. If it should prove acceptable, Feature 4b, with a date of A.D. 1040, would constitute a very early case of Green Corn Ceremonialism in the eastern United States.

Features 5 and 42 (Figure 4). These features are represented by postmold patterns of presumed house structures. They are located in Units III and V. This extensively excavated area proved to be rich in features, notably refuse pits, burnt logs, and obviously truncated middens. Also, Feature 4b, the putative ceremonial pit, is located in this area. Before discussing the two patterns, it should be noted that a sizeable cluster of pits—twelve in number—was discovered directly south of the presumed houses. To the North, East, and West, no pits were located. This may be of significance because at the Baum Site too, pits were found at one side of the "Tepee Site". On the opposite side Baum yielded a series of burials. Although at Blain no burials were found in the corresponding area, it is interesting to note that the plowed surface here produced scattered remains of human skeletons. Apparently burials did exist in this area, but they had been destroyed by the plow. Thus, the internal pattern of the site appears to have been very similar to that noted at Baum (Mills, 1906:56).

The postmold patterns gave evidence of two adjacent structures. Although neither of them is complete, both indicate oval outlines, approximately 23-by-18 feet in dimension. This is in general agree-

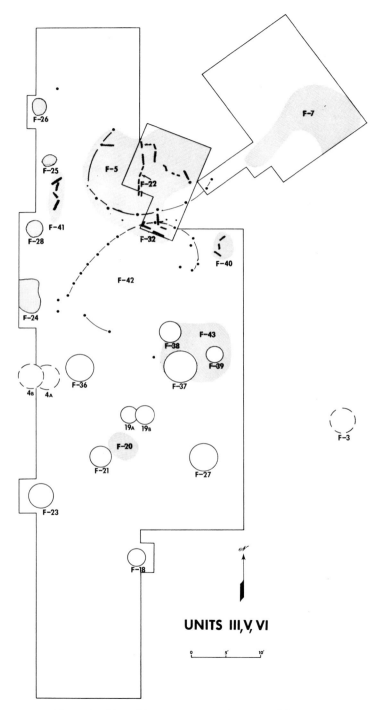

Figure 4. Plan of house patterns and associated features.

ment with the so–called "tepees" at the Baum Site. The spacing of
the postmolds ranges from 18 to 24 inches. In diameter the molds
vary from 4 to 7 inches, the mode being 5 inches. In depth they range
between 6 to 18 inches below the plowzone, the mode being 12 inches.
All posts had been set vertically into the ground; some were pointed
at the base. Apparently they had been shaped by firing, a trait also
noted at Baum (Mills, 1906:57). No center posts were found, although occasional, seemingly random, postmolds were found within
the structures.

Both patterns are especially interesting, because no apparent later
prehistoric disturbances impinged upon their outlines. The pits
alluded to earlier are also located outside of the confines of the postmolds. In the light of our contention that Blain Village was essentially
a single settlement of brief chronological duration, this observation
is obviously of some significance. The two structural patterns do not
intersect, but they are so close to each other as to be virtually
contiguous.

Thus far the discussion has dealt with the general nature of both
features. There are, however, significant differences. They are partly
factual, and partly inferential. Feature 42, the more southerly structure, shows no evidence of its ultimate fate. All that could be traced in
the soil were the postmolds. No sheet midden was associated with
these impressions, nor was there evidence of a distinct living floor.
Furthermore, no traces of charcoal or ashes were found within the
structure. Finally, in terms of relative stratigraphic position below
the plowzone, Feature 42 was massively disturbed by recent agricultural activities.

The evidence for Feature 5 stands in sharp contrast to that of Feature 42. Here the remains were found beneath a relatively sterile soil
zone, 1—5 inches in thickness below the plowzone. Inasmuch as the
postmolds did not appear until the level underlying this soil was
reached, it must be assumed that the latter was deposited on this area
of the site subsequent to the destruction of the putative house. The
best explanation for this situation would appear to be that, shortly
after this event, the remains were covered by a flood deposit. Since
artifacts and other refuse were present in this level, it is here suggested that eddying waters carried cultural materials from adjacent

features into this particular area. Flooding of the site, including localized eddying, which could have produced a similar situation as that just described, was witnessed by Shane during the relatively mild 1968 spring flood.

As far as the structure itself is concerned, there is clear evidence that it was destroyed by fire. All the postmolds were charred throughout their depths. Burnt and charred sections of structural members, presumably posts, were frequently found inside and outside of the feature. There is some evidence, based upon the disposition of the charred remains, that a northwesterly wind was blowing when the fire occurred. Specks of charcoal and ashes are common throughout the area.

From these data it is inferred that the structure, obviously, was consumed by fire. It can further be concluded that the other presumed house, Feature 42, post–dates Feature 5, because its confines are devoid of charred remains. In fact, the very prominent specks of charcoal and ashes noted in the area of the latter, disappear quite abruptly in the area of Feature 42. Notwithstanding recent disturbances by the plow, the delineation of fire–affected versus unburnt areas is so obvious as to suggest that Feature 42 impinges upon Feature 5. On the other hand, the chronological distance between the two features cannot be great because, as noted, no pits or other prehistoric disturbances of any significance have cut into the pattern of either structure. Also, such artifacts as were found in the house areas proved to be entirely homogeneous.

At the risk of sheer speculation we consider it likely that Feature 42 may have been constructed literally within the year following the conflagration and postulated flood. Inasmuch as evidence for ancient and recent flooding throughout the area of the site is abundantly indicated, the combination of two such disasters as befell Feature 5 is not in any sense surprising.

Feature 6 (Figure 5). This feature was located in one of the random test areas which are not part of the regular excavation units. It was not completely excavated. For reasons of time limitations, only two 5-by-5 foot squares were examined. As in the case of Features 5 and 42, the present evidence would seem to indicate the presence of a

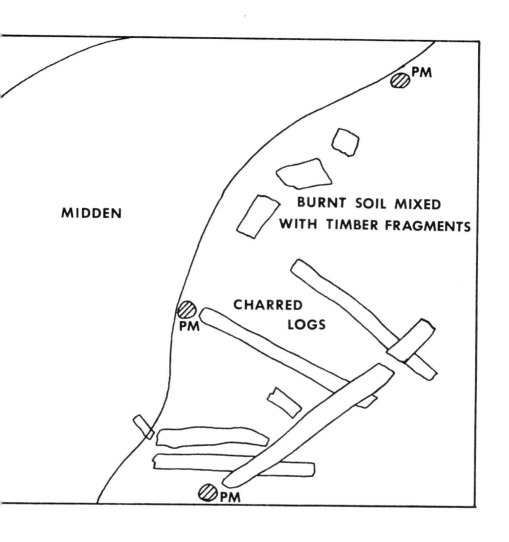

MIDDEN

PM

BURNT SOIL MIXED
WITH TIMBER FRAGMENTS

CHARRED
LOGS

PM

PM

SCALE: 0   1'   2'

Figure 5.   Plan of Feature 6.

house structure impinging on one of the squares. Interestingly, this building too, appears to have burnt down.

Stratigraphically the situation was as follows: beneath the plow-zone, a deeply burnt soil deposit, 8 inches in thickness, was encountered. This area is sharply set off from a dark midden deposit, extending to a depth of 12 inches, which may have been an irregularly shaped pit. Beneath this level, sterile alluvium was encountered. Embedded in the burnt area were found numerous large fragments of completely charred logs, representing collapsed posts. In two instances one end of the post terminates at charred postmolds, 5—6 inches in diameter. This strongly suggests that the molds and adjacent horizontal logs constitute single units. The log diameters are identical to those of the postmolds. The burnt area with charred logs extends beyond the confines of the excavation square. We interpret this situation with some assurance to be indicative of a burnt house structure similar to that of Feature 5. Artifacts were sparse in the presumed house area, but very common in the adjacent midden. They are characteristic of the site as a whole. Feature 6 yielded a radiocarbon date of A.D. 1440 which, on the cultural evidence, is too late. As noted in Chapter 16, the sample was taken from one of the logs found just beneath the plowzone. It may have been contaminated by roots.

Feature 33 (Figure 3b). This is a stratified refuse pit of cylindrical shape. It was located during testing near the western margin of the site; it is not part of a regular excavation unit. Maximum diameter just below the plowzone was 53 inches, and maximum depth, again from the base of the plowzone, 38 inches. The top deposit consisted of a fill, 23 inches in depth, which contained little by way of cultural material. Beneath that occurred a well–defined, but not very productive midden, 5 inches in thickness. This, in turn, was underlain by a 6 inch level of essentially unproductive fill. On one side of this deposit a cluster of fire–cracked rocks was noted. The basal deposit, a midden on the average 5 inches in thickness, contained in the center a mass of fishbones, overlain by quantities of sharply angular, apparently cleaved sandstone fragments, probably manufacturing residue. To the side of this rested two curious, grit–tempered clay cylinders. One of these, 160 mm in height and 130 mm in diameter, was slightly (probably accidentally) fired. The other, measuring 170-by-130 mm, was unfired. Both bore fabric impressions, as if they had been contained in tight bags as well as individual string impressions which had slightly constricted these objects. The total inventory of this pit, in addition to faunal remains, etc., consisted of the following items:

1.	Sherds of *Baum Cordmarked Incised, Var. Blain*	19
2.	Sherds of *Baum Shell-tempered, Var. Blain*	27
3.	True flint blades	1
4.	Flint debitage	21
5.	Worked antler	1
6.	Clay cylinders	2
7.	Sandstone debitage	24
		95

This feature deserves special comment only because of its unusual content. It should be noted that it is the only one in which shell-tempered sherds constitute the majority of the ceramic remains, although, given the poverty of the general assemblage, this is hardly of significance.

Feature 44. This is the burial mound discussed in detail in Chapter 11. Inasmuch as that report primarily deals with the physical anthropology of the skeletons, and only sketchily with the cultural data, the following brief discussion is intended to elucidate the cultural aspects of this structure. For all other details the reader is referred to the relevant chapter.

The mound fill contained occasional sherds of *Baum Cordmarked Incised*, var. Blain and *Baum Shell-tempered, var Blain* pottery, a few projectile points, and faunal refuse. Beneath the floor of the mount similar debris was found, although this cannot be considered to constitute evidence for a sub-mound midden. Apparently the material merely represents a scatter of artifacts on the surface of the area involved.

The burials had all been placed on the mound floor which does not appear to have been specially prepared. The burials themselves did not show any particular plan of disposition. Two individuals were oriented south, three to the east, one to the southeast, and one to the northwest. Six individuals were buried in an extended position, and one was interred lying on the side with bent knees. The specific nature of burial goods association, as well as the distribution of other artifacts, is illustrated by Table 1.

Table 1.   Association of skeletons and burial goods in Blain Mound.

Burial Number	Nature of Objects	Where Found
1	Composite object of 2 shell gorgets and raven beak	On side of left talus
	Traces of red ochre	On trunk
	One triangular projectile point	Under left femoral head
	One projectile point tip	In head of left humerus
2.	One large triangular flint dagger	In right hand resting on right femur
	One triangular projectile point	In left rib cage
3	One Chesser Notched point	Embedded in dorsal aspect of cervicle vertebrae
4.	—	—
5.	One rectangular sandstone bar	Under head
	One large circular ocean shell gorget	On chest
	Two strands of disc shell beads	On wrists
6	One shell spoon	Near right knee
	One limestone elbow pipe	Under left elbow
	One triangular projectile point	In left rib cage
7.	Two strands of cylindrical shell beads	On forearms
	One notched shell spoon	Near skull

Using the evidence of the projectile points in the bodies, it is apparent that three individuals came to a violent end. One individual had been injured by projectile points, although his injuries do not seem to have been lethal. In one instance a mastoid infection may have been the cause of death. The third one of the killed individuals was a small child.

The age distribution suggests the presence of one infant, approximately one year of age, another about two and a half years of age, a fifteen year old adolescent, and four adults about thirty-five years of age. Only the adults could be sexed; they include three males and one female.

The evidence indicates that all individuals were interred at the same time. Whether this constitutes a family group must remain a moot point, although the possibility cannot be excluded. The very position of the mound in a plaza, roughly in the center of the village, does, however, suggest that the individuals here interred were no ordinary folk.

The absence of grave goods with two individuals should be noted. The skeletons involved were those of the youngest child and the adolescent. That youth was not a criterion for the presence or absence of grave furniture is indicated by the fact that the two and a half year old child (Burial 7) had been interred with strands of beads and a shell spoon. In conclusion it may be said that no particular pattern of grave goods disposition emerges from the limited data of the mound.

As far as Griffin's burial trait list is concerned (1943: Table XIV), we note that of the seventeen traits given for Baum and Gartner, six traits were also present at Blain, all associated with the mound. A further trait, "Village Site Burials", may have been present in the vicinity of Features 5 and 42. Finally, the occasional occurrence of burials literally pitched into garbage pits (Griffin, 1943: Table XIV), was also noted at Blain. Among the faunal remains of Feature 17, the fragmentary remains of a new-born infant were found (see page 17).

V

Ceramics

All excavation units and features proved to be rich in ceramics. In addition, surface collecting, undertaken in the course of the initial survey and during the excavations, yielded large quantities of sherds. As a result, it can fairly be stated that at Blain Village ceramics very clearly constitute quantitatively the most productive category of artifacts.

One of the major questions to be resolved was that of the homogeneity of the site. Given the size of the locality, no *a priori* judgment could be made regarding this point. Although there was no question as to the basic affiliation of the cultural remains, there always remained the possibility that the site represented a sequentially multiple occupation during the *Baum Phase*. In order to resolve this question with reasonable certainty, the ceramic finds from the various units were compared internally for consistency in terms of the shell/grit temper ratio. The results of this comparison proved that, as far as pottery is concerned, the excavated units were entirely internally consistent. In addition, the excavated pottery sample was compared in terms of temper ratios with the random surface collection, comprising approximately two thousand sherds. Again, the results indicated the fundamental homogeneity of the site. In no significant way did the ratio of the surface sample differ from that of the excavated sample. Thus, the ceramic evidence supports our general conclusions that Blain Village represents essentially a single component settlement, spanning a relatively brief period of time, during the earliest period of the *Fort Ancient Tradition*.

The present analysis of the Blain ceramics includes the surface and excavated samples, comprising a total of 13,317 sherds. The metric data are based upon actual measurements of approximately 75 percent of the total sample. In order to check on possible between feature and unit metric differences, independent measurements and comparisons were made. No significant differences could be detected.

FORT ANCIENT SERIES
Baum Cordmarked Incised, var. Blain

GENERAL DATA

For previous definitions of *Baum Cordmarked*, see Griffin, 1943; McKenzie, 1967; and for additional data, consult Mills, 1904, 1906.

Apart from Griffin's brief type description of *Baum Cordmarked*, and his additional comments in the textual analysis of the *Baum Focus* (1943: 36–69, 342–343), the only systematic attempt at classifying presumed *Baum Focus* ceramics was made by McKenzie (1967: 68–71).

In the present definition it is recognized that Griffin's and McKenzie's definitions are too simplified to do justice to the ceramics they have called *Baum Cordmarked*. As explained elsewhere in this report, there appear to be at least two distinct ceramic complexes which are lumped by Griffin into a single type. They include the pottery from the classic greater Scioto Valley sites represented by Baum and Gartner, and the material from the Baldwin Site in the Hocking Valley drainage. Graham Village, excavated by McKenzie in 1965, is located in the Hocking Valley. The ceramics from the latter two sites are clearly very similar if not identical. It was on the basis of comparing his materials with the pottery from the Baldwin Site which, in turn, was typed as *Baum Cordmarked* by Griffin, that McKenzie (1967) somewhat uneasily classed the Graham Village ceramics with Griffin's type. The following table illustrates the differences between the two complexes:

Table 2.   Comparison of *Baum Cordmarked* ceramics from the Scioto and Hocking Valleys.

Trait	Hocking Valley	Scioto Valley
Thickness	thin: mean 6.3 mm	thick: mean 7.9 mm
Texture	moderately fine	medium coarse
Range of variation	limited	considerable
Rim appendages	rare: 26 (3.8 percent)	common: 98 (15.9 percent)
Cordmarking style	almost dainty	coarse
Color	medium to light	dark
Temper	fine grit	medium coarse grit
Temper density	medium low	high
Decorative mode	much scratching, little broad incising	broad incising, finger incising
Decorative motifs	limited range	wide range
Plain/decorated ratio	97.0 to 3.0 percent	90.2 to 9.8 percent

It would be unfair to state that Griffin was unaware of the differences between the *Baldwin Component* and other *Baum Focus* sites, for he states the following: "The pottery from the Baldwin site is mainly of the Baum Cordmarked and Baum Incised types. Very few sherds, however, have any incising. In this respect, as well as in other details to be mentioned, this component resembles the Baum site less than the Gartner site, for example, resembles the Baum site. There is a definite resemblance to Woodland pottery, and were it not for certain Fort Ancient cultural attributes, primarily in the rim and decorative treatment, it would be difficult to separate this pottery from that of the Woodland Pattern." (1943:55). The fact, however, remains that Griffin did call these ceramics *Baum Cordmarked* and *Baum Incised*, both being subsumed under a single type definition (1943:342–343), the latter being conceived of as a "companion type" to *Baum Cordmarked* (1943:44). McKenzie too, had some misgivings as to the status of supposed *Baum Focus* ceramics from the Hocking Valley (1967:77–79). The truth is that he was caught in the four–focus pattern of Fort Ancient established by Griffin in the 1930's, a pattern that was perfectly valid at the time when the only available information was both antiquated and based upon dubious field data. Anticipating the discussion of our views on Fort Ancient, we merely want to point out here that the Hocking Valley sites are indeed related to the localities in the greater Scioto Valley. This relationship, however, is broad in nature, a fact that only too easily overshadows the very real regional and presumably ecological differences between the two areas, differences that undoubtedly have more than passing socio–cultural implications.

In line with McKenzie's analysis of the ceramics from the Graham Village site, the definition presented here assumes that the decorated sherds from Blain—and by implication those of other presumed *Baum Focus* localities—do not constitute a separate pottery type, not even a vague "companion type" to *Baum Cordmarked*, as Griffin has suggested. They are an integral part of the type, and, at least in the Blain assemblage, the ratio of decorated to undecorated sherds in conjunction with a consideration of the limited areas that bear decorations on Fort Ancient vessels, strongly suggests that the vast majority of all Blain vessels were decorated.

One further comment is in order. Griffin lumped shell and grit–tempered sherds into his type definition, merely noting the approximate percentage distribution of each. In as much as shell–temper is a Mississippian horizon marker, and in as much as there are indications that the relative proportions of shell to other kinds of temper in any discrete ceramic assemblage may have chronological significance, we are here following McKenzie's example, in excluding shell–tempered sherds from the type definition.

The present definition is based upon the following sample:

Body sherds:		11,982
Cordmarked:	11,009	
Decorated:	973	
Rim sherds:		696
Cordmarked:	421	
Decorated:	275	
		12,678

Basal sherds are included with body sherds because only in rare cases was it possible to state with certainty whether a given sherd was indeed a base; this is a function of the globular shape of the vessels and the generally uniform thickness of body sherds below the neck.

PASTE

METHOD OF MANUFACTURE

Coiled; coil breaks are fairly common.

TEMPER

Baum Cordmarked Incised, var. Blain is by definition grit–tempered. Particles consist of a variety of crushed rocks including quartz, feldspar, and black micaceous particles. These minerals appear to be of generally local derivation. A number of sherds contain admixtures of sand, probably derived from the Scioto River. Particle size ranges from 1 to 4 mm, with 2mm representing the mode. Particle density in any given sherd is high. This factor contributes to the coarse and brittle texture of the sherds.

TEXTURE

Medium–coarse to coarse. Generally uncontorted and unlaminated.

HARDNESS

No hardness measurements were taken; 2.0–3.5 on the Moh scale according to Griffin (1943:342). On the whole the sherds are brittle and crumbly, i.e., hardness is rather low. This is a function of temper distribution and poor firing control.

COLOR

The color spectrum is wide. It varies from black to ochre, the overall impression being that of a rather dark reddish to grey range, with frequent exterior clouds of fire smoking. In line with other Fort Ancient ceramics, interior hues range from grey to black, regardless of exterior values. Core color is in general agreement with the exterior color.

SURFACE TREATMENT

The basic treatment consists of exterior, rather coarse, cordmarking, produced by means of a cordwrapped paddle. The paddle impressions very rarely overlap; application is generally vertical. Some variation in the spacing of cords has been noted, but the overall characteristics are narrow and tight spacing. Overwhelmingly the cords are two–ply. Smoothed interior cordmarking has occasionally been noted.

In all cases, exterior cordmarking covers the entire body of the vessel up to the shoulder and including the base. In most instances, cordmarking also occurs in the area from the shoulder up to the lip. Only on these upper vessel areas has the complete absence of cord-marking been noted. The distribution of smoothing based upon a random sample of 200 cordmarked body sherds is as follows:

No smoothing: 46 percent (92 sherds)
Some smoothing: 33 percent (66 sherds)
Much smoothing: 21 percent (42 sherds)

In addition to cordmarking, 973 body sherds and 275 rim sherds, or 9.8 percent of the total sample have incised decorations, appendages, notches, punctates, or combinations of these elements. Such decora-tions are restricted to two areas, that immediately below the shoulder and/or that above the shoulder to, and including, the lip (Table 4). All appendages are attached to either rims or lips.

The decorations on neck/rim and occasionally shoulder were ap-plied over (a) unsmoothed cordmarking, (b) smoothed cordmarking, (c) a completely plain background, and (d) a differentially smoothed cordmarked background. Mode (c) occurs only above the shoulder. Mode (d) always consists of an incised guilloche design applied onto an initially unsmoothed cordmarked background. Subsequently, the areas above and below the guilloche band were smoothed; how-ever, the areas within the guilloche, outlined by the incised design, were left unsmoothed, i.e. the cordmarking here is fully present.

As noted under *General Data*, the ratio of undecorated to deco-rated sherds, given the limited space allocated by the potters on any given vessel to decorative elements, strongly suggests that nearly every vessel was decorated. This is confirmed by the inspection of sherds from the shoulder and neck areas; nearly all of these show traces of design.

The major decorative technique is broad incising. The incisions are almost always wider than 3mm; they never fall below 2 mm, and the maximum width—excluding finger incisions to be discussed be-low—does not exceed 8 mm. The incisions are between 1 and 2 mm deep. Two technical modes of incising can be distinguished. The more common one is characterized by the use of a well–defined incising tool, presumably a stick or bone object, which was firmly and evenly dragged over the exterior vessel surface. The second technique, represented by 70 sherds, involves what can best be called "finger incising". Dragging a finger, more or less deeply impressed into the clay, over the vessel surface thus produced wide and relatively shallow impressions.

As far as decorative motifs are concerned, tool and finger incised single bands of curvilinear guilloches are the mode. 1,080 decorated sherds, or 86.5 percent of all decorated sherds bear this design, either alone or in combination with appendages, punctates, notches, etc. The remaining designs, once the appendages to be discussed below are excluded, are as limited in their range of motifs as they are few in numbers. They consist primarily of rim decorations such as rows of punctates, parallel incised bands, chevrons, and short parallel incised lines on the lips, and notches on lips. In addition, a very few examples of the incised open triangles on the neck, also noted by Griffin (1943:Pl. III, 1–2, 4–5), and a few isolated sherds with entirely idiosyncratic designs (Figure 6, G; 7, I; Plate II, C; III, D-E) have been noted. Among the sherds with the characteristic incised guilloche, two specimens with a double band of this pattern have been recovered (Figure 6, H). A single sherd with a triple band of guilloches, was also found.

The composition of the guilloche design has four patterns, each defined by the number of lines used in the design. These patterns are here termed single–line, double–line, triple–line, and quadruple–line guilloche. Of the 1,080 sherds bearing the guilloche design, 159 sherds exhibited at least one complete guilloche segment. The distribution of these patterns is as follows:

1-line:	8	(5.03 percent)
2-line:	51	(32.08 percent)
3-line:	94	(59.12 percent)
4-line:	6	(3.77 percent)

Clearly, two-line and three-line guilloches represent the mode.

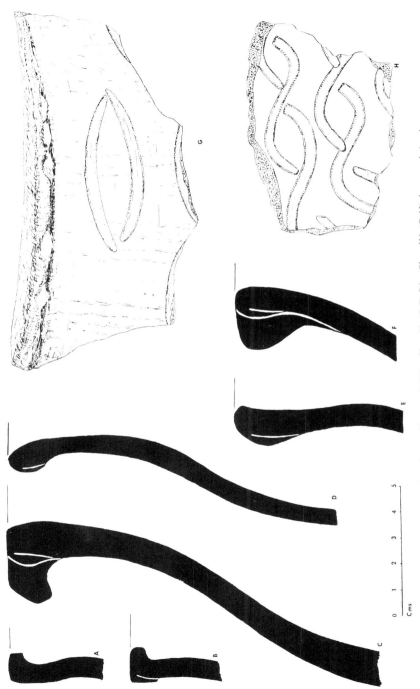

Figure 6. *Baum Cordmarked Incised, var. Blain* rim profiles. (A-B) Rim Class V; (C-F) Rim Class IV; (G-H) decorated sherds.

Inches

Cms

Plate II. (A–C) *Baum Shell Tempered, var. Blain* sherds. (B) *Baum Shell Tempered, var. Blain* sherds.

Plate III. (A-C) *Baum Shell Tempered, var. Blain sherds* (D-E) *Baum Cordmarked-Incised, var. Blain sherds.*

Thirty–three rim sherds bore at least one complete guilloche segment. The association of patterns with rim classes is as follows:

Table 3. Distribution of guilloche types by rim classes on *Baum Cordmarked Incised, var. Blain* ceramics.

Rim Class	1–line	2–line	3–line	4–line	Total
I–a	1	5	1	1	8
I–b	–	–	1	–	1
I–c	1	1	–	–	2
II	–	1	3	–	4
III	–	7	3	–	10
IV	–	3	5	–	8
	2	17	13	1	33

FORM

RIM AND LIP

Taken as a whole, the rim profiles from the Blain Site are quite uniform in shape, ranging from straight and vertical to moderately flared. In some instances the rims are recurvate near the lip. Marked variability occurs only in the lip area as a result of thickening and/or because of the appendages so characteristic of this pottery. This should be noted with some care, because such lip treatment tends to overshadow the overall uniformity of the rim profiles.

In line with the example set by McKenzie (1967) in the Graham Village report, we have subdivided the rim sherds from Blain into a number of classes, based primarily upon rim modifications near the lip. These classes are formal in nature; at present their spatial and temporal significance is not known, although it is expected that rigorous analyses of other Fort Ancient ceramics may shed some light on this.

Rim Class I((Figure 7, A-I). Total sample:195 rims. These rims are straight and vertical to slightly flaring, with unthickened rims and flat or rounded lips. In some instances the lips are exteriorly and/or interiorly extruded, although this has only been noted where the lips are flattened. Occasionally the lip is thinner than the body of the rim (knife-edged).

Figure 7. *Baum Cordmarked Incised var. Blain* rim profiles. (A-I) Rim Class I.

Subclass I–a: total sample: 90 rims. Fifty–four rims are undecorated, and 36 variously decorated; among the latter 11 have appendages. Table 4 shows the distribution of decorative motifs. All rims of Subclass I–a are straight and vertical, the range of lip form varying from round to flat. Vertical, unsmoothed, cordmarking occurs up to the top of the lip. As a rule, the rounded lips are smoothed, whereas the flattened ones bear cord impressions. Mean thickness is 7.78 mm, with a range from 5–13 mm.

Subclass I–b: total sample: 33 rims. Twenty-three rims are undecorated, and 10 variously decorated; among the latter, 2 have appendages. Table 4 shows the distribution of decorative motifs. With the exception of three slightly flaring specimens, all rims of Subclass I–b are similar in profile to those of Subclass I–a. The difference between the two subclasses relates to the surface treatment. In the present series the cordmarking just below the lip is invariably smoothed to form a plain band varying in width from 1 to 3 cms. Frequently wiping marks suggest the use of a piece of coarse cloth for smoothing. Mean thickness is 8.79 mm, with a range from 6–13 mm.

Subclass I–c: total sample: 73 rims. Forty rims are undecorated, and 33 variously decorated; among the latter, 5 have appendages. The rims of Subclass I–c differ from those of the other subclasses in that their profiles form a continuous gradient from straight and vertical to moderately flaring. Furthermore, all rims are either completely smoothed, or were never cordmarked in the first place, above the shoulder. There is a high correlation between this rim subclass and the occurrence of the guilloche design above the shoulder and up to the lip. Table 4 shows the distribution of decorative motifs. Mean thickness is 7.54 mm, with a range from 5–13 mm.

Rim Class II: (Fig. 8, A–G). Total sample: 169 rims. One hundred and four are undecorated, and 65 are variously decorated; among the latter, 4 sherds have appendages. Table 4 shows the distribution of the decorative motifs. This class corresponds to McKenzie's *Class III.* Some of the less distinctive rims in this class from the Blain Site

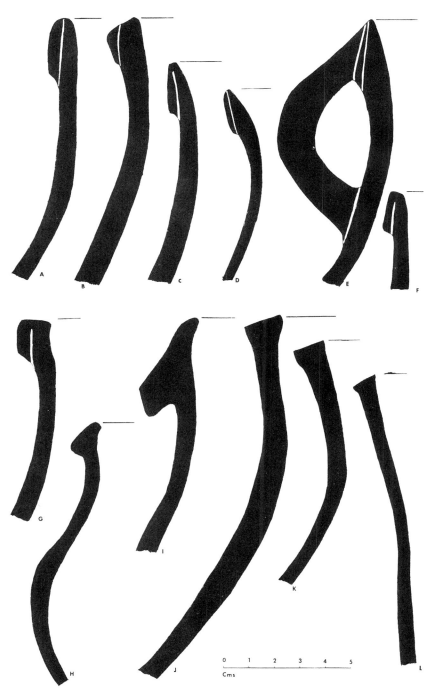

Figure 8. *Baum Cordmarked Incised, var. Blain* rim profiles. (A-G) Rim Class II; (H-L) Rim Class III.

grade into *Class IV* (below), but in the main *Class II* rims are very distinctive indeed.

Class II consists of rims with flat bands of clay attached vertically to the exterior face of the lip. These bands range from 15 to 20 mm in width. Their addition thickens the upper rim and lip area. For purposes of this analysis, the thickened section of the rim will here be considered the lip. In many instances the rim strips are poorly attached to the body of the sherd, so much so that they occasionally peel off, and frequently show a clear "seam" at the lower exterior border of the strip–body junction. In all cases the strip–body joint is clearly discernible in the rim profile. The profile of what is here considered the lip, modified by the addition of the rim strips, varies from straight–vertical exterior–interior faces leading to a rounded or flat lip proper, to an exteriorly rounded, but interiorly straight and vertical face, thus producing a plano–convex cross–section. The rims as a whole are almost invariably straight and vertical; very slight flaring is rare.

Decorations occur on cordmarked, smoothed, or entirely plain backgrounds. Sixty-two rims have cordmarked rim strips. This treatment of the strip can occur independently of the presence or absence of cordmarking below the lip. Mean thickness below the lip is 7.12 mm, with a range from 5–10 mm. Mean thickness of the lips is 10.15 mm, with a range from 8–14 mm.

Rim Class III: Figure 8, H–L Total sample: 127 rims. Sixty-nine rims are undecorated, and 58 are variously decorated; among the latter, 25 sherds have appendages. Table 4 shows the distribution of decorative motifs.

Rims of this class are characterized by lips thickened due to the addition of a horizontally projecting strip of clay. Although the projection is principally on the exterior face, in a number of sherds there is also an additional wedge–shaped projection on the interior. The slant of the lip is always outward, and its form is always flat. Thus, the lip profile is gable–shaped. McKenzie divided these rims into two subclasses (II–a and II–b), the criteria being the presence or absence of the interior projection. In the Blain sample, the morphological fluidity is such that subdivision does not seem to be warranted. The rims as a whole are predominantly straight and vertical; only occasionally has slight flaring been noted.

As far as surface treatment is concerned, all but 4 specimens are cordmarked to just below the lip. One sherd has been smoothed by coarse wiping below the lip, and in all but 4 the lip is either plain or smoothed cordmarked. Mean thickness below the lip is 6.85 mm, with a range from 5–10 mm; mean lip thickness, measured from gable peak to the exterior gable edge is 11.85 mm, with a range from 7–25 mm.

Rim Class IV: (Figure 6, C–F). Total sample: 127 rims. Eighty-three rims are undecorated, and 44 are variously decorated; among the latter 20 have appendages. Table 4 shows the distribution of decorative motifs.

Rims in this class correspond to McKenzie's Subclass II–c. They are here given separate class status, because they are quite distinctive, and at no time within the range of *Class III* (McKenzie's Subclasses II–a and II–b). The rims are straight and vertical or slightly flaring. Thickening consists of an amorphous rim strip molded to the lip. The lip is usually rounded or quite irregular. Although quite distinctive when compared with the other rim classes, the rims here show considerable internal variability and a certain lack of homogeneity. All sherds are cordmarked to the lip, except for 17 specimens which are plain or smoothed cordmarked. No sherd bears cord impressions on the lip. Mean thickness below the lip is 7.21 mm, with a range from 3–10 mm; mean thickness at the lip is 9.83 mm, with a range from 5–10 mm.

Rim Class V: (Figure 6, A–B). Total sample: 4 sherds. None are decorated. Rims in this class are thickened by the addition of a strip of clay to the top of the lip. The lip is flattened so that the exterior face of the sherd is straight up to the lip edge. The flattening process resulted in a sharply defined interior lip projection, in the manner of a T-bar. In profile these rims are straight and vertical. They are cordmarked to the lip, and, with one exception that is smoothed, they are also cordmarked on the flat lip proper. Mean thickness below the lip is 7.00 mm, with a range from 5–8 mm; mean thickness at the lip is 11.25 mm, with a range from 10–14 mm.

Other Rims: a single sherd represents a straight vertical rim with an appliqued-collared lip. Body and lip are plain, with a guilloche design reaching to the lip. Thickness below the lip is 5.0 mm; at lip, 11.0 mm.

BODY AND BASE

The Blain vessels are uniformly rounded jars with rounded shoulders and well defined necks and rims. Only 7 vessels are characterized by rounded bodies and somewhat angular shoulders. The globular shape of these jars is underscored by the absence of any basal sherds other than rounded ones. Inasmuch as body and basal sherds appear to be remarkably uniform in thickness, and inasmuch as bases as well as body sherds are both cordmarked, it proved rather difficult to isolate with certainty more than a few definite basal sherds. Vessel size is relatively uniform. The majority appears to range from 25–55 cm in height; one nearly complete vessel is 25.6 cm in height. The mean thickness of 6,000 sherds is 7.80 mm, with a range from 3–20 mm.

APPENDAGES

Rim and lip appendages are characteristic of the Blain ceramic assemblage. They occur on 99 sherds, representing 14.2 percent of the total rim sample. The following is a typological analysis of these appendages:

Straphandles: (Figure 7, H; 8, E; Plate IV, B–C). Total sample: 8. Two of these are shoddily made, short and thick, almost semi-circular straphandles, attached below the lip. Their perforations are small and irregular. According to Griffin (1943:367) they are commonly found at the greater Scioto Valley sites (Baum and Gartner), but rare in the Hocking Valley (Baldwin). The other 6 straphandles from Blain are elongated and thin, almost trianguloid; they are luted to the lip. Griffin (1943:367) states that this form is rare in the Scioto Valley and absent in the Hocking Valley. McKenzie (1967:71) reports a single straphandle from the Graham Village site in the Hocking Valley.

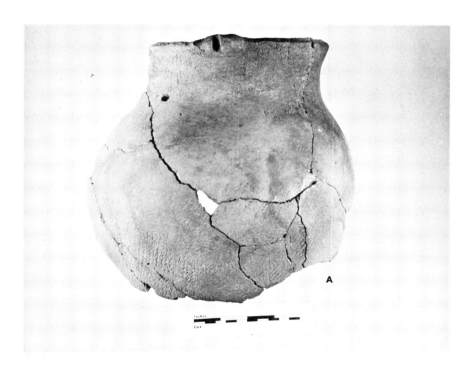

Plate IV.   (A-C) *Baum Cordmarked Incised*, *var. Blain* rims.

Six of the Blain specimens are cordmarked, 2 are plain. Cordmarking is noted as "present" for the Scioto Valley sites, and "rare" for the Hocking Valley. One of the elongated straphandles is decorated with rows of punctates, a feature that is noted as "present" at the Baum site, "rare" at Gartner, and "absent" at Baldwin. Griffin's discussion of Baum Focus straphandles includes the following remarks: "The straphandle is a poor imitation of the Madisonville type. It is usually squat, thick, and poorly shaped, and is most often attached to the lip. It sometimes has two ears. It very rarely has incised lines, or somewhat more commonly horizontal rows of punctates on the outer surface." (1943:342).

It is clear that the Blain straphandles differ somewhat from those reported from other *Baum Focus* sites in the Scioto Valley.

Discrete Lugs: (Figure 6, F; 7, F; Plate IV, A; V, C–E; VI, A). Total sample: 39. These are well-defined, large or small, teat-like attachments to the lip or rim. Commonly they are single lugs (37 specimens); only two cases of double-lugs have been noted. The detailed typology of these appendages is shown in Table 4. The term *discrete* here refers to the fact that these lugs are elements of limited, defined size, rather than attached rim strips that generally widen to become what Griffin called "horizontal ridges at lip" (1943:367), a term which we have replaced here by *continuous lug*. A glance at Griffin's list of discrete lugs from Baum and Gartner (1943:366–367) immediately makes clear the limited range of such appendages on the Blain vessels. Most noteworthy is the fact that some forms such as semicircular ridges with or without ears, noted as common for Baum and present for Gartner have not been found at Blain.

Continuous Lugs: (Figure 6, C, G; Plate V, A; VII, A–C; VIII, B). Total sample: 60. Griffin has provided a description of this form which can hardly be improved upon: "Particularly significant are the lug handles, which can be subdivided into a number of types. The simplest of these may be an elaboration of the thickened upper lip, or it may be the result of copying a technique of another cultural group. This style of lug is a narrow horizontal strip of

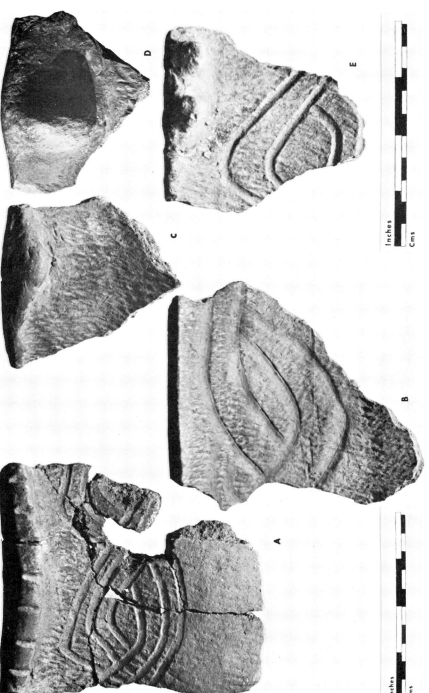

Plate V. (A-E) *Baum Cordmarked Incised, var. Blain* sherds.

Inches

Cms

clay, luted to the vessel just below but contiguous to the lip, or placed on the rim and definitely below the lip. . . . Some of these lugs are relatively short horizontally, . . . others may extend around one–quarter to one–third the circumference of the vessel. . . . The narrowed lips of the lugs are sometimes decorated by vertical notches. . . ." (1943:45). As far as the Blain sample is concerned, this description needs amplification only in regard to the decorative motifs that occur on these lugs. The decorative range (Table 4) at Blain may be somewhat greater than that at the other localities discussed by Griffin. In some cases the strips and lugs are so poorly applied that, in fact, they peel off. In such cases there is evidence that the joints had been cord–roughened prior to the attachment of the lugs. At the Graham Village site (McKenzie, 1967) continuous lugs similar to those from Blain are virtually absent.

Eared Rims: total sample: 5. Four specimens have vertical double ears protruding from the lip; these extrusions are small and narrow, and appear to be similar to the double ears noted by Griffin in conjunction with semicircular lugs (1943:366). However, the Blain examples are definitely not associated with such lugs. The fourth specimen consists of a rim to the exterior lip edge of which flat double ears, similar to the normal, vertical ones, are attached horizontally.

GEOGRAPHICAL RANGE

Directly related ceramics occur only at Gartner near Chillicothe in the Scioto Valley and at Baum, on the Paint Creek, a tributary of the Scioto River. Less well documented are finds of this ware from a series of unpublished localities in the Scioto Valley such as the Higby site and McGraw's Garden site. As a minority ware, *Baum Cordmarked Incised, var. Blain* has been reported from sites of Griffin's *Feurt Focus*, again in the Scioto Valley. In a wider sense, the ceramics from Baldwin and Graham in the Hocking Valley, and the materials from Griffin's Brush Creek component are related to this type, thus extending the range beyond the Scioto drainage. In the strict sense, however, *Baum Cordmarked Incised, var. Blain* does not seem to penetrate beyond the confines of the Scioto Valley proper. This will be discussed in the interpretive sections of this report.

Plate VII.   (A-D) *Baum Cordmarked Incised*, *var. Blain* sherds.

Plate VIII. *Baum Cordmarked Incised, var. Balin* sherds. (A) Undecorated rim; (B) Continuous lug showing seam between lug and rim.

CHRONOLOGICAL POSITION

Probably earliest Fort Ancient, with dates ranging from the 10th to the 13th centuries A.D. For details consult the interpretive sections of this report.

Table 4. Distribution of decorative motifs on *Baum Cordmarked Incised, var. Blain* ceramics.

		I	I-a	I-b	I-c	II	III	IV	V	Sherdlets	Other	Total
1.	Undecorated	-	55	23	41	105	70	83	4	42	-	423
2.	Incised guilloche on neck and rim	-	12	4	18	32	20	15	-	-	1	102
3.	Single horizontal incised band on or just below lip with guilloche on neck	-	-	-	-	1	-	-	-	-	-	1
4.	Single horizontal incised band on or just below lip	-	1	-	-	-	1	-	-	-	-	2
5.	Double horizontal incised bands on or just below lip	-	4	-	1	1	1	-	-	-	-	7
6.	Same as (5) with guilloche on neck	-	2	1	-	6	-	3	-	-	-	12
7.	Same as (5) with incised open triangles on neck	-	-	-	1	-	-	-	-	1	-	2
8.	Triple horizontal bands incised on or just below lip	-	4	-	1	2	-	-	-	-	-	7
9.	Same as (8) with vertical incisions intruding from neck	-	-	-	1	-	-	-	-	-	-	1
10.	Two incised horizontal bands alternating with two rows of punctates on lip.	-	-	-	-	1	-	-	-	-	-	1
11.	Short parallel diagonal lines on lip	-	2	1	1	1	-	-	-	2	-	7
12.	Same as (11) with wide incised triple zigzags on neck, and diagonal elongated punctates on shoulder	-	-	-	-	-	1	-	-	-	-	1
13.	Incised single wavy band on lip	-	-	-	2	-	1	-	-	1	-	4
14.	Same as (13) with guilloche on neck	-	-	-	-	-	-	-	-	1	-	1

Table 4. (*Continued*)

	I	I-a	I-b	I-c	II	III	IV	V	Sherdlets	Other	Total
15. Incised chevrons on lip	-	1	-	-	3	1	-	-	-	-	5
16. Same as (15) with guilloche on neck	-	-	-	-	4	3	-	-	-	-	7
17. Vertical short incisions on exterior lip	-	-	-	-	-	1	1	-	1	-	3
18. Punctates on lip	-	-	-	3	-	3	1	-	-	-	7
19. Punctates on body, neck, lip over incised guilloche on neck	-	-	-	-	1	-	-	-	-	-	1
20. Punctates below lip and guilloche on neck	-	-	-	-	2	-	-	-	-	-	2
21. Notched lip	-	1	-	-	3	2	1	-	-	-	7
22. Incised open triangles on neck to lip with two incised horizontal bands at shoulder	-	-	-	-	-	1	2	-	-	-	3
23. Zig-zag on lip with guilloche on neck	-	-	-	-	1	-	-	-	-	-	1
24. Same as (11) with fine oblique incisions on neck	-	-	-	-	1	-	-	-	-	-	1
25. Single horizontal incised line on lip with single horizontal incised line on neck below notched strip	-	-	-	-	1	-	-	-	-	-	1
26. Undefinable fragmentary decorations	-	-	-	-	1	1	-	-	7	-	9
27. Straphandles, undecorated	3	-	1	1	-	1	-	-	-	-	6
28. Straphandles with guilloche on neck	1	-	-	-	-	-	-	-	-	-	1
29. Straphandles with punctates	-	1	1	-	-	-	-	-	-	-	2
30. Discrete lugs: single small to medium size	-	-	1	-	-	1	1	-	-	-	3
31. Same as (30) with vertical notch on lug	-	1	-	-	-	-	-	-	-	-	1
32. Same as (30) with incised coronae, and guilloche on neck	-	1	-	-	-	-	-	-	-	-	1
33. Same as (30) with incised coronae	-	1	-	-	-	-	-	-	-	-	1
34. Same as (30) with multiple vertical incisions on lug, and guilloche on neck	-	1	-	-	-	-	-	-	-	-	1
35. Same as (30) undefinable	-	-	-	-	-	-	-	-	7	-	7

Table 4. (*Continued*)

	I	I-a	I-b	I-c	II	III	IV	V	Sherdlets	Other	Total
36. Huge discrete oval with single horizontal incised band on edge of lug, and guilloche on neck	-	-	-	-	1	-	-	-	-	-	1
37. Discrete lugs: double, small, with guilloche on neck	1	1	-	-	-	-	-	-	-	-	2
38. Continuous lugs: undecorated	-	-	1	-	3	11	7	-	3	-	25
39. Same as (38) with incised single horizontal band below lip	-	-	-	-	-	-	1	-	-	-	1
40. Same as (38) with double incised bands on lip	-	-	-	-	-	1	-	-	-	-	1
41. Same as (38) with incised ellipse on rim	-	-	1	-	-	-	-	-	-	-	1
42. Same as (38) with guilloche on neck	-	-	-	-	-	1	2	-	-	-	3
43. Same as (38) with chevrons on lip	-	-	-	-	1	2	-	-	-	-	3
44. Same as (38) with short parallel diagonal incisions on lip	-	-	-	-	-	3	1	-	-	-	4
45. Same as (38) with notched lug	-	-	-	-	-	1	4	-	5	-	10
46. Same as (45) with guilloche on neck	-	1	-	-	-	1	4	-	-	-	6
47. Same as (38) with punctates on lug and guilloche on neck	-	-	-	-	-	1	-	-	-	-	1
48. Horizontal double ears at lip	-	1	-	-	-	-	-	-	-	-	1
49. Vertical double ears at lip	-	3	-	1	-	-	-	-	-	-	4
50. Heavy rim locally thickened vertically and horizontally with four incised bands on lip	-	1	-	-	-	-	-	-	-	-	1
51. Unidentifiable fragmentary appendages	-	-	-	-	-	-	-	-	12	-	12
GRAND TOTALS	5	94	34	71	171	129	126	4	82	1	717

FORT ANCIENT SERIES
Baum Shell Tempered, var. Blain

GENERAL DATA

Not previously defined as a separate type, but included with *Baum Cordmarked* by Griffin (1943), and discussed separately, but not formally defined, by McKenzie (1967) for the Graham Village site. A separate, although tentative type is here established, because of the crucial significance of shell–tempered ceramics during the Mississippian Period (Figure 9, A–D; Plate II, B; III, A–C).

Present definition is based on the following sample:

Body sherds:		427
Undecorated:	409	
Decorated:	18	
Rim sherds:		15
Undecorated:	6	
Decorated:	9	
		442

PASTE

METHOD OF MANUFACTURE

Coiled.

TEMPER

Small shell fragments generally not exceeding 2 mm in diameter, with occasional fragments up to 5 mm or more in diameter; a considerable proportion of the tempering material is less than 1 mm in diameter. Temper density is medium to high. In most instances the shell particles are present; leaching out is rare. Consequently, so–called "hole–temper" has been observed in very few sherds.

TEXTURE

Medium fine, generally uncontorted but laminated.

HARDNESS

No measurements were taken. The overall impression is that of a rather soft and flaky ware.

COLOR

Exterior and core color range from buff to light grey. Occasionally darker sherds were noted. Black interior color occurs, but not as consistently as in the case of *Baum Cordmarked Incised, var. Blain.*

SURFACE TREATMENT

Decorated sherds are rare (Table 5). The present limited sample suggests that in terms of technique, quality of execution, and decorative motifs, the shell–tempered sherds duplicate *Baum Cordmarked Incised, var. Blain* ceramics. The basic nondecorative treatment is medium-coarse to fine cordmarking which in 80 percent of the sherds has been smoothed almost to the point of elimination. The remaining sherds are either unsmoothed or slightly smoothed. Cordmarking is vertical, two–ply, and rather tightly spaced. In the case of two vessels the neck and rim areas are plain.

FORM

RIM AND LIP

With one exception, a plain flaring rim with a sharply excurvate lip, the rims are similar to those of *Baum Cordmarked Incised, var. Blain.* Table 5 shows the distribution of rim classes and rim decorations.

BODY AND BASE

Same as *Baum cordmarked Incised, var. Blain*; whether vessel size is similar as well could not be determined on the basis of the available sample. Mean thickness of body sherds is 6.30 mm, with a range from 3–12 mm.

APPENDAGES

The sample consists of two discrete lugs and one straphandle. One of the lugs is in the shape of an undecorated medium–sized teat below the lip of a rim of *Subclass I–a*. The second lug is an example of what Griffin (1943:45) called a "semi-circular rim lug". The straphandle is on a rim of *Subclass I–a*, and is identical to the handles found on *Baum Cordmarked Incised, var. Blain.*

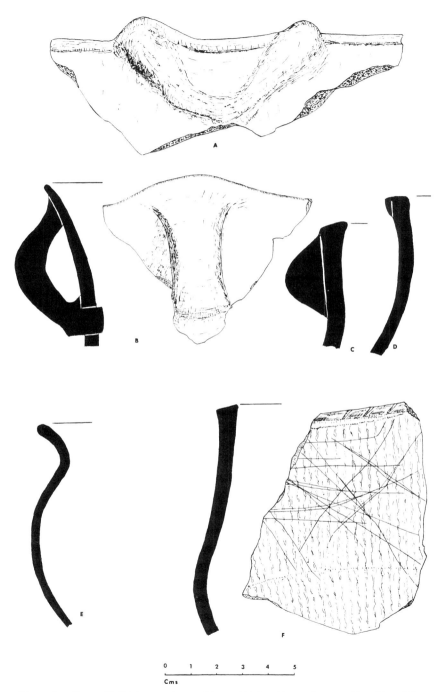

Figure 9. *Baum Shell Tempered, var. Blain.* (A) Semi-lunar lug on Rim Class IV;
(B) Rim Class I; (C) Rim Class III; (D) Rim Class IV. (E) *McGraw Cordmarked.*
(F) Unclassified incised sherd.

GEOGRAPHICAL RANGE

This is a companion type to *Baum Cordmarked Incised*. In the definition of that type it was noted that it appears to be restricted to the greater Scioto Valley, and that the equivalent ceramics from the Hocking Valley, although related, are sufficiently different to warrant separate status. This does not seem to hold true of the shell–tempered sherds. To all intents and purposes there is no regional variation as far as shell–tempered pottery is concerned.

CHRONOLOGICAL POSITION

Same as *Baum Cordmarked Incised, var. Blain*. It may be that this type is ancestral to *Feurt Incised*. At Blain this is a minority type, while at Feurt, *Baum Cordmarked Incised* is in the minority with respect to *Feurt Incised*.

Table 5. Distribution of decorative motifs on *Baum Shell Tempered, var. Blain* ceramics.

DECORATIVE MOTIFS	I-a	I-c	II	OTHER	TOTAL
1. Undecorated	2	-	2	1	5
2. Incised guilloche on neck and rim	-	-	3	-	3
3. Double horizontal incised bands on lip	-	-	1	-	1
4. Punctates on lip	-	1	-	-	1
5. Discrete lugs: single, medium-sized	1	-	-	-	1
6. Diagonal incised lines on rim	-	1	-	-	1
7. Incised chevrons on rim	-	1	-	-	1
8. Straphandle under castellation	-	1	-	-	1
9. Semi-circular lug vertically extending from lip	1	-	-	-	1
	4	4	6	1	15

In addition to the ceramics discussed thus far, Blain Village yielded a number of sherds which do not belong to either of the two types previously defined. They are briefly discussed below.

Peters Cordmarked (Prufer and McKenzie, 1966). These sherds conform to the type definition. They include nine body sherds and six rims. All of these except for two rims from the surface, one rim

A

Inches

Cms

Plate IX. *Baum Cordmarked Incised, var. Blain* sherd.

from Feature 17, one rim from Feature 2, and one body sherd from Feature 4b were recovered from Feature 1. The thickness range for the body sherds is 7—11 mm, with a mean of 7.8 mm. Rim thickness ranges from 6—8 mm, with a mean of 7.3 mm.

Peters Plain (Prufer and McKenzie, 1966). A single body sherd of this type was found in Feature 2. It conforms to the type definition, and measures 9 mm in thickness.

Plain and Cordmarked Limestone-Tempered Pottery. This series includes fifty-five cordmarked body sherds, one plain body sherd, and three rims. One of these has a notched lip and belongs to Rim Class IV. The second rim, belonging with Rim Class II, bears indeterminate finely incised lines; the third rim, of Rim Class IV, is undecorated. These limestone-tempered sherds showed no particular distribution pattern. Their metric attributes are as follows: thickness range of body sherds: 4–11 mm; mean thickness: 7.34 mm. The two measurable rims are 9 mm thick. Except for the thinly incised rim sherds and the plain body sherd this material is indistinguishable from *Baum Cordmarked Incised, var. Blain*. It is here segregated merely on the basis of the temper attribute which consists of large, chalky–white particles. It should be noted that occasional limestone–tempered sherds were also recorded at Graham Village (McKenzie, 1967) and that in Griffin's *Brush Creek Component* of the *Baum Focus* 25 percent of the assemblage appears to have been limestone–tempered (Griffin, 1943:63).

Plain Grit-Tempered Pottery. This series consists of one hundred and one body sherds and one rim. Except for the absence of cordmarking this series is identical with *Baum Cordmarked Incised, var. Blain* and has here been segregated only on the basis of surface treatment. The rim has a small teat-like lug and belongs to Rim Class IV; it is 9 mm thick. The metric attributes of the body sherds are: range 4—11 mm; mean: 7.83 mm. Some plain sherds appear to be characteristic of all early Fort Ancient sites. At Balin their distribution was random.

Plate X. (A) *McGraw Cordmarked* rim; (B-C) *Baum Cordmarked Incised, var. Blain* rims.

In addition to these relatively sizeable sherd series, Blain Village yielded the following unclassified sherds:

1. Three grit-tempered, brushed body sherds. Thickness range is 6—8 mm, with a mean of 7.3 mm.

2. Three grit–tempered rims belonging to Classes Ic, II, and IV. They bear very thin, apparently unpatterned scratched–incised lines. All speciments were found in Feature 1. Thickness ranges from 8—9 mm, with a mean of 8.6 mm (Figure 9, F).

3. Four sand–tempered rim sherds found in as many features. Two of these belong to Rim Class Ib, the remaining specimens to Class II. Thickness ranges from 5—8 mm, with a mean of 6.3 mm. Two of these sherds bear thin incised lines of indeterminate pattern.

4. Six sand–tempered and two grit–tempered, fragmentary miniature vessels with plain or smoothed cordmarked bodies were found in various features. Such miniatures are characteristic of the *Baum Focus*. These vessels are crudely made and cannot easily be described. They appear to have been round based with thinned rims and lips. Rims are either slightly flaring or incurvate. The largest specimen was approximately 100 mm high, the smallest less than 50 mm.

5. Feature 4b yielded seven sherds of a single vessel, apparently a plain miniature specimen which appears to have been unfired. No tempering material could be detected.

Finally, Feature 2 yielded fourteen sherds of a single vessel representing a fragmentary small cordmarked jar with an angular shoulder, excurvate plain rim, and rounded lip (Figure 9, E; Plate X, A). Body and rim thickness average 4 mm. Although the basal section is missing, the extant fragments suggest a sub-conoidal vessel. The temper is fine grit. The fabric is hard and well fired, and the color is orange. This jar does not resemble Fort Ancient ceramics, nor can it be classed with *Peters Cordmarked*. It is however, nearly identical with a vessel from the late Hopewellian Ginther Mound in Ross County, Ohio (Prufer, 1968:43, Figure 7E; 44, Pl.8a), and with a similar vessel from the late Hopewellian Rutherford Mound in Illinois which has yielded a radiocarbon date of 432

RIM CLASSES

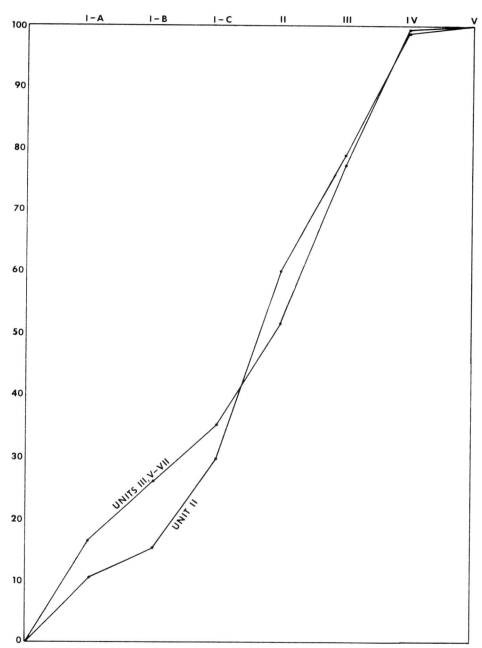

Figure 10. Cumulative frequency polygons for Baum Cordmarked Incised, var.
Blain rim classes from various units.

A.D. (Fowler,. 1957). In connection with this vessel, which we identify as *McGraw Cordmarked* on formal grounds, it should be noted that Feature 2 also yielded *Peters Cordmarked* and *Peters Plain* pottery as well as the earliest date for the Blain site. From the distribution of these sherds in the feature, we must conclude that the vessel in question is part of the primary deposit and must therefore be contemporary with the occupation of the site, notwithstanding its typologically early attribution.

The Blain ceramic assemblage is remarkably homogeneous. The overwhelming majority of the pottery is of one type, *Baum Cordmarked Incised, var. Blain.* In all features and excavation units this type is absolutely dominant. Although it is apparent from the preceding discussion that *Baum Cordmarked Incised, var. Blain* is a complex type which, because of its many and varied attributes, should reveal trends of change, if indeed such trends exist, a statistical analysis of all sherds from all features indicated no significant distributional variations. This proved true for such attributes as rim decoration, rim form, and thickness. Figure 10 shows the distribution of rim classes for Units II, III, and V–VII, the excavation units with samples large enough for meaningful analysis. This chart shows no significant differences between units. From these data we conclude that, on the basis of our excavations, the site is completely homogeneous and that its temporal span was limited indeed. This matter will be discussed in more detail in the chapter dealing with chronology.

The only other ceramic type that was represented in any quantity is *Baum Shell–Tempered, var. Blain.* Again, as in the case of *Baum Cordmarked Incised, var. Blain,* the uniformity of this pottery in type and distribution is consistent and shows no significant trends. The residual sherds constitute too small a sample for significant study. With the exception of the *McGraw Cordmarked* vessel from Feature 2, these residual sherds are neither chronologically nor in a broad cultural sense out of place at Blain Village.

VI

The Flint Industry

The flint industry from Blain Village proved to be extensive and interesting. Before presenting a formal analysis of the artifacts and débitage, a few comments are in order on the availability of comparative materials from culturally related or chronologically contemporary localities in south–central Ohio. Although a large number of such sites have been investigated in the past, their excavation and presentation in print were singularly inadequate. Among the directly relevant localities (Baum and Gartner in Ross County, and Baldwin in Fairfield County, Ohio), the available literature (Mills, 1904, 1906; Griffin, 1943:54) is virtually silent as far as flint artifacts are concerned. Statements and illustrations are usually restricted to the ubiquitous triangular points and to some casual remarks on a few other tools. Statistical data, metric information, and precise provenience data are lacking. Only in Griffin's classic study of the Fort Ancient Aspect (1943) can a few additional details be found as a part of his site summaries. In fact, for the Baldwin Site Griffin's summary constitutes the only information available because this locality has never been formally reported upon. When it is further considered that the older excavations were poorly controlled operations by any standards, and that even in the extant museum collections provenience data are most inadequate, it becomes apparent that nearly all the finds from the classic localities are virtually useless for purposes of comparison.

This leaves us with only two major localities which can profitably be exploited for comparative statements. They are Graham Village in Hocking County, Ohio, excavated in 1965 and published in 1967 (McKenzie, 1967), and Chesser Cave in Athens County, Ohio, excavated and published in the same years (Prufer, 1967a). The former is a village site of vaguely Baum affiliation, the latter is a Late Woodland rockshelter. Both are chronologically within the range of the dates obtained for the occupation of Blain Village. Both localities yielded flint assemblages of sufficient bulk to permit meaningful comparisons. In the following analysis the comparative data will be discussed in the context of the diverse tool categories established for Blain. In the final discussion of this chapter, the overall comparative information will be presented in tabular form. The following table summarizes the basic statistics for the Blain flint assemblage:

Projectile points	376
Fine bifacial knives	59
Drills	50
Other artifacts	417
Cores	202
Specialized chippage	8
Chippage	6626
Total:	7738

To the best of our ability all the chippage was recovered. Excluded from the chippage count are surface chips and chips derived from the plowzone. As far as artifacts and cores are concerned, surface and plowzone material is included in the analysis. In the presentation below, the ratio of *in situ* to surface materials is given for each artifact category. Unless otherwise stated, the within-site distribution of tools proved to be uniform in the sense that it did not indicate potentially significant patterns of either cultural or chronological significance.

A few additional comments are indicated regarding the analysis of the chippage. In recent years much attention has been devoted to the analysis of flint débitage from archaeological sites. We do not doubt the value of such analyses. In the case of Blain Village, however, we have not elected to undertake this time consuming task for the following reasons. Blain Village was shallow; in the main, the original occupation floors were disturbed by plowing and fluvial scouring. Thus all chances of discovering discrete activity areas on the original site surface were eliminated. Clearly, the greatest possible validity of detailed chippage analysis rests upon the study of such undisturbed activity areas. In the case of Blain Village, therefore, the value of a débitage analysis would be reduced to a mere investigation of chipping techniques on a large body of material of doubtful origin and presumably considerable time depth within the site's occupational history. Inasmuch as it is thus impossible to isolate individual activities or evidence for the manufacture of discrete tools, and inasmuch as we must assume that various ways of dealing with flint were used by various people for the production of various tools, an analysis of the available heterogeneous chippage seems to us, under the circumstances, a matter of small significance.

Most of the material recovered occurred in features such as pits and a few minor small sheet middens. With the exception of feature 4b, all of these features represent, in our opinion without doubt, evidence of refuse disposal. It seems to us that such refuse disposal is mostly a matter of a casual sweeping of waste materials, and objects deemed useless by the aborigines, into these "dumps". Also— and the evidence bears this out by inspection—we must assume that the remains of multiple activities were thus disposed of in single features. Therefore we neither expected to, nor did we, find reflections of single discrete activities that might fruitfully be analyzed in terms of chippage. We did, however, carefully examine the débitage from these features and have introduced in the following report detailed discussions of the débitage whenever this seemed to be even remotely warranted.

For raw material the inhabitants of Blain Village relied almost exclusively on locally derived flints and cherts. By far the overwhelming majority of all flint objects was made of pebble flints and cherts obtained from the gravels of the Scioto River. These pebbles were rather small, probably rarely exceeding 15 cms in diameter. Similar pebbles still occur in profusion along the banks of the Scioto and on gravel bars. The ultimate origin of these materials is probably quite heterogeneous. Some of it may have been transported downstream from as far north as central Ohio, while other pebbles may have had their origin in the hilly tracts of southeastern Ohio whence they were carried into the Scioto by some of the tributary streams such as the Salt Creek. Given the small size of the pebbles it is not surprising to find that a high percentage of the débitage consists of decortication flakes. In color the pebble flints and cherts range from dull brown to dull black; yellow and ochre hues also are common.

In addition to these strictly local materials, a fair although not precisely determinable percentage of the flint varieties used at Blain Village consists of Brush Creek and Zaleski flint. The former variety occurs in the Conemaugh member of the Pennsylvanian system, the latter in the Zaleski member of the Pennsylvanian system. Both varieties occur in quantity within twenty-five miles of the Blain Site in Vinton and Jackson Counties. In color and quality these flints are macroscopically quite similar to the pebble flints from the Scioto River. In fact, many of the flint pebbles may represent Zaleski and Brush Creek flint transported into the Valley by the Salt and Little Salt Creeks. Within the context of local prehistoric interaction patterns, all of these flints can probably be conceived of as being locally derived, i.e. their sources are well within easy range of the inhabitants of the central and lower Scioto Valley. There remains to be discussed the question of Upper Mercer flint. This characteristically grey to lustrous black material was extensively used in prehistoric Ohio (Prufer, 1963). It occurs in moderate quantities among the tools and débitage from Blain Village. Its principal source consists of massive outcrops in Coshocton County, Ohio, approximately one hundred miles northeast of the site. Thus, this material can not be considered of local derivation in the Scioto Valley. However, virtually indistinguishable outcrops of Upper Mercer flint occur in southeastern Ohio as well. In the light of this fact it is probably wise ". . .to assume that for a given locality the Upper Mercer flint present came from the nearest known outcrop." (Shane and Murphy, 1967: 334). In the case of the Blain materials such outcrops would be located in Vinton County, well within the range of the other raw materials utilized at the site.

Finally, less than one percent of all flint objects from Blain Village are made of Flint Ridge flint from Licking County, Ohio. This colorful material, which is alien to the local area and which can easily be distinguished from other flint sources, was evidently of little importance to the Blain population, and for that matter, to flint knappers of Late Woodland and Fort Ancient affiliation in general. This stands in sharp contrast to the preceding Middle Woodland cultures whose flint assemblages indicate a very marked preference for Flint Ridge flint. In summary it can be stated that the Fort Ancient people of the Blain Site and other southern Ohio localities of the same cultural affiliation preferred and relied primarily upon local flint varieties for the production of tools. This kind of localism does, in fact, transcend the boundaries of the overall southern Ohio "Fort Ancient Culture Area"; it is even more specific. Just as we can infer on the basis of the Blain evidence that the bulk of flint at this site was derived directly from the river gravels a few hundred yards distant from the settlement, so it is apparent that at Graham Village in Hocking County, Ohio, local Upper Mercer flint outcrops some three miles from the site were used for obtaining raw material (McKenzie, 1967:74).

ANALYSIS OF FLINT TOOLS

Convex-based Triangles (88 specimens; Figure 11, D–F). Nineteen specimens are sufficiently complete for length measurements. In general these points are similar to those from Chesser Cave (Prufer, 1967a: 19–20). However, it should be noted that the Blain specimens are, on the whole, less carefully made. Frequently "humps" occur on one or both faces, where the knapper had not bothered to remove the thick apex of the point. Nonetheless, most of these points are finished specimens. Flint Ridge flint is represented with four points; the remainder of this series is made of local raw material. Of the total assemblage, 35 specimens were recovered *in situ*, beneath the plowzone. Fifty-two specimens represent surface and plowzone material. Neither metric nor qualitative distinctions were noted between the surface and *in situ* points. The following are the metric attributes of convex based triangles:

Length	Width	Thickness
N = 19	N = 76	N = 88
Range: 24—45 mm	Range: 12—30 mm	Range: 3—9 mm
Mean: 34.3 mm	Mean: 18.1 mm	Mean 5.1 mm

One of the Blain points was found embedded in the skeleton of Blain Mound Burial 6. As far as comparative data are concerned, we can merely point out that convex–based points were common at

Chesser Cave. On the other hand, at Graham Village only three such points were found, although this site is chronologically and culturally closely related to Blain. Metrically, the 3 specimens from Graham Village do not warrant comparison with the Blain series. The 24 points from Chesser do, however, permit this. The mean length for 15 measurable specimens here is 29.4 mm, the width of 20 measurable points is 19.2 mm, and the thickness of 22 specimens is 3.6 mm. These data indicate that in terms of length and thickness the two series would seem to be significantly different, whereas in width they are in agreement. The reason for these similarities and differences are apparent only as far as the thickness factor is concerned; the more careless execution of the Blain points, with their frequently occurring apical "humps", can be held responsible for the divergent thickness measurements. At the classic sites of the *Baum Phase*, convex–based triangles occur in some quantity at Baum and Gartner (Griffin, 1943:39, 48), whereas at Baldwin only 2 out of 147 triangular projectile points shared this basal configuration (Griffin, 1943:54). If nothing else, the extreme scarcity of convex-based triangles at the two Hocking Valley sites, as opposed to their common occurrence at Blain, Baum and Gartner in the Scioto drainage, underscores the distinctiveness of these two related culture groups.

Concave-based Triangles (24 specimens: Figure 11, G-I). Only three specimens were sufficiently complete for length measurements. In all essentials these points are similar to convex–based triangles, the differences being merely the matter of basal configuration. One point is made of Flint Ridge flint, the remainder of local raw material. Eleven points were recovered *in situ*, 13 from the surface or plowzone. No specific distribution patterns could be determined for the *in situ* series, nor did the latter show different attributes from the surface series. The following are the metric attributes of concave-based triangles:

Length		Width		Thickness	
N =	3	N =	22	N =	24
Range:	16—40 mm.	Range:	14—29 mm.	Range:	3—8 mm.
Mean:	29.0 mm.	Mean:	19.7 mm.	Mean:	5.1 mm.

Figure 11. Chipped flint.

One of the Blain points was found embedded in the skeleton of Blain Mound Burial 1; another in Burial 2. Concave-based points were common at Chesser Cave but virtually absent at Graham Village. For Baldwin no data are available. At Baum and Gartner concave bases appear to have been absent or very rare. As far as metric differences between points from the three sites with adequate date are concerned, they are less pronounced in the case of these points that in that of the convex-based triangles.

Straight-based Triangles (67 specimens; Figure 11, A–C). Fourteen specimens were sufficiently complete to permit length measurements. As in the case of the previously discussed types of triangular projectile points, the straight-based ones are in all essentials similar to the other variants, except insofar as the basal configuration is concerned. All Blain specimens are made of local flint varieties. Thirty–five specimens were found *in situ*, 31 are of surface or plowzone provenience. No significant distributions could be determined for the *in situ* points, nor were there any determinable typological differences between the latter and the surface specimens. The metric attributes of straight-based triangles are as follows:

Length	Width	Thickness
N = 15	N = 50	N = 67
Range: 22—40 mm	Range: 11—36 mm	Range: 3—8 mm
Mean: 32.8 mm	Mean: 18.9 mm	Mean: 5.0 mm

Although at Blain Village straight–based triangles are somewhat less common than convex–based forms, they are clearly one of the quantitatively most significant point categories at the site. Similarly, it would seem that at all other Fort Ancient sites of *Baum Phase* affiliation this type is either very common or, in fact, the dominant one. On the other hand, at Chesser Cave it is relatively rare. As far as metric data are concerned, straight–based triangles from Blain Village, Graham Village, and Chesser Cave are most similar if compared with the metric data for the other triangular points from these localities.

Unifacial Triangles (3 specimens: Figure 11, J), These tools are in all respects similar to bifacial triangles, except for the fact that they are unifacially chipped on thin flakes. Two of the specimens are concave–based, the third has a convex base. All specimens are made of local flint. The following are the relevant metric data:

Length	Width	Thickness
N = 1	N = 3	N = 3
Range: 33 mm	Range: 16—20 mm	Range: 4—6 mm
Mean —	Mean: 17.7 mm	Mean: 4.7 mm

Two specimens have *in situ* provenience data, the third is a surface find. No comparative data are available.

Coarse Triangles (54 specimens: Figure 11, K–L). These are crudely percussion-chipped morphological equivalents of the triangular pro-jectile points. As a rule they are in all dimensions larger than the fine triangles. On most specimens some fine marginal retouch is present. Although some of the Blain specimens may have been preforms for regular triangles, it can be stated with reasonable certainty that the majority constitutes finished tools. In addition to the marginal re-touching they show signs of utilization in the form of edge batter or mild grinding. The function of these tools is not clear. As far as wear patterns are concerned, there is evidence that some were used at the pointed end, others along the lateral edges, and a few along the basal edge. All specimens are made of local flint. Eighteen coarse triangles have *in situ* provenience data, 36 were found on the surface or in the plowzone. With the exception of one specimen which came from the mound fill, all other documented coarse triangles were found in regu-lar pits. The significance of this is not known. The following are the relevant metric data:

Length	Width	Thickness
N = 42	N = 49	N = 54
Range: 29—56 mm	Range: 17—44 mm	Range: 6—20 mm
Mean: 42.8 mm	Mean: 25.4 mm	Mean: 11.6 mm

Coarse triangles have also been noted at Graham Village and Ches-ser Cave. Although they are not mentioned in the old excavation reports of the classic sites, nor in Griffin's study of the Fort Ancient Aspect (1943), we are certain that they occurred at these sites as well. They are present in the collections from these localities.

Unidentifiable fragments of triangular projectile points (38 specimens). These consist of 32 tip fragments and six mid–sections of fine
triangular points. The numerical discrepancy between these two sub-
categories should be noted. All specimens are made of local flint.
Twenty–two were found *in situ*, 16 on the surface or in the plowzone.
One of the documented fragments was found embedded in the right
femur of Blain Mound Burial 1.

Chesser Notched Points (3 specimens Figure 12, D-F). These tools
fall well within the range of Chesser Notched points as defined by
Prufer (1967a: 21–22). One specimen has *in situ* provenience data;
the remaining two were found on the surface. The single specimen
with secure provenience data was found firmly embedded in the cervical vertebrae of Blain Mound Burial 3, an infant less than two years
of age. Thus, the association of these points with early Fort Ancient
cannot be doubted. This is the more interesting since the type has, to
our knowledge, not been reported from other early Fort Ancient
sites. It certainly was absent at Graham Village. On the other hand it
is a consistent trait at Late Woodland localities. Twenty-nine such
points were found at Chesser Cave; they have also been noted at Stanhope Cave and Rais Cave, both in Jackson County, Ohio (Prufer,
n.d.; Shane, n.d.). They are also present at the Late Woodland sites
of the Cole Complex in central Ohio (R.S. Baby, personal communication). The Blain specimens correspond in all essential attributes to
those of the type series. The following are the relevant metric data:

Length		Width		Thickness	
N =	1	N =	2	N =	3
Range:	58 mm	Range:	24—26 mm	Range:	7—8 mm
Mean:	—	Mean:	25.0 mm	Mean:	7.3 mm

All three specimens are made of local flint.

Small Side-notched Points (1 specimen; Figure 11, M). This small,
rather stubby specimen, made of local flint, was found *in situ* below
the plowzone in Feature 1, associated with typical Baum Cordmarked pottery. It has an expanded trianguloid blade, straight base,
and thick–lenticular cross–section. A slight median ridge is present.

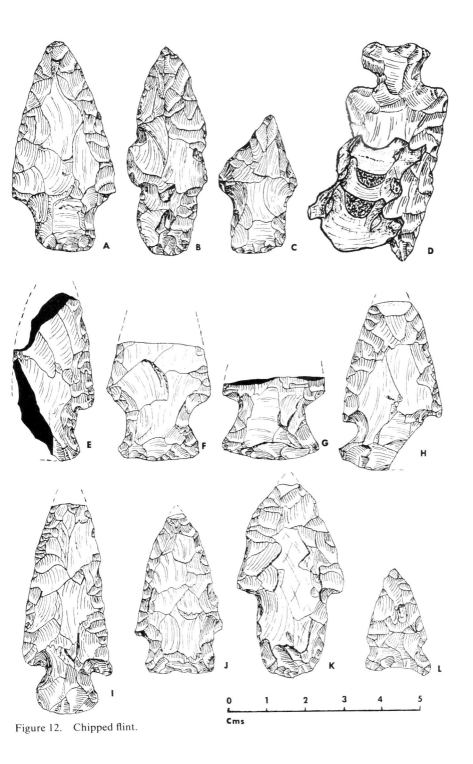

Figure 12.   Chipped flint.

The dimensions are: length: 27 mm; width: 19 mm; thickness: 6 mm. Similar points were found at Graham Village (McKenzie, 1967: 90, Fig, 7, K, L). Presumably many of the "notched points" from the classic sites were similar to this type.

Corner–notched Points (2 specimens). These are round–based, percussion–chipped, small, rather crude, corner–notched points with lenticular cross–sections. Both specimens were found on the surface; one is made of Flint Ridge flint, the other of local raw material. Both specimens are fragmentary, hence length measurements could not be taken. An estimate derived from the more complete specimen suggests that these points did not exceed 45 mm in length. The remaining metric data are as follows:

Width		Thickness	
N =	2	N =	2
Range:	23—26 mm	Range:	7—9 mm
Mean:	24.5 mm	Mean:	8.0 mm

A similar point was found at Chesser Cave (Prufer, 1967a:23). Related if not identical types were recovered from Graham Village (McKenzie, 1967), although they were not illustrated in the final report. As far as other early Fort Ancient sites are concerned no definite data are available; it is here suggested that they may be hidden among the "notched points" of the early excavation reports.

Raccoon Notched Points (1 specimen; Figure 11, N). A single point of this type was recovered from the surface of the Blain site. It is made of local raw material. In all respects it conforms to the type definition (Mayer–Oakes, 1955a: 85–87). Because of the fragmentary nature of the Blain specimen, length could not be determined. The other metric data are as follows: width: 17 mm; thickness: 6 mm. Similar points were found at Chesser Cave (Prufer, 1967a: 22–23) and at Graham Village (McKenzie, 1967, Figure 7m). Whether Raccoon Notched points occur at other early Fort Ancient sites as well is uncertain.

Straight–Stemmed Points (10 specimens; Figure 12, A–C). Typologically these points are difficult to define, mainly because of their crudeness. They are percussion–chipped, rather thick, and roughly thick–lenticular in cross–section. The blades are trianguloid with moderately straight sides, and the stems tend to be wide and massive. The basal configuration ranges from square to rounded. Basal thinning of sorts occurs on five specimens; three points are basally characterized by cortex. Two points are basally broken. Shoulders range from poorly to well defined. All specimens are made of local flint. Without exception they were recovered from the surface. The following are their metric attributes:

Length	Width	Thickness
N = 6	N = 10	N = 10
Range: 38—57 mm	Range: 21—27 mm	Range: 7—14 mm
Mean: 49.5 mm	Mean: 23.4 mm	Mean: 9.6 mm

In the absence of *in situ* provenience data for these points, their cultural attribution must remain in some doubt, the more so since Griffin (1943: Table XIV) does not list stemmed points as a trait of his early Fort Ancient Baum Focus, although in the text he refers somewhat doubtfully to the presence of such tools (1943:40). Four such points were found at Graham Village; they were absent at Chesser Cave. On the other hand, similar specimens occur in collections from Fort Ancient localities that we had occasion to inspect. Inasmuch as this type does not seem to be part of any other known cultural complex, we feel that, notwithstanding the poor provenience of the Blain specimens, they belong in the Fort Ancient complex. Certainly, many of the projectile point tip fragments recovered *in situ*, could well have been part of straight–stemmed points.

Middle Woodland Points (2 specimens; Figure 12, G). These well-made, long and thin expanded–stem points conform in every respect to the type definition (Converse, 1963:114). Both specimens were found on the surface. One is made of white Flint Ridge flint, the other of a light brown glossy material of unknown origin. Since both specimens are broken, length can only be inferred. The more complete specimen exceeded 60 mm in length, an estimate that probably applies to the other point as well. The remaining metric data are as follows:

Width	Thickness
N = 2	N = 2
Range: 24—26 mm	Range: 7—8 mm
Mean: 25.0 mm	Mean: 7.5 mm

In southern Ohio, *Middle Woodland Points* are usually associated with Hopewellian localities. As in the present case, they are usually made of non–local flint varieties, notably Flint Ridge flint. With some modifications, the type survives into Late Woodland times, where its derivative has been named *Chesser Notched* (Prufer, 1967a: 21–22). Similar points have been recovered from early Fort Ancient sites, although their precise context is not clear. Whereas it is well possible that the Blain specimens are intrusive, we do not exclude the possibility that the type was long–lived, perhaps lingering on to the end of the First Millenium A.D.

Middle Woodland Corner–Notched Points (2 specimens; Figure 12, H). These points are closely related to the classic Hopewellian *Synders Point* (Bell, 1958). They are characterized by excellent workmanship, deep corner notches, rounded or straight bases, wide triangular blades with expanding sides, and flat-lenticular cross-sections. Both Blain specimens are made of Flint Ridge flint which is the characteristic raw material for the type in Ohio. Both specimens were found *insitu*, one in Feature 1, the other in the Blain Mound fill. The relevant metric data are as follows:

Length	Width	Thickness
N = 1	N = 1	N = 2
Range: 62 mm	Range: 36 mm	Range: 6—8 mm
Mean: —	Mean: —	Mean: 7.0 mm

Although clearly a Hopewellian affiliated Middle Woodland type, these points have a disturbing habit of occurring in early Fort Ancient contexts. Under controlled conditions they were found at Graham Village (McKenzie, 1967: Fig. 7j). At the Baldwin Site in Fairfield County, Ohio, they occurred in good contexts (Griffin, 1943: Plate XIV, 3a), and they have been reported from other localities as well. In the light of the consistent recurrence of a few of these points in what would seem to be good contexts, we feel reluctant to reject them on typological grounds alone, the more so since at some of the localities in question no Middle Woodland components were noted whence these specimens might have been derived. The main argument, however, is the consistency with which the type occurs at early Fort Ancient sites. Thus, with some hesitation, we here consider the Middle Woodland Corner Notched points as part of the original assemblage of Blain.

Miscellaneous Projectile Points (6 specimens; Figure 12, I–L). This category includes a series of points which are definitely not part of the early Fort Ancient complex, and a few points which, being single specimens of undefined type, defy any kind of assured cultural attribution. Among the extraneous points a single *Brewerton Eared Notched* point (Figure 12, L) and one *Kirk Serrated* point are obviously of Archaic origin. Both specimens are surface finds; they conform to the type definition (Ritchie, 1961: 17, Coe, 1964:67). The Brewerton point, which is made of a white chert of unknown origin, is 30 mm wide and 7 mm thick. Being broken, no length measurements could be taken. The Kirk point is made of local flint. It is so fragmentary that no meaningful measurements could be obtained. In addition to these Archaic tools, a typical *Adena Ovate Base Stemmed* projectile point (Figure 12, K) was recovered from the surface. It is made of a yellow chert of unknown origin, and conforms in all respects to the type definition (Dragoo, 1963:178). The metric data are as follows: length: 51 mm; width: 28 mm; thickness: 9mm.

In addition to these definitely extraneous points, Blain Village yielded three untyped ones that may or may not be part of the original assemblage. The first of these is a stemmed, rather flat, square–based point with a triangular straight–sided blade (Figure 12, J). It is made of white Flint Ridge flint, and was found in Feature 1 below the plow-zone. The relevant metric attributes are as follows: length: 42 mm; width: 23 mm; thickness: 6 mm. The second specimen is a fragmentary, rather large, corner–removed point with a rounded base. The blade appears to have been expanded–tranguloid, and the cross–section thin–lenticular. Basal grinding and lateral grinding in the haft area are present. The workmanship is excellent. The raw material is Flint Ridge flint. The relevant metric data are: width: 27 mm; thickness: 6 mm. The point was found in Feature 15, below the plowzone. The third specimen is a fragmentary, long and slender, deeply corner–notched point with a markedly thinned and rounded base. In cross–section it is lenticular; the blade is straight–triangular. The raw material is local flint (Figure 12, I). The relevant metric data are as follows: width: 23 mm; thickness: 9 mm. This specimen too was found in Feature 15, below the plowzone. No comparative data for these points are available.

Unidentifiable Non–triangular Projectile Point Fragments (75 specimens). This category consists of 64 tip fragments, nine mid–sections, and two small basal fragments. Thirty–six specimens have *in situ* provenience data, 39 were found on the surface or in the plowzone. All but one specimen, which is made of pink Flint Ridge flint, are made of local raw material.

Trianguloid Bifacial Knives (24 specimens; Figure 13, N–O) These objects are morphologically similar to the straight and convex–based triangular projectile points. The latter variant is represented with 19, the former with four specimens. In addition, there is one knife with an irregular, sinuous base. These objects differ from triangular points in two respects. They are somewhat larger than the points, and they exhibit marked grinding or delicate chipping along one or both lateral edges. Also, their qualitative range is somewhat less uniform than that of the true points. All specimens are made of local flint. Eight specimens were found *in situ*, 16 on the surface or in the plowzone. The relevant metric data are as follows:

Length		Width		Thickness	
N =	2	N =	23	N =	24
Range:	30—48 mm	Range:	13—29 mm	Range:	4—11 mm
Mean:	39.0 mm	Mean:	21.2 mm	Mean:	6.8 mm

Similar knives occur at all early Fort Ancient sites. They have not been reported from Late Woodland contexts in southeastern Ohio.

Fine Bifacial Ovate Knives (35 specimens; Figure 13, M). These are moderately well chipped, bifacial ovates with fine marginal retouch which, for want of a better term, are here identified as knives. In cross–section they are lenticular. All but one specimen, which is made of Flint Ridge flint, are made of local raw materials. Eight of these objects were found *in situ,* 27 were recovered from the surface or

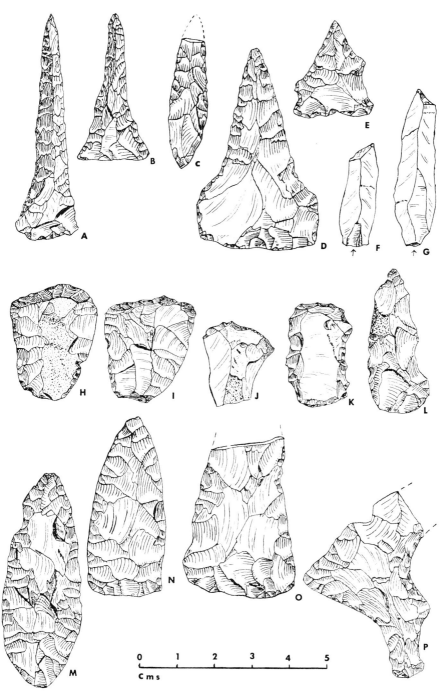

Figure 13. Chipped flint.

plowzone. The following are the relevant metric attributes:

Length		Width		Thickness	
N =	16	N =	26	N =	27
Range:	21—58 mm	Range:	16—35 mm	Range:	5—14 mm
Mean:	41.8 mm	Mean:	24.9 mm	Mean:	10.1 mm

Tools similar to these have been noted at all early Fort Ancient and Late Woodland sites, although they are not necessarily reported in the relevant literature.

Crude Bifacial knives (36 specimens; Figure 14, C). These tools are crudely percussion–chipped, thick, bifacial objects, ranging in shape from roughly ovate–trianguloid to discoidal. In some cases, there is evidence of at least partial consecutive marginal retouch. All specimens are made of local flint. Fourteen were found *in situ*, 48 on the surface or in the plowzone. The function of these objects is not clear, although scraping and rough cutting are suggested in many instances. They give the impression of having been manufactured rather casually. No metric data were taken because of the fragmentary condition of most of the specimens. By way of a general statement on dimensions it should be noted that, on the whole, these tools are rather small, with a suggested length range from 30—70 mm and width range from 10—25 mm. Although such objects are rarely reported in the literature, they appear to be present at all Fort Ancient and Late Woodland sites in the area.

Small Lozenge–shaped Bifaces (8 specimens; Figure 15, A–B). These are thick but narrow and elongated, lozenge–shaped tools with lenticular to diamond–shaped cross–sections. They show signs of considerable utilization along both lateral edges and tips. In five cases both ends taper to rough points, in three cases the presumed base is square and had been thinned on both faces. Much of the terminal and lateral wear consists of moderate to pronounced grinding. All specimens are made of local flint; two specimens were found *in situ*, the remainder was found on the surface or in the plowzone. The function of these tools is not clear. The following are the relevant metric data:

Length		Width		Thickness	
N =	7	N =	8	N =	8
Range:	36—47 mm	Range:	13—19 mm	Range:	5—10 mm
Mean:	41.3 mm	Mean:	16.6 mm	Mean:	7.7 mm

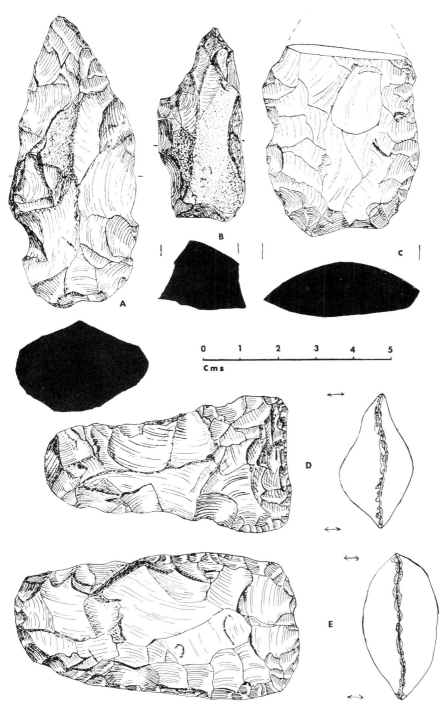

Figure 14.   Chipped flint.

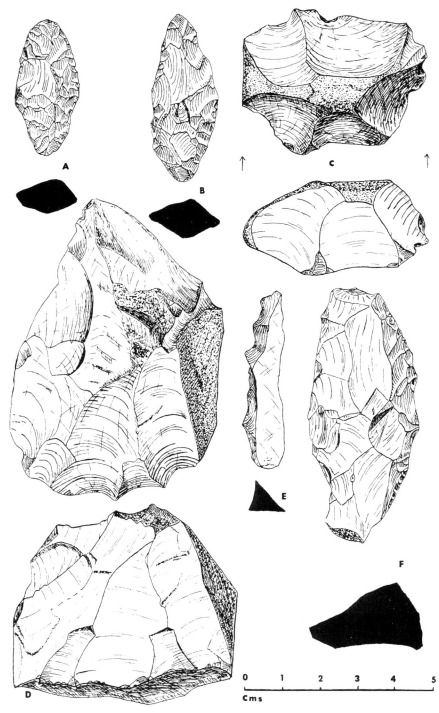

Figure 15.   Chipped flint.

Lozenge–shaped bifaces were found neither at Chesser Cave nor at Graham Village. On the other hand they occur at Scioto Valley Fort Ancient sites, although they are not specifically reported in the literature.

Drills (50 specimens; Figure 13, A–E). The following drill types were recovered from the Blain Site:

Trianguloid drills	21	(2 unfinished)
Drills with expanded rectangular bases	8	
Drills with expanded trianguloid bases	2	
Drills with expanded bases	5	(1 unfinished)
Drills with straight bases	3	
Side–notched expanded base drills	1	
Bi–pointed drills	1	
Drills, fragmentary and unidentifiable	9	(3 unfinished)
	50	

This classification is based on Leslie (1954). The trianguloid drills show the same range of basal variation as the triangular projectile points. Eight specimens are convex–based, seven are straight–based, four are concave–based, and two are indeterminate. The drill points were fashioned by constricting the triangle above the base. As a rule, the drill points above the base are diamond–shaped in cross–section, with sharp median ridges on both faces. This is true of the drill points on all other types as well. Most of the drills are carefully made. Many specimens show signs of extensive wear at the tip. All drills but one, which is made of Flint Ridge flint, are made of local raw materials. Twenty–four specimens were found *in situ*, 25 were found on the surface or in the plowzone. The following are the pooled metric data for all drill types; unfinished specimens are excluded from the measurements:

Length	Width	Thickness
N = 18	N = 36	N = 38
Range: 25—61 mm	Range: 8—32 mm	Range: 4—9 mm
Mean: 37.3 mm	Mean: 16.8 mm	Mean: 5.4mm

Comparative data for drills are somewhat better than in the case of other flint tool categories. Among the four drills at Graham Village, all but one type, the T–shaped drill, are also represented at

Blain. At Baum, the "...most common types were the cylindrical single and double–pointed specimens;" (Griffin, 1943: 40). No specific data are available for Gartner. At Baldwin drills are similar to those from Blain and Graham Village (Griffin, 1943: Plate XIV). It is interesting to note that the most common drill types at Baum are very scarce at the Blain Village. At Chesser Cave, T–shaped drills, absent at Blain, are well represented.

True Parallel–sided Blades (18 specimens; Figure 13, F–G). These tools are entirely similar to the numerous plain blades and blade tools from Chesser Cave (Prufer, 1967a:28–29). They conform to the standard definition of unifacial blades well known from the Old World Upper Palaeolithic, and recently defined in the context Middle Woodland Hopewellian blades by Pi–Sunyer (1965; 60–62). As in the case of Chesser Cave, the Blain specimens are somewhat cruder than Hopewellian blades. In cross–section they are triangular, i.e. they have a single median ridge on the upper face. All specimens show signs of utilization. Five blades have intentional "nibbled" marginal retouch which, in two instances, is on the pointed tips. One blade is made of Flint Ridge flint, the remainder of local raw material. Thirteen specimens were found *in situ*, five on the surface or in the plow-zone. The following are the metric attributes of blades:

Length	Width	Thickness
N = 11	N = 18	N = 10
Range: 21—47 mm	Range: 7—19 mm	Range: 2—5 mm
Mean: 30.9 mm	Mean: 12.1 mm	Mean: 3.2 mm

As stated above, blades similar to those from Blain are very common at Chesser Cave. They have also been noted at Graham Village (McKenzie, 1967:74). The situation at other early Fort Ancient sites is not clear. At Baum, numerous true blades and corresponding cores, both made of Flint Ridge flint, were found (Griffin, 1943:40). These, however, are clearly Hopewellian in origin. Their presence at Baum is not surprising since the village was located within the confines of the spectacular Hopewellian Baum earthworks. The blades and cores are obviously intrusive. Griffin (1943:49) also notes blades from Gartner without specifying whether these are similar to those from Baum; if so, they certainly are not common at this site. We know of no Fort Ancient site with truly controlled data which produced Hopewellian–type blades as part of the original assemblage. We are thus inclined to reject the proposition that Hopewellian blades survived into Fort Ancient times; the more so, since they have not been recovered from any Late Woodland site. As stated, at Baum the situation is fairly clear. If indeed the blades mentioned by Griffin for Gartner are typologically Hopewellian, we suggest here too the presence of a Middle Woodland locus which could be held accountable for these tools. Such a locus would not be surprising since the Gartner site is located in that stretch of the Scioto Valley which produced the densest clusters of Hopewellian occupations and ceremonial centers.

In no sense can the blades from Blain, Graham, and Chesser Cave be compared with Hopewellian blades. Although they are typologically true blades, they are quite different; they were probably produced by a somewhat different technique of striking blades, and they are almost never made of Flint Ridge flint, the overwhelmingly preferred raw material for Middle Woodland blades.

Bifacially Chipped Endscrapers (12 specimens; Figure 13, H–I). These tools are small to medium–sized endscrapers on flakes. They are trianguloid in outline, and plano–convex in cross–section. The distal, functional end is universally wider than the proximal, non–functional end. The former is delicately chipped from the flat ventral face at a moderately steep angle. Ten of the Blain specimens are made of local flint, two of Flint Ridge flint. Three scrapers were found *in situ*, the remainder on the surface or in the plowzone. The following are the relevant metric attributes:

Length		Width		Thickness	
N =	11	N =	12	N =	12
Range:	29—58 mm	Range:	17—30 mm	Range:	6—19 mm
Mean:	39.0 mm	Mean:	22.7 mm	Mean:	10.2 mm

Neither Graham Village nor Chesser Cave produced endscrapers similar to those described. Nor is there anything in the older literature on the classic localities that suggests the presence of such tools.

On the other hand, collections from numerous Fort Ancient sites which we have had occasion to inspect show that such scrapers are fairly common constituents of these assemblages.

Endscrapers on Unifacial Flakes (4 specimens; Figure 13, J–K). These are very poorly made tools on small unifacially worked flakes. The rounded scraping edges are minimally retouched. In all respects these tools are similar to those from Chesser Cave (Prufer, 1967: 27–29). All specimens are made of local flint. *In situ* provenience data are available for two specimens. The following are the relevant metric attributes:

Length	Width	Thickness
N = 4	N = 4	N = 4
Range: 19—44 mm	Range: 17—28 mm	Range: 4—13 mm
Mean: 28.0 mm	Mean: 22.0	Mean: 7.5 mm

No endscrapers on unifacial flakes were found at Graham Village. If they occurred at other early Fort Ancient sites, this cannot be determined from the literature. Only Griffin (1943: 40, 54) notes that scrapers in general were rare and, specifically, that a single thumb–nail scraper was found at Baldwin.

Endscrapers on Core Chunks (2 specimens; Figure 16, D). These are well–defined endscrapers made on relatively amorphous core chunks. The lack of special shaping on these objects in general is sharply set off by the care that was taken in chipping the rounded scraping edges chipped from the flat basal face. Both specimens are made of local flint, and both were found *in situ*. The following are the relevant metric attributes:

Length	Width	Thickness
N = 2	N = 2	N = 2
Range: 39—41 mm	Range: 27—31 mm	Range: 11—18 mm
Mean: 40.0 mm	Mean: 29.0 mm	Mean: 14.5 mm

No comparative data are available. These tools were not noted at Chesser Cave and Graham Village.

Discoidal Scrapers (1 specimen). This fragmentary tool was made on a roughly discoidal–pyramidal, flat–based core chunk of local flint.

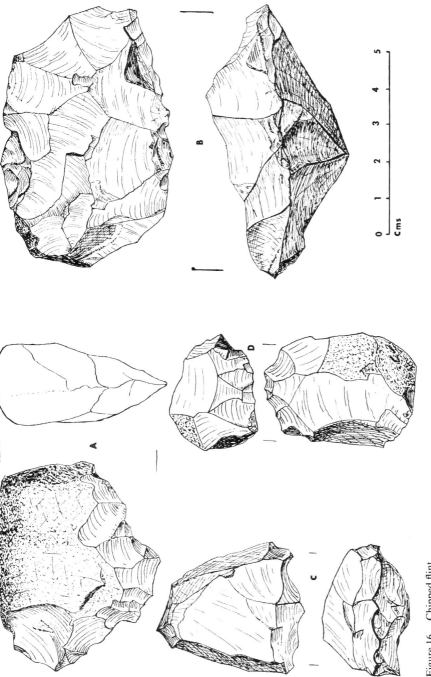

Figure 16. Chipped flint.

Originally the functional retouch flaking encompassed the entire edge of the tool. It was found *in situ*. The metric data are as follows: maximum diameter: 43 mm; thickness: 17 mm. No comparative data are available.

Perforators (2 specimens; Figure 13, L). This category consists of one thin, ovoid biface, the narrow end of which was worked into a fine perforator point. The second object is a unifacial, trianguloid, decortication flake with a similarly worked point. Both specimens are made of local flint, and both are surface finds. Their metric attributes are as follows:

Length		Width		Thickness	
N =	2	N =	2	N =	2
Range:	31—39 mm	Range:	21—26 mm	Range:	6—9 mm
Mean:	35.0 mm	Mean:	23.5 mm	Mean:	7.5 mm

No comparative data are available.

Chipped Celts (10 specimens; Figure 14, D–E). These are bifacially percussion–chipped core tools with rounded and finely chipped wide polls, and tapering, often almost pointed bits. The cutting edge at the poll–end invariably shows signs of considerable utilization. In cross–section these tools are lenticular. Maximum width is invariably near the poll. All specimens are made of local flint. Five were found *in situ*, the remainder on the surface or in the plowzone. The following are the relevant metric data:

Length		Width		Thickness	
N =	9	N =	10	N =	10
Range:	49—84 mm	Range:	31—49 mm	Range:	10—27 mm
Mean:	72.2 mm	Mean:	40.9 mm	Mean:	18.2 mm

No chipped celts were found at Graham Village. On the other hand they do occur at least at some other early Fort Ancient sites (Griffin, 1943:49). The specimens from Chesser Cave (Prufer, 1967a: 32–33), are much cruder and less well-defined than those from Blain Village.

Core Picks (5 specimens; Figure 14, A–B). These are medium–sized, crudely percussion–chipped, elongated core tools. The distal ends have been worked to a pick–like point; the proximal ends are thick; and in all but one case, which is chipped, the butt–ends preserve the original pebble cortex. All specimens are made of local flint. Three were found *in situ*, two on the surface or in the plowzone. The following are the relevant metric data:

Length		Width		Thickness	
N =	5	N =	5	N =	5
Range:	46—77 mm	Range:	19—37 mm	Range:	15—22 mm
Mean:	56.8 mm	Mean:	30.2 mm	Mean:	18.6 mm

Similar picks were found at Chesser Cave. They did not occur at Graham Village. The literature does not mention picks from other early Fort Ancient sites.

Choppers (25 specimens; Figure 16, A–C). These tools are made on more or less amorphous core chunks; occasionally real cores were modified so as to serve as choppers. The chopping edge is invariably bifacial along one edge. In a number of cases the chipping along the functional edge alternates thus creating a sinouus or wavy working edge. All specimens are made of local flint. Fifteen choppers were found *in situ*, the remainder was recovered from the surface or plow-zone. The following are the relevant metric attributes:

Length		Width		Thickness	
N =	25	N =	25	N =	25
Range:	34—97 mm	Range:	26—57 mm	Range:	15—40 mm
Mean:	52.8 mm	Mean:	38.8 mm	Mean:	22.7 mm

Similar choppers were found at Graham Village, although they are not listed in the published report. They also occurred at Chesser Cave. They are not listed for the classic early Fort Ancient sites. However it is clear from the extant collections that these tools did occur there as well; they were simply not recognized.

Sidescrapers (1 specimen; Figure 15, F). A single large sidescraper made on an elongated core chunk was found on the surface. The raw material is local flint. This specimen is roughly plano–convex in cross –section. The functional edge is steeply and delicately retouched along its entire length. The tool is very distinctive. Its metric attributes are: length: 68 mm; width: 31 mm; thickness: 17 mm. No comparative data are available.

Undefinable Tools on Core Chunks (99 specimens). This category consists of amorphous, obviously shaped tools, of indeterminate function and typology. These objects occurred in roughly equal proportion in all features and on the surface. As a rule one or more edges were more or less crudely and casually retouched. Evidence of utilization is present on many specimens. Measurements are obviously not significant beyond maximum and minimum dimensional ranges. The smallest object is 27 mm in maximum diameter; the largest measures 78 mm. All specimens are made of local flint. Similar tools are common at all Fort Ancient and Late Woodland sites, although they are not necessarily reported in the literature. No particular effort was made at Blain to collect them systematically from the surface. Hence the present sample is not as representative as that of other tool categories.

Retouched Flakes (161 specimens). Both the excavated units and the surface produced numerous, amorphous, retouched flakes, ranging from 19 mm to 51 mm in length. These objects all exhibit more or usually less consecutive fine, marginal, retouch clearly suggesting deliberate application. Beyond noting their existence, little more can be said regarding their function. They suggest casual utilization of an impromptu nature. Two specimens are made of Flint Ridge flint; all others consist of local raw material. No attempt was made to collect them systematically from the surface. As a result the overwhelming majority in the present collection came from excavated features where the tools did not show a specific pattern of distribution. Although they are not always reported in the literature, they are obviously present at all Fort Ancient and Late Woodland sites.

Core Tools with Ground Working Edge (1 specimen). This object is fundamentally a flat–based core. The original striking platform was modified by fine chipping, and its edge was subsequently heavily ground either by use or intention. This tool is made of local raw material; it was found *in situ*. The metric data are: length: 47 mm; width: 55 mm; thickness: 27 mm. No comparative data are available.

Flint Hammerstones (3 specimens). All 3 hammerstones are small, none exceeding 50 mm in maximum diameter. They are made of local flint. Two specimens were found *in situ*, one on the surface.

Miscellaneous Special Tools (2 specimens; Figure 13, P; Plate XI, E). The objects in this category are presumed to be ceremonial objects. The first of these is a large, triangular, bifacial tool, found near the right hand of Blain Mound Burial 2. Its position in relation to the skeleton suggests that it originally was equipped with a short handle; presumably it served as a dagger. The chipping is carefully executed; marginal retouch on both faces is delicate and prominent. The raw material is local. Metric data ard as follows: length: 136 mm; width: 67 mm; thickness: 14 mm. Similar dagger–like tools were found at the Voss Mound in Franklin County, Ohio, where, however, they were interpreted—erroneously, as we believe—as Late Woodland (Baby, Potter, and Mays, 1966).

The second object in this category is an eccentric bifacial object. It is made of local flint and was found in Feature 10. Although it is fragmentary, its curious shape could be reconstructed. Inasmuch as the shape cannot easily be described, the illustration Figure 13, P) will have to serve *in lieu* of a detailed description. The object is carefully chipped. Along all edges it is ground to a moderate extent. No comparative data are available.

Cores (202 specimens; Figure 15, C–D; 16, B). The Blain site yielded three types of cores. The most common variety is the *standard, flat–based core*. Its shape was largely controlled by the available raw material which is pebble chert or flint from the local Scioto gravels. Almost invariably these pebbles were small, probably not exceeding 120 mm in diameter. In the case of the standard flat–based cores from the site, the smooth flat pebble cortex provided a natural striking platform. Thus no platform preparation was necessary in most cases. This

Plate XI. (A) Bi-pitted stone; (B-D) Concretion cups; (E) Flint dagger from Burial 2.

is in sharp contrast to generally similar cores from Chesser Cave. Here the raw material was "mined" from flint deposits, and consequently the striking platforms had to be prepared by cleavage. For reasons that are only partly understood, but which almost certainly relate to the vagaries in cleaving striking platforms, core rejuvenation was frequently necessary. Hence, rejuvenation flakes are common at Chesser Cave. At Blain the natural pebble platforms rarely necessitated this; hence rejuvenation flakes are as uncommon as rejuvenated cores. In general the standard flat–based cores were worked to a point where further utilization proved no longer profitable. In other words, most cores recovered are exhausted.

A total of 190 standard flat–based cores was recovered from the Blain site. One of these is made of Flint Ridge flint, one is made of Elkhorn Creek flint from Kentucky, and the remaining 188 specimens consist of local raw materials. As in the case of retouched flakes and worked core chunks, no particular attention was given to the collection of surface specimens. As a result 122 cores in the present sample have *in situ* provenience data; while only 66 specimens were recovered from the surface or plowzone. As in the case of the Chesser Cave specimens, approximately one third of the entire series consists of cores that were secondarily used as core scrapers, the striking platform edge forming the functional edge. The only other aspect of these cores that should be commented upon is the fact that at Blain as well as at Chesser Cave and Graham Village these cores were frequently not only struck from a single platform, but from double and multiple platforms. These multiple platforms were achieved by a simple twist of the core to a point where an area suitable for use as a platform was present. On some of the cores the twist amounted to 180 degrees, resulting in what can best be called pseudo–bipolar cores. The metric data on a sample of 50 standard flat–based cores are as follows:

Vertical–Length		Basal Width		Basal Thickness	
N =	50	N =	50	N =	50
Range:	20—85 mm	Range:	10—63 mm	Range:	8—44 mm
Mean:	37.5 mm	Mean:	36.1 mm	Mean:	21.2 mm

No data on cores from the classic early Fort Ancient are available in the literature. The cores from Graham Village, although they are not discussed in the site report (McKenzie, 1967), are similar to the cores from Chesser Cave which, in turn, differ from the Blain cores only in the matter of the nature of the raw material.

The second type of core found at Blain is the *Conical Core*. This type is worked around the entire basal edge, rather than along one segment of the striking base only. In the case of the three Blain specimens, all platforms were prepared by cleavage. All conical cores are made of local flint, and all were found *in situ*. The metric data are as follows:

Vertical Length   Basal Diameter

N =   3   N =   3
Range: 24—51 mm   Range: 18—42 mm
Mean: 36.6 mm   Mean: 27.6 mm

No similar cores have been reported from any other early Fort Ancient or Late Woodland site.

The third type of core found at Blain Village is the *Biconical Core*. Such cores are roughly discoidal chunks of flint that were alternately reduced on both faces. Nine biconical cores were found at Blain; all are made of local flint. Two specimens were recovered *in situ*, the remainder from the surface or plowzone. The metric data are as follows:

Vertical Length   Basal Diameter

N =   9   N =   9
Range: 24—71 mm   Range: 25—50 mm
Mean: 38.8 mm   Mean: 32.4 mm

No comparative data are available from either early Fort Ancient or Late Woodland sites.

Core Trimming Flakes (8 specimens; Figure 15, E). These flakes, resulting from the rejuvenation of standard flat–based or conical cores, have been described at length in the report on Chesser Cave (Prufer, 1967a: 37). The Blain specimens, although few in number, conform entirely to the type description. They are made of local flint, and they were all found *in situ*. No measurements were taken, because metric data were deemed insignificant in the case of these objects.

Chippage (6,626 specimens). The chippage from Blain is remarkably uniform as to size and raw material provenience. The overwhelming majority of the chips is less than 25 mm in maximum diameter; chips exceeding 50 mm in diameter are exceedingly rare. Wherever flotation was used as a means of separating artifacts from the soil, very small chips were found. Since this technique was used only in the case of features that deserved this treatment on grounds other than the recovery of chippage, it is here assumed that the "actual" majority of the débitage originally present in the excavated areas was less than 15 mm in diameter. Inasmuch as the local flint pebbles used at Blain are small in size, the metric attributes of the débitage are not surprising.

We have designated as chippage all those flint objects which cannot readily be classified as either artifacts or cores. Thus, the chippage not only includes presumed waste flakes *sensu structu*, but also such amorphous core chunks as might have resulted from the primary breaking up of flint pebbles. On the whole, true flakes considerably predominate over core chunks. Decortication flakes are common; this is undoubtedly a reflection of the pebble raw material and its size.

More than 99% of all the raw material is of local derivation in the sense of the definition presented in the introductory section to this chapter. Among the demonstrably non–local flint varieties represented in the Blain débitage, only two chips could not be identified as to raw material origin. The remainder consists of Flint Ridge material.

Two further observations on the chippage are in order. Flakes of bifacial retouch, i.e. flakes struck off finished tools or semi–finished preforms, are rare. The same is true of flakes with "overhanging" striking platforms which Fitting, (1967) considers characteristic of the soft hammer technique.

In the main it can be said with some assurance that the débitage (and of course the presence of numerous cores and decortication flakes) indicates that all stages in the manufacture of flint artifacts are well represented at Blain Village. This observation implies that the differences noted in the typological composition of the flint tools from Blain and such contemporary sites in the hilly sections of southeastern Ohio as Chesser Cave, are real indeed, for these differences are paralleled by differences in the nature of the débitage and cores as well. Although this was not stated in the Chesser Cave report (Prufer, 1967a) because of the lack of controlled comparative assemblages, the nature of the waste material at Chesser Cave is very different from that of Blain. Suffice it to say here, by way of contrast, that at Chesser flakes with overhanging striking platforms were very common whereas at Blain they are rare. By the same token, at Chesser true blade tools and blade cores were of frequent occurrence. At Blain these elements are only sparsely represented. Finally, medium–sized to large flakes abound at Chesser, but are rare at Blain.

The chippage from Graham Village consists of 1,409 chips and core chunks. As noted, on the whole the débitage from this site is larger than that from Blain Village. In composition it is similar to that of Blain. The size difference between the two assemblages is probably a function of different types of raw material: pebble flint at Blain and quarry flint at Graham. As far as size is concerned, the same argument holds true for Chesser Cave.

As previously noted, particular attention was given to such chippage from Blain that might reflect discrete activities. The closest evidence for this came from Feature 11 which contained among its sparse collection of débitage thirty-two small chips of Flint Ridge flint obviously struck from a single core. A few of the chips could be reassembled. They indicate with their plain striking platforms and well developed bulbs of percussion the application of what Fitting (1967) has called the hard hammer technique. Five of these chips were decortication flakes removed from a slab–like piece of flint. In the absence of the actual core and the ultimate end–product of the manufacturing process, nothing further can be said about this material. None of the flakes exceeds 30 mm in maximum diameter.

DISCUSSION

The most striking aspect of the flint tools from Blain Village is the absolute preponderance of triangular projectile points. Within the total series of points (N = 376) triangles constitute 72.87 percent of the assemblage. Only 27.13 percent (N = 102) consist of other point types. With the exception of the coarse ones (N = 54), the triangles are almost certainly arrow points. It is obviously not clear whether they were predominantly used for hunting or war. It is, however, suggestive that among the five projectile points found embedded in the skeletons of the Blain Mound, four specimens were triangles. Neither in general terms nor in terms of the various types of triangles, as defined by basal configuration, could specific distribution patterns be established within the features of the site. This is also true of other flint artifacts. In other words, triangles occurred everywhere. The only exception is the *Coarse Triangle*. Nearly all *in situ* specimens of this type were found in pits. Fracturation patterns on broken triangular projectile points reveal a number of cases with torsion fractures as opposed to clean impact breaks. The same pattern was noted at Chesser Cave (Prufer, 1967a: 38).

The non–triangular projectile points present certain problems. If we exclude the Archaic and Early Woodland points which are obviously not part of the legitimate Blain assemblage (although they might have been secondarily used by the Blain people), we are left with fourteen points which are sufficiently complete for purposes of discussion. Among these, some have previously been found in Fort Ancient and/or Late Woodland contexts. Notably the *Chesser Notched* type should be mentioned here. Although this kind of point had thus far only been reported from Late Woodland localities, its occurrence at Blain, embedded in the cervical vertebrae of Blain Mound Burial 3, constitutes incontrovertible evidence that this type is part of the legitimate assemblage of the site. Other types, such as the straight–stemmed, small side–notched, and *Raccoon Notched* points, are entirely in context. On the other hand, the diverse Middle Woodland types would at first glance seem to be out of place. It should be noted, however, that such points occur at nearly all early Fort Ancient sites as a consistent minority type. This is especially significant in the cases of Blain and Graham, where they were recovered *in situ*. On the basis of these facts, we consider these points to be part of the original assemblage, notwithstanding the typological questions they raise.

One surprising aspect of the non–triangular projectile points is the fact that only 14 such specimens (excluding the three extraneous ones) were sufficiently complete for any kind of identification. The remaining 73 specimens consist of otherwise unidentifiable tips and mid–sections. This is in sharp contrast to the triangles where only 38 specimens were found to be too fragmentary for further identification. It should be noted that this pattern holds true at Chesser Cave as well; there unidentifiable triangles are represented by seven specimens, whereas the non–triangular tips and mid–sections amount to 176 specimens. On the basis of this evidence we would argue that at both sites, regardless of the different cultural affiliations involved, the function to which these different point categories were put, must have been quite similar. One further comment is in order. At Chesser Cave as well as at Blain, the ratios of mid–sections to tips among the non–triangular points are very similar:

Table 6.   Distribution of projectile point tips and mid-sections from Blain and Chesser Cave.

	Tips	Midsections
Blain	64	9
Chesser	111	75

The same holds true for triangles at Blain; here tips outnumber mid–sections by a ratio of 32:8. Since Chesser Cave yielded only seven fragmentary triangles, no meaningful comparative statement can be made for this site. Because of the over–all paucity of fragmentary points at Graham, the material from this site is excluded from this discussion.

At Blain none of the tip sections could be matched with basal or medial fragments. As in the case of Chesser Cave (Prufer, 1967a: 38) we take this to imply that tip sections may have been accidentally retrieved from the carcasses of hunted animals after the former had been brought back into the settlement for processing and consumption. In contrast, basal and medial sections of shattered points were probably discarded "in the field", when broken points were replaced on the shafts of arrows and spears.

To speculate on the function of the flint tools other than projectile points is a fruitless enterprise. In some instances, such as with hammerstones and drills, obvious functions are suggested. In the case of the roughly made tools no attempt at interpretation is made in this report, beyond noting that the diversity of tool types involved is probably a function of differential utilization.

As far as comparative statements are concerned, it should be kept in mind that because of the inadequate data available for the materials from the classic sites, no attempt has here been made to match these diverse assemblages with Blain. This restricts comparison to Chesser Cave and Graham Village. In terms of absolute quantity and typological diversity it is interesting to note that Blain and Graham, which represent closely related facets of early Fort Ancient in comparable valley bottom locations, are very dissimilar. Graham Village is almost impoverished by comparison with Blain. On the other hand, Chesser Cave, a Late Woodland cave occupation, is in many ways quite closely related to Blain as far as flint is concerned. The following table illustrates this point:

Table 7. Distribution of flint artifact classes from Blain, Graham, and Chesser Cave.

	Blain	Graham	Chesser
Projectile points	376 (42.15%)	101 (58.05%)	348 (37.37%)
True blades	18 (2.02%)	7 (4.02%)	80 (8.59%)
Fine knives	59 (6.61%)	5 (2.87%)	— —
Endscrapers	18 (2.02%)	— —	115 (12.35%)
Drills	50 (5.61%)	4 (2.30%)	10 (1.07%)
Other tools	371 (41.59%)	57 (32.76%)	372 (40.60%)
	892	174	925

Chippage and cores are omitted from the above table because the large quantities of objects in these categories would have obscured the percentage differences among the tools proper. The following table illustrates the site–to–site differences between the débitage categories:

Table 8. Distribution of flint debitage categories from Blain, Graham, and Chesser Cave.

	Blain	Graham	Chesser
Chips	6,545 (96.89%)	1,409 (99.09%)	32,930 (99.66%)
Cores	202 (2.99%)	13 (0.91%)	80 (0.24%)
Rejuvenation flakes	8 (0.12%)	— —	31 (0.10%)
Total	6,755	1,422	33,041

Finally the artifacts from the three sites were considered in terms of numbers of classes present at each locality:

Table 9. Distribution of numbers of flint artifact classes from Blain, Graham, and Chesser Cave.

	Blain	Graham	Chesser
Projectile points	15*	10	14
True blades	1	1	1
Fine knives	2	1	—
Endscrapers	3	—	1
Drills	7	3	4
Other tools	14	4	19
Cores	3	1	1
Chips	2	2	2
Total	47	21	42

We are, at this time, in no position to interpret these differences and similarities in a meaningful way. The significant questions to be asked are: (1) How can the impoverished flint industry from Graham Village be explained (2) Why is this site so dissimilar from Blain, notwithstanding the fact that the excavations were of comparable scope? (3) Why are Chesser Cave and Blain seemingly so much more closely related, even though they actually are culturally disparate and ecologically quite differently adapted? Chesser was a winter hunting station in the hills, whereas Blain clearly was a full–blown agricultural village. The only constant at both sites is that they are on the same time horizon.

There is one other formal comparison that should be presented here. This pertains to the ratios of triangles as opposed to non–triangular projectile points from the three sites. The following table presents the relevant data:

Table 10. Distribution of triangular and other projectile points from Blain, Graham, and Chesser Cave.

	Blain	Graham	Chesser
Triangles	274 (72.90%)	86 (85.15%)	86 (24.71%)
Other points	102 (27.10%)	15 (14.85%)	262 (75.29%)
Total	376	101	348

It is apparent from this table that the data from Blain and Graham are in close agreement. At both sites triangles predominate; while at Chesser Cave this is not true. There is nothing unexpected about

*Excluding the obviously extraneous points.

this situation. The explanation is probably largely a matter of culture history. In Ohio triangular points are known to occur in Late Woodland assemblages, although they are always in the minority. On the other hand, at Fort Ancient localities triangles constitute invariably the overwhelming majority of all projectile points. We are convinced that to some extent these differences between Mississippian and Late Woodland sites, especially in the case of contemporary sites culturally differentiated as a function of ecological isolation, are a reflection of differential adaptations.

Differences and similarities between the three industries which are not reflected in the above formal tables, can be summarized as follows. At all sites predominantly local raw materials were used. Qualitatively the projectile points from the three localities differ somewhat, especially if Blain and Chesser Cave are compared. Metrically, significant differences have been noted between the Blain and Graham assembleges on the one hand, and the Chesser materials on the other hand. This is especially true of the coarse core tools. It does not solely appear to be a function of different types of raw material—small pebble flint versus quarry flint—because at Graham, where quarry flint was used, the tool dimensions are generally in line with those from Blain where pebble flint predominates. The coarse tools at Chesser are bigger and more massive than their counterparts from the other two sites. To some extent these differences would seem to reflect cultural selection, probably related to differential function. Finally, the chippage must briefly be considered. As pointed out earlier in this report, there are quantitative differences in the ratios of chip types from Blain and Chesser. By the same token, the chip categories at the latter site and at Graham are very similar in composition; this is in agreement with the postulated close cultural relationships between the two localities. As far as dimensions are concerned, the chippage from Chesser and Graham sites which relied on quarry flint, is statistically larger than that from Blain, where primarily small flint pebbles were used for raw material.

VII

Stone Artifacts

This category includes all stone tools and modified stone objects excluding chipped flint. Such artifacts occurred in all units and features of the site. Unless otherwise indicated, no specific distribution patterns were noted within the archaeological deposits. As far as raw materials are concerned, the Blain stone tools are all made on rocks which occur locally. To the extent to which this can be verified, this is also true of the stone tools from other early Fort Ancient sites. In terms of comparative trait distribution, the Blain assemblage does not seem to differ from those of other early Fort Ancient localities. Even those traits which are not specifically listed by Griffin (1943) could in nearly all cases be duplicated from our own knowledge of local collections and from data contained in various publications such as Converse (1966). As in the case of other artifact categories, Graham Village in the Hocking Valley constitutes the only well–known contemporary Fort Ancient locality which did not yield many of the traits here discussed as typical of the period. Unless otherwise stated in the following analysis, such traits were absent at this site. Excluding the widely diffused, angular sandstone fragments, the stone artifact category includes 148 objects.

Celts (20 specimens; (Plate XIII, A)). The ground stone celts from Blain vary considerably in size and shape. Eighteen specimens are made of hard base rock, two are made of slate, and one of limestone. The dominant type (Plate XIII, A) appears to be similar to that described by Griffin for the Gartner Site: "The most characteristic

Plate XII.   (A) Marine shell gorget and (B) strand of disc shell beads from Burial 5.
(C) slate gorget; (D–E) slate pendants.

shape is oval, with a wide bit and sides which gradually converge to a narrowed poll." (1943:50) Mills illustrates similar celts from Baum (1906:83), and they have also been noted at Baldwin. In cross–section they are thick–elliptical. The surfaces are ground near the bit, and smoothed over the rest of the body. Three complete specimens of this type were found. They are quite uniform in size. The following table gives the relevant metric data:

Table 11.   Metric data for selected celts from Blain.

Provenience	Material	Length	Width	Thickness
Feature 4a	Base rock	90	39	26
Surface	'' ''	88	51	27
Surface	'' ''	89	44	27

Two entirely fragmentary bits of this type were found in Feature 3 and on the surface.

Rectanguloid flat celts are represented by two specimens. One of these, found on the surface, is made of limestone. Its fragmentary condition permits only minimal measurements: length: 78+ mm, width: 44 mm, thickness: 21 mm. The second specimen is the poll end of a large flat celt found in Feature 1. Originally it was considerably longer than 100 mm; its width is 61 mm and thickness 19 mm. Both specimens were smoothed and ground in a manner similar to that of the type discussed above.

A single trianguloid slate celt was recovered from the surface. It is flat in cross–section. The surface was pecked and chipped. Its general condition is battered. Minimal grinding occurs at the bit. Maximum measurements are as follows: length: 75 mm; width: 38 mm; thickness: 15 mm.

Finally, there are twelve fragmentary specimens which either do not fit any of the types, or which are too fragmentary to permit meaningful identification. One specimen from the surface, was a large, fully polished celt with sharp lateral angles. Another, also from the surface, is represented by a sharply tapered poll–end; all extant surfaces are smoothed. Yet another surface specimen is represented by a markedly rounded and well–polished bit; the body was left fundamentally unaltered beyond some casual pecking. In addition to these more or less

describable specimens, there are nine entirely fragmentary, rather
large celts. The single slate specimen in this series was recovered
from Feature 23; it is ground on all extant faces. Among the remaining eight entirely fragmentary specimens, six were found on the
surface, one in Feature 1, and one in Feature 36.

As far as the typologically identifiable specimens are concerned,
the Blain celts are entirely in line with those from other early Fort
Ancient sites. The limited data on Late Woodland ground stone tools
suggest that celts from these complexes are typologically different
from Fort Ancient forms (Prufer, 1967a: 40).

Chisels (1 specimen; Plate XIII, B). This battered specimen, which
was recovered from Feature 2, is made of a granitic base rock. It is
narrow and slender, with a thick elliptical cross-section. The surfaces
are ground and pecked. The bit is narrow, and the poll comes to an
angular end. The chisel is 127 mm long, 31 mm wide, and 23 mm
thick. It is not reported in Griffin's Fort Ancient trait lists. On the
other hand, Converse (1966: 135) discusses such objects as of Mississippian derivation, noting that they are extremely rare. Nothing
similar has been reported from local Late Woodland sites.

Discoidal Stones or Chunkeys (2 specimens; Figure 17, E). One of
these is a fragmentary, apparently unfinished specimen recovered
from the surface. The depressions on the two faces were pecked out.
Neither the surfaces nor the depressions had been smoothed by grinding when the object was discarded. It is made of a coarse-grained
granitic rock. Its maximum diameter is 81 mm, and its maximum
thickness is 34 mm; minimum diameter at the center of the depressions is 10 mm. The second specimen was found in Feature 21. It is
made of grey, fine-grained granitic rock. The depressions and outer
circumference were carefully pecked out and smoothed. The dimensions are: diameter: 62 mm; thickness: 26 mm; minimum thickness at
the center of the depressions: 7 mm. Griffin notes that Chunkey
Stones are not particularly common in the *Baum Focus* (1943: 41).
They do not seem to occur east of the Scioto River. They are definitely not part of Late Woodland assemblages.

Bi–pitted Stones (3 specimens; Plate XI, A). These are flattened, round to oval, sandstone pebbles which bear on each flat face a more or less well–defined, pecked–out shallow depression. Along the edges they have well–defined battered areas, suggesting that these objects were used as hammerstones. Two of the specimens were found on the surface, the third in Feature 4b. Maximum diameters are 60, 87, and *Gorgets* (7 specimens; Figure 17, C–D; Plate XII, C, E). All of these objects are made of slate. Four were found *in situ*, and three were recovered from the surface. The most elaborate specimen were found in Feature 4b, where it was part of the presumed ceremonial bundle. (Figure 17, C; Plate XII, E). It is bell–shaped, with a single perforation drilled from one face near the apex, and a serrated lower edge. Both faces bear incised lines which do not, however, form a coherent pattern. The metric data are as follows: length: 35 mm; width: 24 mm; thickness: 4 mm. Unit III yielded a fragmentary, flat, bi–pointed gorget (Figure 17, D); there are no traces of perforations. On one face this specimen bears a few incised designs. A similar but undecorated fragment was recovered from the surface. Feature 27 yielded a rough, unperforated slate preform, sub–oval in shape. This object was apparently intended to become a gorget; it is 91 mm long, 58 mm wide, and 11 mm thick. Other surface specimens include a rectanguloid gorget with tapered sides and a sharp, axe–like lower edge (Plate XII, C). It has a single perforation, drilled from both faces, near the upper edge. At this edge too, there is a fractured perforation, indicating that this specimen had been reworked. The metric data are: length: 64 mm; width: 41 mm; and thickness: 7 mm. Finally, the surface and Feature 14 yielded one entirely fragmentary gorget each. No shapes can be determined. The specimen from Feature 14 was perforated. How typical any of these gorgets are for early Fort Ancient is not apparent from the literature. This statement also holds true as far as Late Woodland is concerned. Lastly, a comment may be in order regarding the raw material. All specimens are made of a grey–black slate. There is no evidence for the use of green banded slate so characteristic of earlier periods and cultures in Ohio. It should be noted that green banded slate is not indigenous to southern Ohio. The use of local black slates at Blain, serves to underscore the remarkable reliance of the Fort Ancient people on purely local raw materials, a

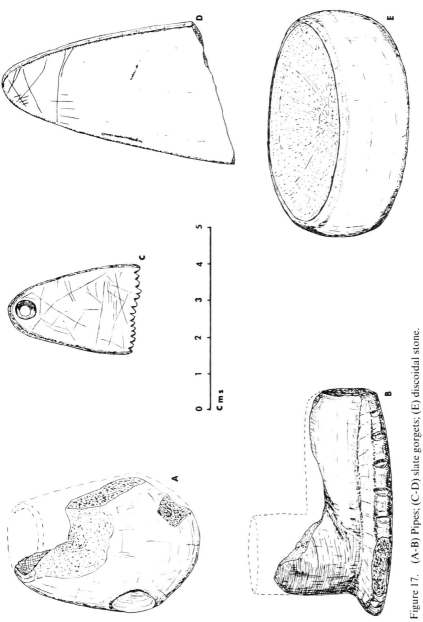

Figure 17. (A-B) Pipes; (C-D) slate gorgets; (E) discoidal stone.

point that has also been made in regard to the flint varieties used by the Fort Ancient folk (see p. 79).

Slate Pendants (1 specimen; Plate XII, D). This thin, plummet-shaped pendant is made of black slate. It has two notches for suspension near the apex, and was found in Feature 37. The metric data are as follows: length: 47 mm; width: 22 mm; thickness: 2 mm. No comparative data are available.

Slate Residue (56 specimens). This category consists of flat slate fragments that would appear to represent the residue from the manufacture of slate gorgets. All specimens are obviously altered, and many show traces of grinding along the edges. They were found in nine different features. Only three of these (Features 2, 5, and 6) yielded single fragments. Feature 23 had two fragments; Features 3 and 15 produced three specimens each; Feature 16 had four pieces, and two specimens were found in the general excavations. Feature 1 is represented with twenty-two fragments, and Feature 14 with seventeen. Some of the specimens could be fitted together. The fairly consistent multiple occurrence of such slate residue suggests that they are reflections of specific activity loci in the vicinity of the features involved.

Cup Stones (6 specimens). These are angular chunks of sandstone into one or both faces of which one or more cup–like depressions had been ground. Four of the Blain specimens were found *in situ*, the other two were recovered from the surface. None exceeds 280 mm in maximum dimension. The following table illustrates the distribution of cups on these stones:

Table 12.   Distribution of 'cup stones' from Blain.

Provenience	"Cups": Upper Face	"Cups": Lower Face
Feature 4b	3	2
Feature 4b	3	–
Feature 7	1	–
Feature 10	2	–
Surface	1	–
Surface	1	–

The depth of the depressions and their quality are variable, ranging from shallow and shoddily executed to deep and well-defined. Only one specimen deserves special comment. This is the cup stone with three depressions on one face only, found in Feature 4b. It is roughly rectangular and measures 280-by-170-by-80 mm in maximum dimensions. The "cups" are very well defined, and are up to 30 mm in depth. The specimen was found in the center of the pit, resting upside-down on the first massive charred walnut and corn deposit of this feature. Charred nuts and corn kernels were found to adhere to both the "cupped" face and to the inside of the depressions. This suggests that cup stones may have served some special purpose connected with processing food. In the light of the endless speculations as to function, which these rather drab objects have generated in the literature (Cf. Sheldon, 1925), this evidence is of some interest. Although Griffin (1943) does not list cup stones as a Fort Ancient trait, they occur in local collections from relevant sites. They have also been noted in Late Woodland assemblages (Prufer and McKenzie, 1966).

Sandstone Hoes (3 specimens). These are thin and flat, roughly oval slabs of sandstone which are crudely chipped along the edges. Such objects are usually interpreted as hoes. Typically the sandstone variety used for hoes is strongly silicified. Of the Blain specimens, however, only one hoe is made of this material; the others consist of local unsilicified rock. Two of the hoes were found on the surface, the third in Feature 17. The latter also happens to be the only unbroken specimen. It is 116 mm long, 96 mm wide, and 13 mm thick. Stone hoes are a characteristic trait of Fort Ancient. Thus far they have not been reported from Late Woodland localities.

Sandstone Mortars or Metates (2 specimens). Both specimens are fragments of flat sandstone slabs, the upper faces of which had been carefully ground to a slight concavity. The fragments suggest that originally both were square or rectangular in shape, probably not exceeding 300 mm in maximum dimension. They were found in Feature 4b in association with the charred vegetable remains that characterized this pit. Typologically they probably correspond to

Griffin's category of "Mortars." No data are available for the Late Woodland occurrence of these artifacts.

Sandstone "Palettes" or Whetstones (19 specimens). These are flat sandstone slabs not exceeding 150-by-100-by-30 mm in maximum dimensions. In shape they range from rectangular to irregularly oval. Grinding occurs on both faces and along the edges. Inasmuch as many specimens show traces of yellow or red pigment (ochre?) adhering to the surface, it is surmised that these objects probably were palettes. All specimens were found *in situ*. Significant clustering was noted only in the case of Feature 1 which yielded seven specimens. As far as site distribution is concerned, palettes were widespread. Similar objects occur at many Fort Ancient sites; they appear to be identical with Griffin's category of "Whetstones." Under controlled conditions a single specimen was found at Graham Village. They have not been reported from Late Woodland sites.

Sandstone Headrest (1 specimen). This is a perfectly symmetrical, carefully ground, rectangular, sandstone bar which had been placed under the head of Burial 5 of the Blain Mound. The specimen measures 670-by-80-by-50 mm. A similar bar was found at the Gartner site (Mills, 1904: 139). It should be noted that Burial 5 was the most elaborate burial of the mound, characterized, in addition to the sandstone headrest, by a large ocean shell gorget, and two bracelets made of shell beads.

Sandstone Fragments (ubiquitous). Sharply angular, large and small, sandstone fragments were found throughout the excavations. They would seem to represent the residue from the manufacture of sandstone objects. The sharply defined cleavage planes on these rock fragments indicate that they cannot be interpreted as fire–cracked rocks; they would seem to reflect deliberate modifications of the material. In Feature 33 they were found in considerable numbers, placed in a heap at the base of the pit.

Concretion Cups (15 specimens Plate XI, B–D). These objects are small, hollow concretions that were altered by minimal grinding to serve as small containers, probably paint cups. The majority—twelve specimens—are made of hematite concretions. Two specimens are made of limestone, and one of sandstone. In one of the limestone specimens, traces of yellow ochre were noted. Alterations of the natural objects are restricted to grinding along the rims and the interior hollows. Seven of the Blain specimens are complete. The range in maximum diameter from 26–50 mm, with a mean of 38.6 mm. The trait is common at Fort Ancient sites, and has been specifically described by Converse (1966:130). Concretion cups have also been noted at Late Woodland localities.

Utilized Pebbles (11 specimens). This category includes a series of nine pebbles of crystalline rock and two sandstone specimens. All show signs of utilization in the shape of grinding marks and/or batter, suggesting that at least some of the bigger specimens were used as hammerstones. Because of the grinding marks and because of the size and shape differential, it must, however, be assumed that some of these objects served other purposes. Possibly they were used for smoothing pottery. Broadly speaking, these rocks fall in three categories: medium-sized, round cobbles (four specimens), not exceeding 105 mm in maximum diameter; circular to oval flat pebbles (four specimens), not exceeding 65 mm in diameter; and very small round quartz pebbles with obvious traces of smoothing (three specimens). The last-named do not exceed 25 mm in maximum diameter. Localized batter is restricted to the large cobbles. All specimens were found *in situ*. No specific distributions were noted. The cobbles undoubtedly correspond to Griffin's category of "Round Hammerstones."

Abrading Stones (1 specimen). This is a multiple faceted, small piece of very coarse sandstone, 60 mm in maximum diameter, which bears several grooves, apparently the result of abrading or grinding. The nature of the grooves suggests that this object may have been used to shape bone tools, probably awls. It was found in Feature 4a. Abrading stones are a common Fort Ancient trait.

DISCUSSION

Nothing particularly meaningful can be concluded from the artifacts discussed in this chapter. As far as general distribution is concerned,

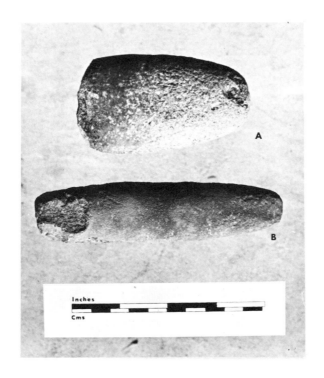

Plate XIII.   (A) Ground celt; (B) Ground chisel; (C) Clay cylinder from Feature 33.

these tools show little significant clustering. In terms of homogeneity the stone tools are all in harmony with their counterparts from other Fort Ancient sites. Only in regard to specific activities is it possible to draw some tentative conclusions. The slate refuse indicates clearly that slate objects, presumably gorgets and pendants, were manufactured at the site. The numbers of gorgets recovered, when compared with the amount of refuse, would seem to indicate a reasonable artifact/debitage ratio. In other words, the amount of refuse suggests a moderate production of such objects locally used and discarded. The widespread sandstone debitage is not quite in agreement with the quantities of sandstone artifacts recovered. From this we conclude that the sample of artifacts made of this material and recovered from the excavations, is not as representative as it might be. The debitage far exceeds expectations based upon the incidence of tools. The implications of this are not clear.

VIII

Pipes

Blain Village yielded four smoking pipes. Two of these specimens were found on the surface, one was associated with Burial 6 of the mound, and one specimen was found in Feature 10.

The pipe associated with Mound Burial 6 (Plate XIV, A) is an elbow pipe made of limestone. The round bowl rises at an angle of approximately sixty degrees from the flattened–tubular, short stem. The latter projects by 2 mm beyond the bowl, so that the vertical line from the rim of the bowl to the base of the stem is not straight but slightly set-in at the junction of bowl and stem. The pipe is undecorated except for a fine, double-incised line surrounding the top of the bowl just beneath the rim. Maximum height of the specimen is 53 mm; the bowl is 34 mm high. Maximum length is 44 mm. Exterior bowl diameter is 28 mm, and the interior diameter at the rim is 17 mm. Maximum width at the base measures 28 mm, and the diameter of the bore at the mouthpiece amounts to 12 mm. This pipe is typical of Fort Ancient, and corresponds to Griffin's short-stemmed elbow pipes. Closely related pipes were also found at the Voss Mound in Central Ohio (Baby, Potter, and Mays, 1966).

One of the surface pipes and the specimen from Feature 10 (Figure 17, A) are fragmentary stemless, conoidal pipes made of sandstone. They are entirely undecorated. Because of their broken condition, only height measurements could be taken; both specimens are 48 mm high. This type is similar to Griffin's "Conoidal Pipe."

Finally, a single fragmentary platform pipe made of Ohio pipestone was recovered from the surface. This specimen has a basal length of

Inches

Cms

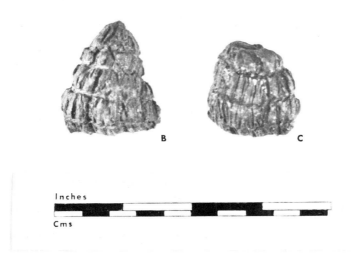

Inches

Cms

Plate XIV. (A) Limestone pipe from Burial 6; (B-C) Bituminous fabric-marked objects from ceremonial bundle in Feature 4b.

60 mm. (Figure 17, B). In shape the platform is oval and has notched edges. The bowl appears to have been round and cylindrical. It is placed near the distal end of the platform, and connects at right angles with a cylindrical tube which, in turn rises out of the platform and terminates at the mouthpiece. Thus, this specimen is essentially an elbow pipe, the base of which expands into an oval platform. We know of no parallel to this specimen. Although it is clearly a platform pipe in a descriptive sense, it does not resemble in any sense the classic Hopewellian platform pipes of the Middle Woodland period.

IX

The Bone Industry

Bone and antler artifacts occurred in abundance at the Blain Site. A total of 257 such tools was found in the course of the excavations. Occasionally they showed significant feature distributions. In the following discussion, Griffin's trait categories will be adhered to wherever possible, in order to facilitate comparison.

BONE TOOLS

Whole Bone Awls (25 specimens; Plate XV, M–O, R–S; XVI, C–D). All of these awls are made on mammalian bones, mostly deer. Quantitatively the most common single awl type was made on the lateral margin of a deer scapula; seven such specimens were found. They range in length from 114 mm to 116 mm. Four awls, all of which are fragmentary, were made on the proximal ends of deer ulnae. Ten awls are represented by unidentifiable mammalian fragments, nearly all of which appear to represent deer bones; and one small awl, 92 mm long, is made on the proximal end of a raccoon radius. Two further complete awls, 87 mm and 78 mm in length respectively, are made on the fibulae of red fox. Finally a single awl, 73 mm in length, is made on the baculum of a raccoon. All specimens were found *in situ*. They do not differ from awls found at other Fort Ancient sites; only Graham Village did not produce a single whole bone awl similar to those discussed here.

Turkey Metatarsal Awls (4 specimens; Plate XV, P–Q). All of these specimens were found *in situ*. The three complete awls have a length range from 83–102 mm, and a mean length of 90.66 mm. The type is common at early Fort Ancient sites, although it has not been reported from Graham Village.

Splinter Bone Awls (13 specimens; Plate XV, F–L; XVI, C). Qualitatively the range of these tools is considerable. Although in all cases the body of the awl is simply splintered longitudinally, there is considerable variability in the degree of care taken to produce the awl point proper. Eleven specimens are made on splinters of mammalian bones, probably deer, and two specimens are made on bird bones, apparently turkey. In the latter cases the bones had been split lengthwise, and the longitudinal edges were ground right up to the functional tip. All specimens were found *in situ*. Eight specimens are sufficiently complete for length measurements. The relevant metric data are: range: 84–145 mm; mean: 108.12 mm. Splinter bone awls are common at all Fort Ancient and Late Woodland sites. Only five such tools were found at Graham Village.

Double-pointed Pins or Gorges (2 specimens; Plate XV, T–U). Both specimens are made on mammalian bones, probably deer. They were found *in situ*, and their metric data are as follows: length range: 60–66 mm; mean: 63.00 mm. This type of bone tool is common at all Fort Ancient sites; it has been noted neither at Graham Village nor at the Late Woodland localities of southeastern and south–central Ohio.

Utilized Raccoon Penis Bones (2 specimens). Both specimens were found *in situ*. They show signs of considerable polishing. Their function is unknown. Similar objects are known from all Fort Ancient sites, with the exception of Graham Village; they have not been reported from Late Woodland localities.

Cut and Polished Mammalian Ribs (3 specimens). These are fragmentary deer or elk ribs which show signs of polishing along the narrow edges, as well as cutting marks on one or both faces. Their function is unknown, although they might have been used as knives. This type of tool is not reported in the list of bone tools for any of the Fort Ancient phases, nor did it occur at Graham Village. It is also unknown from local Late Woodland localities.

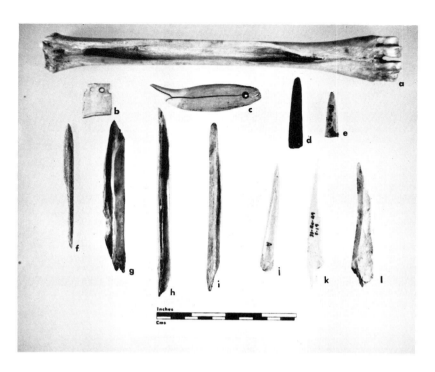

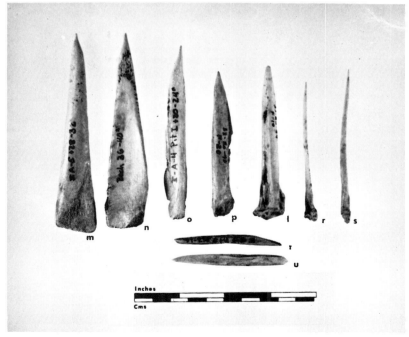

Plate XV.   (a-u) Bone tools.

Beaver Tooth Chisels (2 specimens; Plate. XVI, M). Both Blain specimens were found *in situ*. Similar objects are common at all Fort Ancient sites excepting Graham Village. They do not seem to occur in Late Woodland assemblages.

Bone Tubes (1 specimen; Figure 18, G). This is a longitudinally split bone tube, 76 mm in length, made on a bird bone, presumably turkey. The extant face is finely polished, as are the beveled terminal edges. The specimen was found *in situ*. This type has been reported from all Fort Ancient foci. It did not occur at Graham Village, and it has not been reported from local Late Woodland sites.

Shoulder Blade Knives (1 specimen). This object consists of a juvenile deer scapula which had been elaborately cut so as to form a bone knife. This was achieved by the removal of the muscular fossa immediately dorsal to the lateral margin. Furthermore the object was deeply grooved along the lateral margin between the glenoid fossa and inferior angle. The specimen was found *in situ*. Similar tools have been reported from other early Fort Ancient sites, although none was found at Graham Village. At Late Woodland localities they are absent.

Fishhooks (6 specimens; Figure 18, H–J; Plate XVI, I). Three specimens are fragmentary completed fishhooks. The other three represent stages in the manufacture of these objects. Two of the unfinished specimens consist of the convex part of a rectangular shaft section of mammalian bone. The lower edges are rounded and ground. On the upper faces attempts were made to scrape out the central area of the bone. Had this process been completed " . . . until a central open space was produced, one could make two fishhooks from this one bone section by cutting the bone at opposite ends." (Griffin, 1943:51). The third unfinished specimen from Blain had that process completed when it broke and was discarded. Fishhooks manufactured in this manner are characteristic of early Fort Ancient localities. Only at Graham did they not occur. The Blain specimens were all found *in situ*. There is no evidence for fishhooks from local Late Woodland sites.

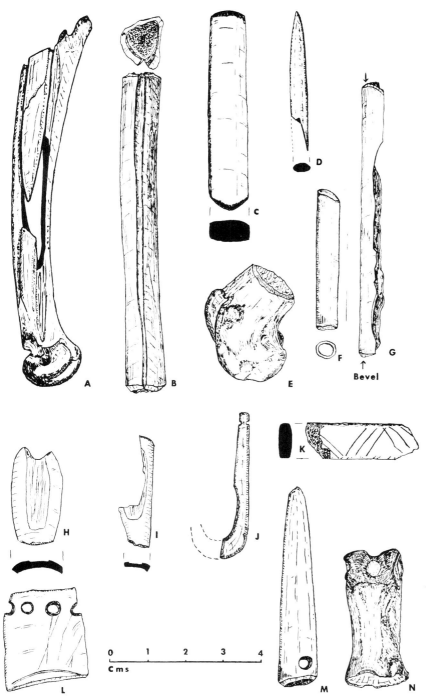

Figure 18.   Bone tools.

Beamers (36 specimens; Plate XV, A; XVI, A, R). Beamers are all made of deer metatarsal bones. In the Blain series three specimens proved to be complete, 15 specimens are represented by fragmentary mid-sections, three are distal ends, and 14 are proximal fragments. The ratio of distal to proximal sections is astonishingly disparate. On the basis of the available data no meaningful guess can be made as to its significance. One of the complete beamers, found in Feature 4b, deserves special discussion because it was extensively modified into three different tools. The specimen consisted of several fragments which partly represent accidental fractures and partly deliberate alterations. The original beamer was a singularly well–made, very highly polished specimen. Modification of this object proceeded in the following manner. As is well–known, beamers consist of deer metatarsals from the posterior aspect of which a longitudinal section was cut out of the shaft between the condyles. This was achieved by a grooving process resulting in bevelled facets along the two edges from between which part of the shaft had been removed. The widest and deepest part of the gap in the shaft invariably is at the mid-length of the shaft. It narrows and sharply decreases in depth near the condyles. The bevelled edges appear to have been the functional edges of this tool; they are always polished and longitudinally striated. In the case of the present specimen, the proximal condyle was removed by slicing the bone along each of the bevelled edges. Thus two awl–like segments, including parts of the proximal condyle, were detached. Both of these fragments were, in fact, used as awls: their distal ends have polished tips. The original beamer, now modified to terminate at the junction of the shaft and condyle, was further altered by a diagonal cut at the terminal end, thus producing an oblique scraping or rubbing edge which shows considerable signs of wear. Also, there is polish along the edges from which the two awls–to–be had been removed along the bevels of the original beamer. Since all fragments of this beamer were recovered, it was possible to re–assemble the component tools into their original condition. Subsequent to the modifications described, the main body of the beamer was exposed to intense fire; the two awls show minimal evidence of such exposure.

Of the total series 33 specimens were found *in situ*, one was found in the mound fill, and two represent surface finds. Beamers are characteristic of all Fort Ancient sites. They were, however, absent at Graham Village. They have never been reported from Late Woodland sites of southern Ohio.

Cut Mountain Lion Metatarsals (2 specimens; Figure 18, A). On the last page of the classic Baum report (Mills, 1906:136) there is an illustration of a longitudinally grooved mountain lion metatarsal. Obviously this represents a bone in the process of alteration for the manufacture of an implement. Two such specimens were found *in situ* at Blain. Since one of these is in an advanced stage of alteration, permitting certain inferences to be made as to the tool manufacture involved, a detailed description of these objects is in order.

The first specimen is identical to that illustrated in the Baum report. It is 110 mm long. The anterior aspect bears a slight longitudinal groove covering the entire length of the bone shaft. The posterior aspect bears a similar but deeper groove which partially cut through the bone proper into the medullary canal. The walls of the groove show distinctive cutting marks in the form of longitudinal striations.

The second specimen was originally somewhat longer than 100 mm; in its present condition the proximal end is partially broken off. The bone shaft bears on its posterior and both lateral aspects deep grooves similar to those on the specimen already described. Each of the grooves cuts through the bone into the medullary canal. The grooves on the posterior and one of the lateral aspects resulted in a bone ridge between them. Toward the mid-length of the shaft this bridge had been cut through; by leverage, the proximal part of this bridge was fractured out of the body of the shaft, thus producing a bone sliver. This operation also led to the more or less accidental removal of the proximal end of the bone. The sliver itself, which was found together with the remainder of the metatarsal, was altered to form a splinter awl. For some reason, perhaps the sliver proved too short (41 mm), the tool was never completed beyond the rough grinding out of the awl tip. It could be fitted back, without difficulty, into the original metatarsal.

The method of bone tool manufacture reflected in the two altered mountain lion metatarsals, is reminiscent of the groove–and–splinter bone working technique known from the Old World Upper Palaeolithic. Among the worked bone fragments to be described below under *Varia*, there are several long bone fragments with grooves that seem to represent evidence for the same technique.

Perforated Deer and Elk Phalanges (7 specimens; Figure 18, N; Plate XVI, N–O). Six of these specimens represent phalanges of deer, one of elk. These objects are longitudinally perforated at the distal end; in addition, their proximal ends are trimmed off. All Blain specimens were found *in situ*, with a significant clustering of three specimens in Feature 4b. In the literature they are sometimes referred to as tinklers or jinglers. Guilday (1963) has shown convincingly that these objects are part of the Cup–and–Pin Game which still survives among some North American Indian tribes. As far as Fort Ancient is concerned, they appear to occur exclusively in the *Baum Phase*. They were absent at Graham Village and have not been reported from local Late Woodland localities.

Laterally Perforated Deer Phalanges (1 specimen). This unique object which was found in Feature 1, consists of a deer phalange which was crudely perforated through the body of the bone near the proximal end. It has no parallels in the literature.

Turtle Shell Spoons or Cups (10 specimens). These are box turtle carapaces which had been modified into dishes or spoons by grinding the interior attachments to a more or less smooth surface. All specimens were found *in situ*, with a significant clustering of four in Feature 4b. These objects are a characteristic trait of the *Baum Phase.* They also occurred at Graham Village and in various local Late Woodland contexts.

Long Flat Needles (2 specimens; Figure 18, D). Both specimens were found *in situ*. They are flat bone needles, one representing a highly polished tip section, the other a long mid–section. Inasmuch as both specimens are lacking the base, it cannot be determined whether they were eyed. If they were, they would be similar to the flat needles listed by Griffin as a characteristic trait of all Fort Ancient phases. They were absent at Graham Village. No data are available for local Late Woodland sites.

Canine Teeth Pendants (7 specimens; Plate XV, C; XVI, H, J). All specimens are drilled at the root end of the teeth. Two specimens represent bear, the remainder are the teeth of smaller carnivores including raccoon, fox and probably dog or wolf. In one case the fractured perforation was re-drilled; one of the teeth is longitudinally split. Six specimens were found *in situ*, the seventh is a surface find. Drilled canine teeth are a common trait of all Fort Ancient phases. However, it was absent at Graham Village; nor does it occur at local Late Woodland localities.

Plain, Long and Short Tubular Bone Beads (10 specimens; Figure 18, F; Plate XVI, K). All of these specimens are tubular beads made on bird bones. The majority is highly polished. All were found *in situ* although, curiously, none was associated with the burials in the Blain Mound. Such beads are characteristic of all Fort Ancient phases. A single specimen was found at Graham Village. None have been reported from local Late Woodland sites. The Blain specimens have a length range of 18—80 mm, with a mean of 41.00 mm.

Decorated Awls (or Pins) (1 specimen; Figure 18, K). This is the midsection of an awl or pin, 9 mm in width and 3 mm in thickness, found in Feature 34. It is highly polished, and bears on one face an incised design of triple chevrons. Related "special" pins are characteristic of the *Baum Phase.* The trait has also been noted at Graham Village. Nothing similar has been reported from local Late Woodland sites.

Ceremonially Utilized Bird Beak (1 specimen; Plate XVI, P; XVII, C). This object is a fragmentary raven mandibula which was found in association with two small shell gorgets and the completely decayed remnants of the raven maxilla, near the lower left leg of Mound Burial 1. The beak and the gorgets evidently formed a single composite object, perhaps a ceremonial pendant. Although none of the classic

Fort Ancient sites nor local Late Woodland assemblages have yielded anything similar, it is worth mentioning that a burial of the Voss Mound in Franklin County, also produced a bird beak. Baby, Potter, and Mays (1966) consider this mound to be of Late Woodland affiliation; it is our opinion that the Voss Mound and Village are fundamentally early Fort Ancient expressions of central Ohio.

Varia (29 specimens; Figure 18, B, E, L). All of these objects were found *in situ*. They are about equally divided between bird and mammalian bones. In no case can their precise artifactual nature be determined. Some of them may be the completely fragmented remnants of awls. Others would seem to be the residue of bone tool manufacture. A few permit some additional comments. First, there is a series of four long bones with circular cutting marks around the shafts' circumference. They may represent residual fragments from the manufacture of bone tubes. Second, two longitudinally grooved long bones should be noted; they are similar in appearance to the mountain lion metatarsals discussed earlier and would thus seem to provide additional evidence for the groove–and–splinter bone working technique. The fill of the Blain Mound yielded a large bear canine which had been altered near the root by cutting and polishing. Two worked bones represent fishes; one of these is a basally cut and somewhat polished gill–rake of a medium to large–sized fish, the other is a marginally polished vertebral disc. Finally a stylus–like, highly polished fragmentary bone staff, and a fragmentary, flat piece of bone with multiple perforations along the margins should be noted. The latter object may have been similar or related to the kind of flat bone pendant found at Baum (Mills, 1906:116, Figure 62).

Antler Arrow Points (13 specimens; Figure 18, M; Plate XV, D–E; XVI, F). These objects are made from the hollowed-out tines of deer antler. All specimens are well finished, and many are carefully polished. Only three are sufficiently complete for length measurements. One of these, which also appears to have been the longest point in the series, has a hole in the side wall near the lower margin. Griffin has suggested that such points may have been harpoon heads (1943:41). All specimens were found *in situ*. Of the total series four specimens were found in Unit III, within the confines of what we presume to have

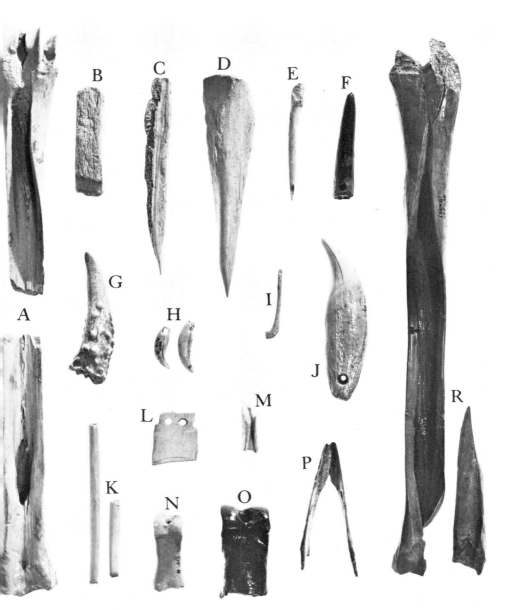

Plate XVI.   (A-R) Bone tools.

been house structures. The remainder were recovered from pits with never more than a single point per feature. The length range for the three complete specimens is 26–54 mm, with a mean of 38.00 mm. Antler projectile points are a common trait of all Fort Ancient phases. They did not, however, occur at Graham Village. Whether they also are a Late Woodland trait is uncertain. At Chesser Cave (Prufer, 1967a: 41–42) some of the worked antler fragments may have been the residue from the manufacture of such points.

Antler Flakers or "Drifts" (4 specimens; Figure 18, C; Plate XVI, B). These are straight, more or less flattened, roughly rectanguloid segments of antler which had been polished on all faces and both ends. Antler flakers of this type are a common attribute of all Fort Ancient phases. A single such specimen was recovered from Graham Village. The trait has also been noted at local Late Woodland sites. The length range of the Blain specimens is 43–54 mm, with a mean of 50.25 mm.

Antler Punches (3 specimens; Plate XVI, G). These are hollowed out antler tines which differ from antler projectile points only inasmuch as the latter are straight whereas the former are curved; it is difficult to see how they could have been used as projectiles. All specimens were found *in situ*. Although such objects are not specifically mentioned in the literature, it is clear from the extant collections that they are common at Fort Ancient as well as Late Woodland sites. Only at Graham Village did they definitely not occur.

Antler Spear Points (1 specimen). This fragmentary specimens is in all respects similar to the antler arrow points, except that it is very considerably larger. In its present condition it is 72 mm long; prior to breaking it was clearly longer than 100 mm. Antler spear points are a common Fort Ancient trait. Only at Graham Village was it conspicuous by its absence. No data are available for Late Woodland sites. The Blain specimen was found *in situ*.

Antler Scrapers (1 specimen). This object is made on a rather flat antler tine. The tip has been artifically rounded and flattened in order to serve as a scraping or rubbing edge. It is 75 mm in length and was found *in situ*. Although not identical with Griffin's 'antler celtlike scrapers', the Blain specimen is clearly related to that class of common Fort Ancient artifacts. Nothing similar has been reported from either Graham Village or local Late Woodland sites.

Antler Beams and Tines with Circular Cutting Marks (24 specimens). These objects are the residue from the manufacture of antler projectile points and punches. Most of the Blain specimens represent fragments discarded after the tine had been detached. One specimen is a tine proper; the intended tool was never finished. Finally there is a complete beam showing circular cutting marks near the tines which are fractured off. All specimens were found *in situ*. Similar specific antler working residue has been noted at all Fort Ancient sites (excepting Graham Village) and in many local Late Woodland assemblages.

Antler Beams and Tines with Generalized Cutting Marks or Grinding (45 specimens). These are antler fragments showing a variety of non-specific cutting and grinding marks. Obviously they represent the residue of antler working. Some of the Blain features contained as many as four such specimens, often in addition to antler tools and residue of the category previously discussed. Such residue is common in all Fort Ancient and Late Woodland assemblages.

DISCUSSION

It can fairly be stated that the Fort Ancient Aspect, as defined by Griffin in 1943, is characterized by rich and diversified bone industries. This is true as much of the Aspect as a whole, as it is true of the early Baum Focus. Of the 37 antler and bone traits listed (Griffin, 1943: 368–369), twenty-four were definitely noted at Blain. Nearly half of the traits absent at this locality, are primarily ceremonial traits derived from burials. Inasmuch as Blain could only boast seven burials from the mound, the absence of many of these traits is perhaps not surprising. On the other hand, the lack of certain other traits is somewhat more difficult to explain. Included here are such "functional" traits as *antler section hoes* and *arrow–points made of deer phalanges*. Such tools appear to have been common at the classic Baum and Gartner sites. Barring such differences, however, the Blain bone tool assemblage is remarkably similar to those from the classic localities. As in the case of non–ceramic artifact categories, the jarring note is struck when Blain is compared with Graham Village. The latter site is almost devoid of bone tools, the total assemblage comprising only eleven artifacts. Typologically, however, the Graham bone tools are in line with those from the *Baum Phase* sites.

One of the major distinctions between Early Fort Ancient and local contemporary Late Woodland assemblages is the non-comparability of the bone industries. Neither in terms of absolute quantities nor in terms of typological diversity do Late Woodland bone tools resemble their Fort Ancient counterparts. One might say with considerable justification, based upon four excavated Late Woodland localities, that their bone industries are almost impoverished. Thus bone tools can serve as a major indicator of cultural differentiation between Late Woodland and Fort Ancient.

As far as internal bone tool distribution at Blain is concerned, a few significant statements can be made. In general, those features which are characterized across the board by large quantities of artifacts, also yielded large numbers of bone tools. Conversely, those features which produced few artifacts in general were also relatively devoid of bone implements. Feature 1 yielded the highest concentration of such tools; the assemblage included 41 artifacts, representing fifteen classes. Among the remainder only three features produced more than ten bone tools (Feature 14 = 10 tools; Feature 37 = 16 tools; Feature 4b = 19 tools).

Significant clustering of specific tool types was noted in relation to beamers, turtle carapace dishes or spoons, awls, perforated deer phalanges, and bone and antler residue. Thus, Feature 1 yielded eight beamers, eight awls, and an unusually large amount of worked bone and antler residue. This feature also contained three drilled canine teeth. Perforated deer and elk phalanges were found in groups of two and three specimens in Features 37 and 4b respectively. Four turtle carapace dishes or spoons were recovered from Feature 4b. Antler working residue is common in nearly all features; the largest number of such specimens was found in Feature 37.

There is no correlation between numbers of antler artifacts and antler residue as far as feature distribution is concerned. Finally, it should be noted that one of the elaborately worked mountain lion metatarsals was found in Feature 38 which also produced several other elements of the feet of this animal.

X

Shell Artifacts

A total of 392 shell artifacts was recovered from the Blain Site. Most of these proved to be beads associated with the mound burials. Both freshwater pelecypods and marine shells are represented in the assemblage. As far as internal distribution is concerned, little of significance can be said. Once the shell ornaments and tools associated with the mound are eliminated from the discussion, the remainder of the assemblage is too scanty—21 specimens—to reveal any meaningful pattern of distribution. All shell artifacts but one were recovered *in situ.*

Shell Gorgets (4 specimens; Plate XII, A; XVII, A–B, F). All of these objects are circular. One is made on a marine shell, the others on local freshwater bivalves. The largest gorget was found in association with Mound Burial 5. It is made on a large ocean shell, presumably derived from the Gulf Coast. It consists of a convex disc, 114 mm in diameter, with a large central perforation, 63 mm in diameter. There are two small perforation along the margin.

A second specimen of this type was found in Feature 1. It is smaller than the gorget found with Burial 5, and it is made on a freshwater bivalve. The diameter is 63 mm, and the central perforation measures 30 mm.

The remaining two specimens were found in Mound Burial 1 as part of a composite object that also included the beak of a raven. Both shell objects are small discs, 24 mm in diameter each, with single small central perforations. Both are made on freshwater pelecypods.

Gorgets of both types found at Blain are an attribute of Fort Ancient. They were found at the Baum and Gartner sites (Griffin, 1943: 43,52), but they have not been reported from the eastern Hocking Valley sites, nor from the western *Brush Creek Phase*. Thus it would appear that such gorgets were restricted during early Fort Ancient times to the *Baum Phase* of the Scioto drainage area. During middle Fort Ancient, shell gorgets of the types here described appear to have a universal distribution; the same seems to be true of the late *Madisonville Phase*. None of the Blain specimens could be identified as to species.

Shell Beads (367 specimens; Plate XII, B). Two types of shell beads were found with the following distribution:

Table 13. Distribution of shell beads from Blain.

Type	Provenience	Quantity
Cylindrical	Mound Burial 7	14
Disc	Mound Burial 5	352
Disc	Surface	1
		367

The cylindrical beads are made of marine shell columella segments. They were found in two strands of seven beads each around the forearms of Mound Burial 7. In length they range from 8–18 mm, with a mean of 11.6 mm.

With the exception of s single surface find, the disc beads were all found in the form of two strands of 170 and 182 beads, on the wrists of Mound Burial 5. They have a mean diameter of 4 mm, and do not exceed 3 mm in thickness. They are made on marine shells. Both types are common Fort Ancient traits.

Shell Spoons with Notched Edges (1 specimen). This specimen was found with Mound Burial 7. It is made on a valve of *Lampsilis Ovata ventricosa*. Three V-shaped notches had been cut into the margin adjacent to the hinge. As far as early Fort Ancient is concerned, Griffin reports this trait only for the Baum Site (1943: Table XLV).

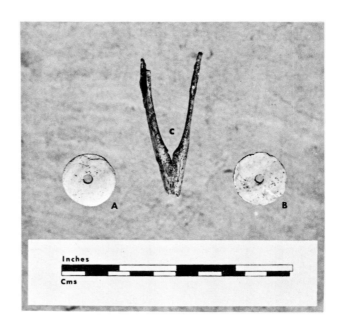

Plate 17. (A-C) Raven beak and two small shell gorgets from composite object with Burial 1. (D) Shell spoon; (E) shell hoe; (F) freshwater shell gorget.

The only other Fort Ancient occurrences were noted for the late *Madisonville Phase.*

Plain Cut Shell Spoons (5 specimens; Plate XVII, D). These are long-oval pelecypod valves with cut margins diagonally opposite to the hinge. The only species represented is *Amblema Costata* (Raf.). One specimen was found with Mound Burial 6; the others occurred in various features. The mound specimen was too badly damaged for preservation and species identification. This type of shell spoon is common throughout the Fort Ancient sequence.

Shell Hoes (12 specimens; Plate XVII, E). These are robust pelecypod valves with single central perforations, on the average 15 mm in diameter. Such objects are commonly referred to as hoes, although neither experimentation with fresh shells (Prufer, 1965:93) nor the wear patterns along the edges would seem to bear out this interpretation. The following species have been identified:

Cyclonaias tuberculata (Raf.)	2
Amblema costata (Raf.)	8
Actinonaias carinata (Barnes)	1

All shell hoes occurred in features. The type is common throughout the Fort Ancient sequence.

Shell Scrapers (1 specimen). This is a robust pelecypod valve of *Amblema costata* (Raf.) found in Feature 1. Apparently it had been used as a scraper. The edges of this well–preserved specimen are dorsally nicked and splintered along the entire circumference excluding the hinge area. Griffin (1943: Table XIV) reports shell scrapers, but in the absence of illustrations it is not possible to determine whether they are identical to the Blain specimen.

Cut Shell Residue (2 specimens). Two cut fragments of freshwater shells were found in Feature 4b. Species identification could not be determined.

DISCUSSION

The shell artifacts and ornaments from Blain Village are all in line with the evidence from Fort Ancient as a whole, and Griffin's Baum Focus in particular. In a more specific sense only the circular gorgets with a central performation seem to diverge from the general pattern inasmuch as they have been reported thus far only from early sites in the Scioto drainage area. This seems to indicate that during the initial period of the *Fort Ancient Tradition* they were restricted to the *Baum Phase*. As a further observation it should be noted that, based upon available data in the literature, the Blain shell assemblage seems to be somewhat impoverished both in terms of absolute quantity and numbers of traits. Griffin (1943: Table XIV) lists fourteen shell traits for the Baum Focus; excluding the shell manufacturing residue, Blain yielded only eight of these traits.

By way of comparison with Graham Village, it should be stressed that this site did not produce a single shell artifact. Roughly contemporary Late Woodland sites in south–central Ohio have thus far not produced a single shell artifact comparable to the early Fort Ancient series.

XI

Varia

In addition to the artifact categories discussed so far, Blain Village yielded a number of other artifacts which might best be classed under the general heading of varia. All of these items were found *in situ.*

Modified and Unmodified Fossils (6 specimens). This category includes three worked and three unworked small fossils, mostly coral. The modified objects consist of two cylindrical beads and one perforated small conical fossil fragment. The remaining three specimens are entirely unmodified. Although fossils are not listed in Griffin's trait list, they appear to be fairly common in Fort Ancient, since they occur frequently in local collections from relevant sites. The trait was not observed at Graham Village.

Bituminous Pear–shaped Objects (2 specimens: Plate XIV, B-C). These objects were part of the presumed ceremonial bundle in Feature 4b. They are small, black, pear–shaped masses, 34 × 34 × 25 mm and 42 × 35 × 23 mm in maximum dimensions. They are made of some bituminous material and appear to have been burnt. Both specimens bear wide–meshed fabric impressions suggesting that each was originally contained in a tight little bag. Both objects were X-rayed in order to determine whether they contained some extraneous matter. The X–ray evidence proved negative. The specific function of these curious items is not known; they do not appear to have parallels in the Fort Ancient literature.

Tempered Clay Cylinders (2 specimens; Plate XIII, C). Feature 33 produced two grit–tempered cylindrical masses of clay. One of these was slightly, probably accidentally, fired. It measures 160-by-130 mm; the other specimen is unfired and measures 170-by-130 mm. Both objects bear textile impressions suggesting that they had been wrapped tightly in a cloth or bag–like container. In addition, these cylinders bear constrictions caused by coarse string impressions. Similar objects were found in association with burials at the Gartner Site (Mills, 1904: 134). They appear to represent mixed clay for pottery–making.

Wattle. Numerous fragments of wattle were found throughout the deposits of Feature 3. They range in size from very small to large pieces 150 mm in diameter. All specimens show reed and other fiber impressions. They are moderately burnt, suggesting that they are the remains of a structure that was consumed by fire. Feature 3 is located in the vicinity of one of the burnt house structures (Feature 5). It is possible that the wattle fragments from Feature 3 represent structural refuse from this conflagration.

Red and Yellow Ochre. With the exception of the burials which revealed only one instance of ochre traces associated with Burial 1, all features and units of the Blain site produced lumps of red and yellow ochre. Some of these had facets that appear to have resulted from rubbing or abrading; others showed no such modifications. None of the specimens exceeds 50 mm in maximum diameter. Traces of what is presumed to be ochre were also found on the ground sandstone palettes and in some of the small concretion cups. All the evidence points to the conclusion that ochre was extensively used for pigments. Although it has not been noted as a specific Fort Ancient trait by Griffin (1943), ochre has been found at many Fort Ancient localities. The trait is absent at Graham Village and at local Late Woodland sites.

XII

The Blain Mound

C. Owen Lovejoy and Kingsbury G. Heiple

The Blain Mound was excavated during the summer of 1966. It was an integral feature of the Blain Village Site, a large Fort Ancient locality in Ross County, Ohio. The coordinates of this site are 39° 18' 49" north latitude and 82° 56' 16" west longitude. The present report describes the excavation of the mound and presents an analysis of the skeletal remains found at its base. In view of the fact that it is part of the general site configuration, the cultural context of the mound and the artifacts recovered from it have been considered elsewhere (Prufer and Shane, in this volume).

The height of the Blain Mound was determined, using a transit and stadial rod, to be approximately eighteen inches at its apex. The structure of the mound indicates that it was never very high and that recent plowing has probably not reduced its height by more than eight to ten inches. Flood drainage and scouring had occurred around the circumference of the mound in an east-west direction (giving it a slightly elliptical shape) so that only the generalized extent could be determined. Again, by means of transit and stadial rod, the diameter of the mound was estimated to be seventy feet.

Excavation. Excavation of the Blain Mound was begun with a 70-by-2½ foot test trench through the approximate center of the mound on an east-west datum (Figure 19). This trench was divided into seven 10 foot test units. Excavation of this series of test units revealed two

Figure 19.   Plan of Blain Mound.

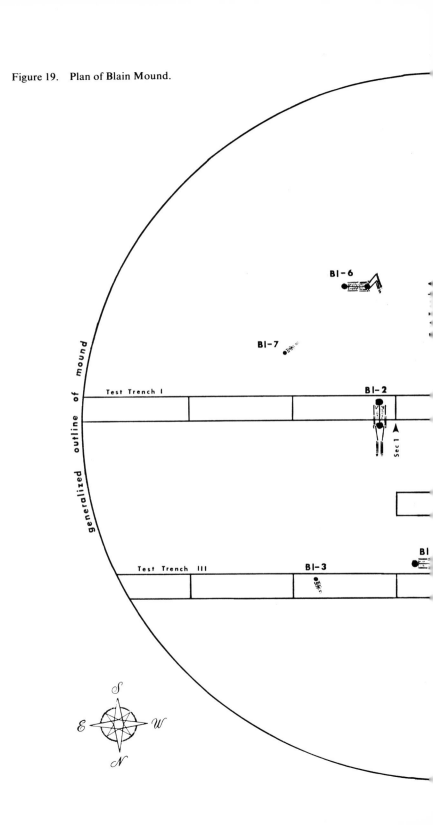

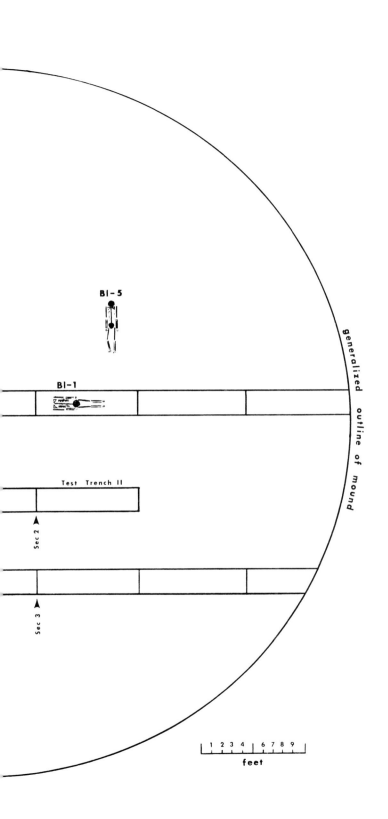

adult skeletons (Burial 1 and Burial 2). Following completion of this trench, Test Trenches II and III were excavated (Figure 19); the former was a short trench, primarily for the purpose of obtaining more definitive stratigraphy, and the latter was another full-length exploratory trench. Test Trench III revealed a third skeleton (Burial 3), that of a young child. A fourth test unit, Test Trench A, was excavated on a north–south datum, bisecting trenches I and II. This unit revealed no new skeletal material.

Careful excavation of the mound by means of these test units in four–inch arbitrary levels revealed very little by way of cultural debris in the fill. A few sherds and some fauna were recovered. The preliminary surface survey had indicated this lack of cultural material in the area of the mound.

Once the stratigraphy and construction of the mound had been satisfactorily determined, the mound was carefully scraped by mechanical equipment along east–west data at two–inch vertical intervals. This procedure completed the excavation of the mound to its natural floor and exposed four additional skeletons (Burials 4, 5, 6, 7). No sub–floor features were found, nor were there any indications of a house structure over the area occupied by the mound.

Stratigraphy and Structure. The way in which the Blain Mound had been constructed was given careful attention during excavation. In Test Trench I, Burials 1 and 2 were found to lie upon a base of organic soil. Covering this stratum was a light yellow, sandy soil with dark lensing which originally was considered to represent "basket-loading" of soils from the immediate vicinity of the mound. Further stratigraphic sections revealed similar soil profiles in the central area of the mound, but more definitive strata were identified by means of horizontal and vertical stratigraphic sections further away from the apex (Figure 20; Plate XVIII, B). These sections indicated the following: the mound lay upon a natural rise of the grey, clayey alluvial subsoil of the site. Upon this base, organic soil of generally uniform thickness formed the first stratum of cultural origin. There were no indications that this midden layer was other than that characteristic of the site as a whole, i.e., that this stratum was an intentional importation for the construction of the mound. All seven

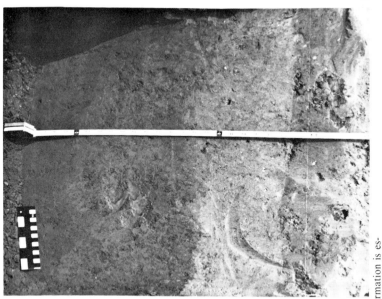

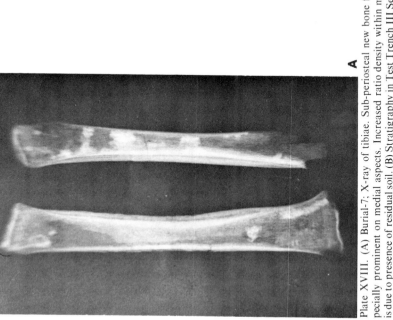

Plate XVIII. (A) Burial-7: X-ray of tibiae. Sub-periosteal new bone formation is especially prominent on medial aspects. Increased ratio density within medullary canals is due to presence of residual soil. (B) Stratigraphy in Test Trench III Section-3.

burials lay upon this layer which contained occasional shell fragments, animal bones, and a limited number of *Baum Cordmarked
Incised, var. Blain* sherds. This level was in turn overlain by a
distinct layer of unmixed yellow sand.

It is our opinion that this unmixed yellow sand originally covered
the entire mound prior to recent farming disturbance. Deep plow
cutting in the central area of the mound has resulted in the lensing of
this layer (in the central area plow scars were deep enough to reach
into the midden soil on which the skeletons lay, and it is therefore
simple good fortune that prevented Burials 1 and 2 from complete
destruction prior to excavation). This conclusion is further supported
by the full length profiles to the north and south walls of Test Trench
I which show that the yellow sand zone is distinct at either end but
grades slowly into the mottled condition obtaining around the apex
of the mound as plow scarring gradually deepens, finally reaching all
the way through to the midden level in the approximate center of the
mound. A similar profile was obtained for Test Trench A, but a
profile of the north and south walls of Test Trench III, on the other
hand, displays an intact stratum of unmixed yellow sand for the
entire length of the trench, gradually fading (through mixture with
topsoil) at the east and west extremities of the mound.

If this hypothesis is correct, the remaining problem is whether this
feature (i.e., the yellow sand), which constitutes the actual mound,
was intentionally collected or whether its unmixed condition was
only accidental and therefore an unintentional aspect of the mound
structure.

Obviously, since the mound was constructed on an already existing base of organic soil containing refuse from the village site,
the mound was not simply constructed by "basket-loads" of soils
from the actual site itself, nor could it have been constructed until
after the site had been in existence for some time. However, the yellow sand of which it is composed is no more than a local alluvium
which would have been readily available at various areas in close
proximity of the site. Since this material is in no way extraordinary
and would not have been difficult to obtain (involving hardships of
transfer, etc.), the available evidence is insufficient for adequate
resolution of the question posed above.

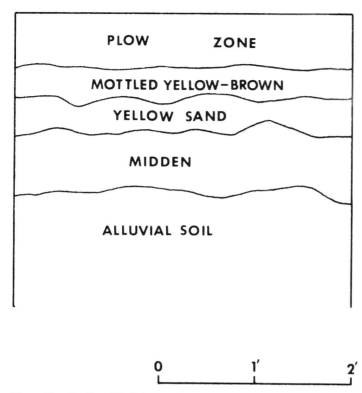

Figure 20.   Profile of Blain Mound.

The Skeletal Series. Preparation of the Blain Mound skeletal material for presentation involved the problems of the relevance and differential importance of data obtainable from small skeletal series.
The post–natal etiology of skeletal variation has been a well understood and documented phenomenon for some time (Bardeen, 1905;
Murray, 1936; de Beer, 1937; Gluckman, 1942). However, analyses
of skeletal populations have tended to rely, for the most part, upon
osteometric data as being of the greatest significance in judging
population affinities, while variability resulting from remodeling reaction to various stress and function patterns in the living, and general skeletal reaction to such factors as climate, nutrition, pathology, and culture have only recently been more fully considered in
discussions of extinct populations (Hughes, 1968). The evidence now

available requires a reassessment of the value, relevance, applicability, and reliability of osteometric data in estimating affinity among skeletal series (Hiernaux, 1963; Kaplan, 1954; Pratt and McCance, 1958; Walker, 1957). There can be no doubt that osteometric analysis is important and appropriate for large skeletal series, especially where there is evidence of population uniformity. Such analyses are valuable in determining skeletal variability and in establishing correlations between various ecological factors and skeletal development. For the small series, however, osteometric data can provide little information of analytical value at the present time. Consequently, only the basic osteometrics suggested by Brothwell (1963) have been included for the adult material in this report.[1]

In recent years, increasing emphasis has been placed on the use of discontinuous or non–metrical features in the analysis of skeletal series. This methodological approach, however, is often also subject to the phenomenon of skeletal plasticity. A case in point is the frequently reported septal aperture (perforation 'of the olecranon fossa floor) of the humerus. This is certainly to be regarded as a non-metric variant, but recent reports have satisfactorily attributed this feature to general robustity of the humerus and to the morphology of the olecranon process (Benfer and McKern, 1966; Benfer and Tappen, 1968). Thus this non–metrical feature is subject to the same conditions of variability that render osteometric analysis of indeterminate value. Thus a basic problem inherent in the use of non-metrical data is the lack of adequate genetic investigations and analysis, and therefore a non–metric feature is, in many cases, of no more value in establishing population affinities independent of skeletal plasticity than is the well–defined osteometric information.[2] The advantage of non–metrical features lies at present more in the fact that they are presence–absence traits and can be readily identified

[1] Post–cranial osteometrics are presented in Table 15. No cranial measurements were included in this report because of the fragmentary condition of all adult crania from the mound.

[2] We do not wish to imply that the majority of non–metrical variations are not of genetic etiology. Rather, such variations should not be assumed to be of genetic origin until such an hypothesis has been supported by familial investigation or proper statistical evidence.

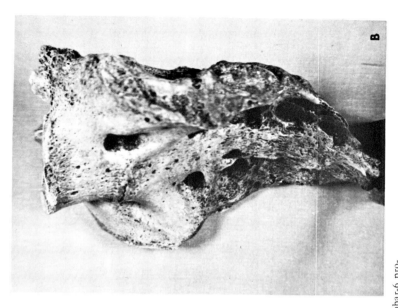

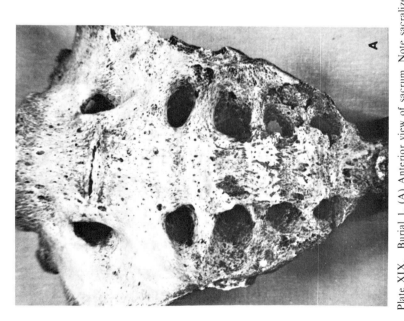

Plate XIX. Burial 1. (A) Anterior view of sacrum. Note sacralized lumbar-6 projecting above alae of sacrum, and complete lateral fusion. (B) Left oblique view of sacrum.

and characterized. What is required for their establishment as reliable genetic indicators are investigations into the nature of their origin—whether genetic or phenotypic. Various authors have listed series of non–metric variations readily identifiable in earlier skeletal populations (Laughlin and Jorgensen, 1956; Brothwell, 1963; Montagu, 1933; Anderson, 1968; Berry, 1968; Brothwell and Powers, 1968). Reporting the presence or absence of each of these for a small skeletal series would be laborious and not necessarily of significant value for the reasons outlined above. Rather, the procedure has here been adopted of reporting all non–metric variations noted but *not* the absence of those observed in other populations. Again, for the large population, it would prove to be of necessity to report the total

Table 14. Occlusal attrition index.

STAGE	DESCRIPTION
A	No evidence of attrition
B	Attrition of enamel only Wear facets on cuspal planes with no dentine exposed
C	Attrition extends through the enamel into the dentine in cuspal and incisal areas Cusp pattern maintained
D	Total exposure of dentine Occlusal surfaces are worn flat Inverted cusp pattern present
E	Attrition is sufficient to expose the pulp Rate is greater than secondary dentine formation
F	Attrition responsible for the total loss of the crown

absence of a discontinuous variant. For the purposes of small series analysis, however, this would be of impractical value.

In reporting the Blain material, a third factor has been given primary consideration: the frequent absence of reliable indicators of demographic variables in small populations. In the large population, problems of variable expression of dimorphic traits (with consequent overlapping of sexual features) and the variance in expression of age indicators can be overcome (See, for example, Miles, 1963). For the small skeletal series, however, more qualitative assessments must be relied upon. Consequently, the criteria upon which demographic data are based have been included within the body of this report, since such demographic data will continue to be of primary importance in small skeletal series until the genetic background of both osteometric and non-metric variation can be more adequately established.

Finally, in the analysis of dental attrition, a scale based on that devised by Fanno (1967) and similar to that developed by Brothwell (1963) was employed. This scale is given in Table 14.

Skeletal Analysis

BURIAL 1

EXCAVATION DATA

Burial Position: Full Extension.
Position in Mound: Near the apex in Test Trench I (Figure 19).
Orientation: Due east.

Depth from Surface: Varied between 6 and 10 inches.

Associated Artifacts: A concave-based triangular projectile point lay beneath the left femoral head. Red ochre was faintly present about the trunk. Two large circular shell gorgets and the beak of a large bird (Raven) were found eight inches north of the left talus. The tip of a projectile point was imbedded in the head of the left humerus (Plate XX, C.-D). One *Baum Cordmarked Incised, var. Blain* sherd was recovered from the fill.

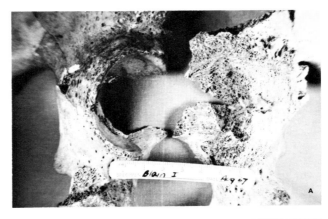

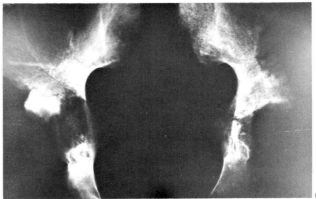

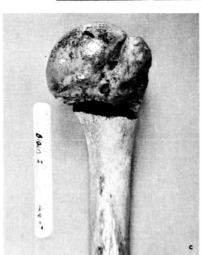

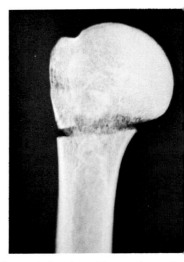

Plate XX. Burial 1. (A) Gross destruction of left acetabular rim with superior and lateral osteophyte formation as marginal repair reaction. Note marked porosity of left side, probably resulting from disuse atrophy and local resorption secondary to infection. (B) X-ray of innominates. Note chronic reaction to infection on left side. (C) Humerus viewed posteriorally. Broken projectile point is flush with bony surface of posterior neck. Rounded margins of impact defect indicate that the injury occurred sometime before death. (D) X-ray of humerus. Note projectile point just above post-mortem fracture.

Condition: Condition was very poor. Plow damage was extensive, as was damage by roots.

Completeness: No skull was present. Several skull fragments were found in the fill, but it could not be determined if these were the remains of Burial 1. Considering the damage by plow to the rest of the skeleton, the skull could hardly have survived since it would naturally lie at a higher level than the postcranial skeleton. Preservation in the cervical region was very poor, and adds nothing to solving the problem of whether the loss of the skull was aboriginal or a result of more recent damage. Bones severely broken by plow cuts included the right humerus, left radius and ulna, left femur, and the vertebral column (thoracics and cervicals). The left innominate and left tibia were crushed.

PHYSICAL ANTHROPOLOGICAL DATA

Age: Components of the skeleton indicative of age were scarce, especially the absence of the skull and pubic symphysis. The clavicle was not available for observation, but all epiphyses present showed complete union. Features most indicative of a ceiling age are the absence of osteoarthritic change in any of the well-preserved lumbar vertebrae, and the absence of laminal spurs. Although these features are erratic they are not without some value in establishing approximate age limits (Stewart and McKern, 1957). A medial gap was present between the sixth lumbar and the first sacral centra in the anomalous sacrum (see below). Stewart and McKern attribute "delayed unions" (in normal sacra) to variances in the intersegmental spaces. The anomalous condition of this sacrum certainly limits the value of such a gap for age estimation, but it should be noted that ossification appears to have been proceeding toward full union (Plate XIX, B). The auricular surfaces of the sacrum showed early signs of roughening and erosion. The skeleton, on the basis of the above indications, was assessed at 35 years ± 5 years.

Sex: Muscular impressions are massive on the femur, tibia, and ulna (all intact). Below the sacralized lumbar, the sacrum displays an even curvature with maximum depth at the third segment. The auricular surface is massive and extends well on to the fourth sacral body

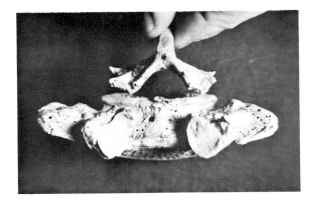

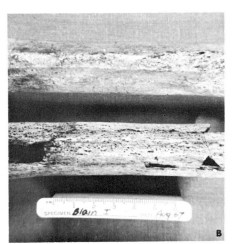

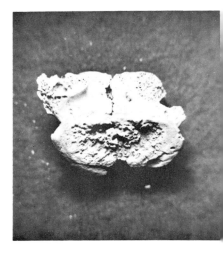

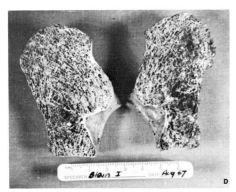

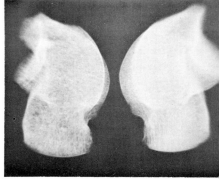

Plate XXI. (A) Burial 5: Spondoloysis of lumbar-5. (B) Burial 1: Posterior mid-shafts of femurs. Left side (below) is grossly osteoporotic compared to right, with loss of normally well-developed ridge of linea aspera. (C) Burial 6: Inferior surface of lumbar-5. Note penetration (hiernation) of intervertebral disk through end plate cancellous body of vertebra. (D) Burial 1: Os calci sectioned anterior-posteriorally. Note loss of bone mass in life calcaneus (right picture). (E) Burial 1: X-ray of (D) above. Left talus has participated in universal atrophy of left lower extremity.

(third in the normal sacrum). Six segments are present in addition to the sacralized lumbar. The sciatic notch of the right innominate is deep and narrow. Articulation of the right and left innominates with the sacrum is still sufficiently complete to indicate a male configuration, with lower segments of the sacrum and ischial spines jutting well into the pelvic canal. Maximum diameter of the femoral head was 50.5 mm. Total morphological pattern (especially the android pelvis) provided the basis for assessment of this skeleton as male.

Pathology: Three pathological conditions may be noted in this burial. The first is a dual anomaly of the vertebral column. Six lumbar vertebrae were present, the most caudal of which was sacralized bilaterally (Pl. XIX, A). Sacralization is not an uncommon anomaly in modern material, and its presence is often reported in Amerindian material (Trotter and Lanier, 1945). This condition has a reported incidence of 4 percent in Whites and 1.5 percent in American Negroes (Trotter and Lanier, 1945).

A projectile point tip was noted in the posterior aspect of the right humerus, flush with the bony surface of the posterior neck. The rounded margins of the impact defect in the cancellous bone of the neck indicate that the intrusion was present months to years prior to death (Plate XX, C-D).

Although the right acetabulum is completely normal in this skeleton, the left acetabulum is grossly eroded, with consequent loss of the superior and inferior rims, and with obvious loss of subchondral bone of the acetabular surface (Plates XX, A-B). Osteophytosis is present above the posterior-superior rim, and most likely resulted from infectious arthritis in young adult life, probably as a result of trauma. This reaction must have occurred between one and five years before death because, although there has been time for osteophyte formation, there is no evidence of eburnation and sclerosis, a condition to be expected after a remote infection and long-term post-infectional arthritis. It should be noted that a fragment of a projectile point was recovered beneath the left femoral head during removal of this skeleton, and this could possibly have been the trauma initiating this extensive arthritic reaction.

The left femoral shaft was found broken *in situ*. Reconstruction of the shaft shows obvious increased porosity (Plate XXI, B) consistent with decreased weight-bearing on this extremity for some time. Measurements of the circumference of the bone compared with the opposite femur did not indicate any significant difference, although a trend toward lessened circumference was evident. The left femoral head was unfortunately absent (post-mortem), but osteophytosis is obvious on the femoral neck.

The left calcaneus, in the light of the above evidence, was sectioned anterior–posteriorly. In comparison with the right, it shows osteoporosis of the internal trabecular architecture, loss of subchondral plate of the posterior facet, and a reduction of surface density in the calcaneal sulcus (Plate XXI, D). Roengentograms of the tali also show osteoporosis on the left side (Plate XXI, E). These observations are again consistent with the reduced weight-bearing capacity of the left lower extremity.

Indications are that this condition must have caused the individual extensive discomfort, and immobilization of the hip almost certainly would have been employed to reduce pain. Observations of modern clinical material indicate that this is almost always accomplished by flexion and adduction of the thigh, which over a period of time results in a neurogenic contracture, making the position more or less permanent (Hollinshead, 1963). The position of this skeleton *in situ* is fully commensurate with such a clinical picture. The left femur is adducted so that the femoral condyles (destroyed by plow) would have rested upon the right femur. Although the left tibia and fibula have been extensively fragmented by plow, the position of the fibula is abnormally high; this is indicative of some medial rotation which would naturally occur in the situation described above. In the living individual such adduction and flexion contracture results in the left leg's crossing anteriorly to the right, and pelvic rotation (also evidenced in this skeleton) is required to bring the leg into as suitable a weight–bearing position as possible. Walking must have been considerably awkward and painful, almost certainly necessitating a crutch or staff.

In association with this evidence, the curious position of the bird beak and shell disks found with this burial (Plate XXV, A) should be considered. Of all the artifacts in the mound, this assemblage is the only case in which the artifact(s) found were not in immediate association with a skeleton. Since it is likely that this individual walked with some artificial aid, and since the assemblage was found 8 inches south of the left talus, there is a distinct possibility that these artifacts were attached to some walking aid (staff?) and that this was included in more or less "anatomical position" with the individual. Soil conditions and age of the site negate the possible preservation of such a staff since it would have most certainly been made of wood or some other equally perishable material.

Cause of Death: Undetermined. The absence of the skull leaves a significant hiatus in the sources of evidence, since trauma is also evident from other remains in the mound. The remote infection in the left hip would not, of itself, have been a sufficient cause of death.

Non-metric Variation: None noted in addition to those already reported above.

BURIAL 2

EXCAVATION DATA

Burial Position: Full extension.

Position in Mound: Near the apex in Test Trench I (Figure 19).

Orientation: Due south.

Depth from Surface: Varied between 6 and 10 inches.

Associated Artifacts: A large, ceremonial, triangular blade was found on the right femur. The terminal phalanx of the thumb lay beneath the blade, while the four remaining terminal phalanges lay atop it, indicating that it had been placed in the hand of the deceased. A concave-based triangular projectile point lay in the upper left quadrant of the rib cage. One *Baum Cordmarked Incised, var. Blain* sherd was recovered from the fill.

Condition: Very poor. Plow damage was extensive, as was damage by roots.

Completeness: Only a portion of the occipital and left parietal remained of the skull. The long bones were fragmentary. The right humerus, pelvis, vertebral column, and rib cage were shattered by plow cuts.

PHYSICAL ANTHROPOLOGICAL DATA

Age: Age estimation was made somewhat difficult by the absence of reliable age criteria. There was complete union in all epiphyses. The inferior half of the right pubic symphyseal face was present and showed definite rarefication and granulation. The face was smooth and flat, and devoid of billowing. Although scoring by means of the Stewart–McKern system was, of course, impossible, evidence from this condition is generally indicative of third decade age (Mc-Kern and Stewart, 1957). There were no intact sutures on the calvarium, The long bones were free of osteoarthritic change, and such change was minimal or absent in the lumbar and thoracic vertebrae. There were no laminal spurs. Although the sacrum was absent, the auricular surfaces of the innominates were crisply defined with minimal age changes. In the absence of further age criteria this skeleton was assessed at 33 years ± 4 years.

Sex: The bony ridge above the auditory meatus was classified as intermediate (Keen, 1950). The skull displayed a strikingly large nuchal area and external occipital protuberance. No other features of dimorphic significance were noted in the fragmentary skull. Although both innominates were present, they were incomplete and there was no sacrum. The sciatic notches were of intermediate width, but tended toward the narrow configuration. The ischial spines were very well developed and showed marked medial convergence. The auricular surfaces of the *os coxae* were large and robust. Long bones were robust but not strikingly so. Maximum diameters of the femoral heads were 48.2 mm on the left and 48.0 mm on the right. On the basis of the above evidence, this skeleton was assessed as male.

Pathology: An external communication was present on the posterior aspect of the left mastoid process. This is a possible indication of mastoid infection or mastoiditus. Although this type of pathology was no doubt serious in precolumbian Indian populations, a more likely cause of death is noted below.

Dentition: No teeth were recovered from this burial.

Cause of Death: The triangular projectile point discovered in the upper left quadrant of the rib cage was most probably the cause of death of this individual.

Non-metric Variations: None noted.

BURIAL 3

EXCAVATION DATA

Burial Position: Semi-flexion.

Position in Mound: In the north-east quadrant of the mound in Test Trench III (Figure 19).

Orientation: 15° east of due south.

Depth from Surface: 14 inches to top of skull.

Associated Artifacts: A side–notched projectile point was found imbedded in the dorsal aspect of the cervical vertebrae. One *Baum Cordmarked Incised*, var. *Blain* sherd was recovered from the burial fill.

Condition: Very poor. There were no intact long bones. The skull was fragmentary.

Completeness: Very poor. No epiphyses were found during excavation and the post–cranial skeleton was very incomplete.

PHYSICAL ANTHROPOLOGICAL DATA

Age: No epiphyses were available for observation. The vertebral column was fragmentary, but all vertebrae available for observation were fused at the apex, while none was fused to a centrum. No other evidence was available from the skull or post–cranial skeleton. Evidence from the dentition (see below), in addition to the above indications, provided the basis for assessment of this skeleton at 28 months ± 3 months (Massler and Schaur, 1944; Scott, 1954).

Pathology: No abnormal conditions were noted.

Plate XXII. (A) Burial 5: Tarsal anomalies are visible bilaterally. (B) Burial 6.

Dentition: Teeth recovered from this burial included: upper and lower right first permanent molars; a complete complement of left deciduous molars; two deciduous lower lateral incisors; one deciduous upper lateral incisor; one lower left deciduous canine; and, one permanent lower central incisor. All deciduous incisors were fully developed. The root of the canine was broken. The roots of the first upper deciduous molar were approximately 70 percent complete; those of the second were approximately 40 percent complete. The roots of the first lower deciduous molar were approximately 80 percent complete; those of the second were approximately 50 percent complete. The crowns of the permanent molars were approximately 90 percent calcified; that of the permanent incisor was approximately 60 percent calcified.

Cause of Death: The projectile point imbedded in the dorsal aspect of the cervical vertebrae (condition was too poor for more accurate location), although not entering the vertebral canal, was doubtless the cause of death of this individual (Figure 12, D).

BURIAL 4

EXCAVATION DATA

Burial Position: Full extension (Plate XXV, B).

Position in Mound: On north-south line just south of Test Trench III (Figure 19).

Orientation: Due east.

Depth from Surface: 15 inches to top of skull.

Associated Artifacts: Three *Baum Cordmarked Incised, var. Blain* sherds were recovered from the fill. No other artifacts were found.

Condition: Fair. The burial was too deep for plow damage to have occurred, but a rodent burrow had damaged the skull and removed proximal sections of the humeri, scapulae, and cervical vertebrae.

Completeness: The skeleton was complete except for the bones noted above as fragmentary. There was no mandible and no palate.

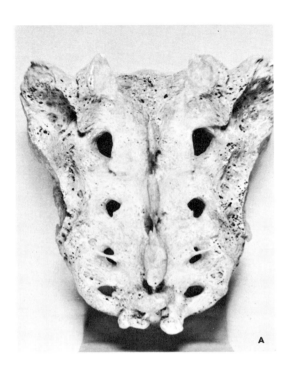

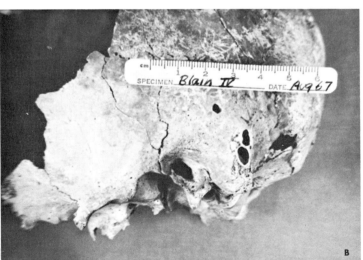

Plate XXIII. (A) Burial 5: Posterior aspect of sacrum. Note bony septa dividing third sacral foramina. This anomaly probably reflects division of the fourth sacral nerve (normally post-foraminal) within pelvis. (B) Burial 4: View of left mastoid. Note large perforations with rounded sclerotic margins indicative of chronic infection.

PHYSICAL ANTHROPOLOGICAL DATA

Age: All epiphyses of the fibula, tibia, os calcis, femur, radius, and scapula (coracoid) were separate, as were the acetabular margins of the ischium, ilium, and pubis. Complete fusion had occurred bilaterally for the conjoint distal epiphyses of the humeri, although the medial epicondyles were still open. Recent fusion had occurred between the olecranon and the diaphysis of the left ulna, although the right ulnar shaft and olecranon showed no fusion. Age was assessed at 15 ± 1 year, with emphasis on the earlier date in light of the absence of union in the pelvis and those unions commonly associated with fusion in the distal humerus.

Pathology: Infection was present in the left mastoid process, with pre–mortem perforations on the interior and exterior aspects of the skull (Plate XXIII, B). There was possible, pre-mortem infectious perforation of the right frontal sinus.

Dentition: No teeth were available for analysis.

Cause of Death: It is possible that death could have resulted from acute mastoid infection indicated by internal cranial perforations (see above) with subsequent brain abscess.

BURIAL 5

EXCAVATION DATA

Burial Position: Full Extension (Plate XXII, A).

Position in Mound: In south–west quadrant of mound south of Test Trench I (Figure 19).

Orientation: Due south.

Depth from Surface: 14 inches to top of skull.

Associated Artifacts: The skull rested upon a long, rectangular sandstone bar. This "headrest" had been carefully smoothed on the top and the under surface. A large shell gorget rested atop the manubrium and below the mental eminence. On both wrists (around the

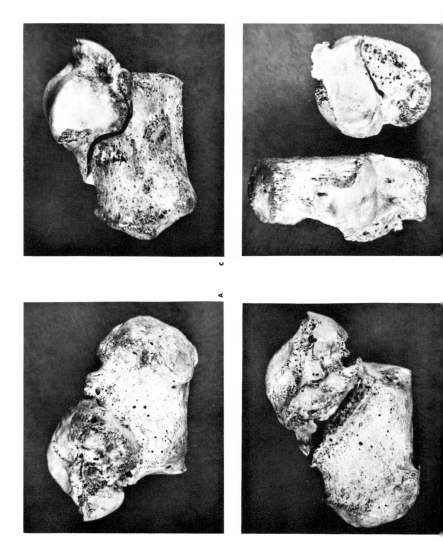

Plate XXIV. Burial 5. (A) Medial aspect of right talus and calcaneus. Bones are fused across sustentacular joint. (B) Lateral aspect of (A) above. Subtalar joint is open but narrow. Note arthritic reaction on neck of talus. (C) Medial aspect of left talus and caleaneus. Note marked arthritic changes and abnormal sustentacular joint. (D) Note open articulating surfaces of left calcaneus and talus, and vascular foramina crossing the abnormal sustentacular facet. Marked arthritis of posterior facets of calcaneus and talus.

metaphyseal flares of the radius and ulna) were a large number of small circular shell beads (n = 352). Their position *in situ* indicated that they had probably constituted two separate strands. Two *Baum Cordmarked Incised, var. Blain* sherds were recovered from the fill.

Condition: With the exception of the skull and pubic bones the skeleton was in very good condition. The skull was badly broken by a deep plow cut, although the maxilla, mandible, and the posterior aspect of the cranium were intact.

Completeness: With the exception of a portion of the pubic bones, and those areas of the skull noted above, the skeleton was complete.

PHYSICAL ANTHROPOLOGICAL DATA

Age: All epiphyses (including sternal clavicular) were completely ossified. A slight medial gap persisted between the first and second sacral centra. A portion of the right pubic symphyseal face was available for observation. It showed considerable rarefication of the demi-face with a definite plateau and dorsal margin. There were no osteoarthritic changes in the vertebral column. Dentition was uniformly indicative of third decade age (See below). The sagittal suture was in late stages of closure both ectocranially and endocranially while the lambdoid exhibited complete closure endocranially (considered anomalous) and ectocranial closure of about 2.5 mm. The auricular surfaces of the sacrum were crisp with quite regular margins. On the basis of these indications the skeleton was assessed at 34 years ± 2 years.

Sex: The articulated pelvis was demonstrably android with marked medial convergence of the ischial spines and marked projection of the lower sacrum into the pelvic canal. The sacrum displayed even curvature, and the auricular surfaces were large and robust, extending well onto the third segment. The post-cranial skeleton displayed robust muscle insertions. The femoral heads were large (maximum diameter left: 50.1 mm; maximum diameter right: 51.2 mm). The posterior roots of the zygomatics were robust, the nuchal area massive, and the mastoids large and projecting. On the basis of the above indications the skeleton was assessed as male.

Plate XXV. (A) Burial 1: Raven beak and shell gorgets during excavation. (B) Burial 4: Note rodent burrow between skull and thorax.

Pathology: Spondoloysis was present in the fifth lumbar (Plate XXI, A) with evidence of only minimal anterior slip of the fifth lumbar on the first sacral centrum. Although a genetic etiology was suggested for this condition by earlier observers, Thieme (1950; See also Stewart, 1953) has extensively reviewed the literature and shown that this condition is most likely a result of mechanical stress in early childhood.

The tali and os calci showed severe arthritic involvement of the talo–calcaneal joint and slight involvement of the calcaneo–cuboid joint. The medial aspect of the right talus and the medial aspect of the right calcaneus are fused where the sustentaculum tali should normally occur (Plates XXIV, A-B), a condition commonly referred to as a talo-calcaneal bridge. The left foot shows an incomplete form of the medial bridge between the talus and calcaneus (Plates XXIV, C-D). The juncture on this side was apparently a syndesmosis or synchondrosis rather than a complete fusion. This condition can produce a variety of painful secondary defects in the foot with commensurate arthritic reaction and loss of motion, especially eversion and inversion. Although the etiology of this specific disorder is unknown, its bilateral occurrence and the familial pattern of occurrence of similar disorders involving the tarsus (Pearlman, Edkin, and Warren, 1964; Wray and Herndon, 1963) point to a possible genetic origin (For a more extensive treatment of this disorder and its occurrence in this skeleton, see Heiple and Lovejoy, 1969).

Dentition: The complete dentition of this burial was available for analysis. Dental wear in both the maxilla and mandible exhibited Grade C condition (see Table 14). There were no unusual cusps in the lower or upper teeth. Although the upper teeth were free of cavities, caries was present in the lower left first and third molars. The right lower second and third molars were absent pre–mortem. Alveolar indications were that this loss was probably a result of abcess. Calculus was present on all teeth, with severe involvement of the incisors and canines.

Cause of Death: Unknown.

Non–metric Variations: Small medial–laterial septa were present across the posterior aspect of the dorsal sacral foramina (Plate XXIII, A). This condition appears to have been previously unreported; its bilateral expression and probable non-functional etiology are possible indicators of a genetic origin. Communications between the coranoid fossa and olecranon fossa of the humerus were present bilaterally. No other non–metric variations were noted in addition to those already reported above.

BURIAL 6

EXCAVATION DATA

Burial Position: Semi–flexion (Plate XXII, B).

Position in Mound: In south–east quadrant of mound east of Test Trench A (Figure 19).

Orientation: Due east.

Depth from Surface: Varied between 13 inches and 16 inches.

Associated Artifacts: A large, fresh-water bivalve spoon was found adjacent to the right knee. A limestone elbow pipe was found beneath the left elbow. A concave–based triangular projectile point was recovered between the sixth and seventh ribs on the left side. No other artifacts were found.

Condition: Very poor. The skull had been struck by a deep plow cut. Although the remainder of the skeleton had not been damaged by plowing, the bones were fragmentary and badly eroded.

Completeness: The skeleton was complete with the exception of major portions of the skull including the maxilla.

PHYSICAL ANTHROPOLOGICAL DATA

Age: All epiphyses showed complete union including the left medial clavicle. There were no intact sutures on the fragmentary calvarium. The lumbar centra showed minimal arthritic involvement, although in the centra of lumbar–5 and sacral–1 there is evidence of moderate arthritic change including penetration of the disk material through the end plates and into the vertebral bodies (early Schmorl's node, (Plate XXI, C). The cervical vertebrae were completely normal, while the thoracics showed incipent laminal spurring on the superior borders. The auricular surfaces of the innominates showed early signs of erosion and roughening. The symphyseal faces of the pubic bones were too damaged to permit observation. Evidence from the dentition (see below) was indicative of third decade age. Based upon the above indications this skeleton was assessed at 35 years ± 5 years.

Sex: The pelvis could not be articulated because of the fragmentary condition of the sacrum. The sciatic notches were of medium width. The ischial spines were not well developed, and in an articulated pelvis would probably have diverged considerably. Supraorbital ridges were minimally developed, although the forehead was only moderately vertical. There was a pronounced gonial angle in the mandible (135°). The mastoid processes and ridges above the auditory meatus were classified as intermediate. Long bones were large (See Table 15) but not robust. The auricular surfaces of the innominates were not extensive. The maximum diameters of the femoral

Table 15. Osteometric data.*

BURIAL	BL-1	BL-2	BL-5	BL-6
Femur: Max. Length (FeL_1)		R:471 L:477	R:460 L:456	
Tibia: Max. Length (TiL_1)	L:391		R:393 L:392	
Humerus: Max. Length (HuL_1)		L:334	R:316 L:320	R:322
Radis: Max. Length (RaL_1)		L:269	R:261 L:261	
Ulna: Max. Length (UlL_1)	R:287	R:289 L:287		L:286

*All measurements in millimeters

heads were 45.9 (left) and 46.1 (right). On the basis of the above indications this skeleton was assessed as female.

Pathology: Other than the Schmorl's node (Plate XXI, C) noted above, no other pathological conditions were observed.

Dentition: Only the mandible was available for observation. There were no unusual cusps. There had been one tooth loss (left first molar) shortly before death. No caries were noted. Dental wear was assessed at Grade C (see Table 14). A small amount of calculus was present on all teeth, although the lower right canine showed extensive involvement.

Cause of Death: The projectile point recovered from the rib cage was probably the cause of death of this individual.

Non–metric Variations: None noted.

BURIAL 7
EXCAVATION DATA

Burial Position: Semi-flexion.

Position in Mound: In south–east quadrant of mound, south of Test Trench I (Figure 19).

Orientation: Due north-east.

Depth from Surface: Varied between 12 inches and 14 inches.

Associated Artifacts: Two strands of eight cylindrical ocean shell beads each were found on the right and left forearms. Near the skull a notched, fresh–water shell spoon was recovered. No other artifacts were found.

Condition: Very poor. Only one long bone could be removed intact.

Completeness: Epiphyseal centers were almost all absent due to soil conditions and mechanical damage by an unknown agent. The skull was fragmentary, as was the post–cranial skeleton.

PHYSICAL ANTHROPOLOGICAL DATA

Age: The coracoid epiphyses were present and intact bilaterally but were not uniform in size and development, indicating recent ossifi-

Table 16. Summary of Physical Anthropological data.

BURIAL	AGE	SEX	PATHOLOGY	CAUSE OF DEATH	NON-METRIC VARIANTS
BL-1	35 +/- 5 yrs.	Male	Osteoarthritis of left hip with commensurate osteoporosis in left lower limb. Projectile point fragment in right humerus	Unknown	Six lumbar vertebrae present Sacralization of 6th lumbar
BL-2	33 +/- 4 yrs.	Male	Mastoiditis	Cultural trauma	None noted
BL-3	28 +/- 3 mos.		None observed	Cultural trauma	None noted
BL-4	15 +/- 1 yr.		Mastoiditis with possible brain abscess	Brain abscess?	None noted
BL-5	34 +/- 2 yrs.	Male	Spondololysis of 5th lumbar. Talo-Calcaneal bridging with commensurate osteoarthritis of both tarsi.	Unknown	Bilateral septa across sacral foramina. Septal apertures in both humeri
BL-6	35 +/- 5 yrs.	Female?	Early Schmorl's node in L-5/S-1	Cultural trauma	None noted
BL-7	12 +/- 2 mos.		Bilateral osteitis of tibiae	Unknown	None noted

Table 17. Summary of Archaeological data.

BURIAL	ORIENTATION	BURIAL POSITION	GRAVE ARTIFACTS	DEPTH FROM SURFACE
BL-1	Due east	Full extension	Red ochre, two circular shell gorgets with bird beak (raven?)	6" - 10"
BL-2	Due south	Full extension	Large ceremonial triangular blade	6" - 10"
BL-3	15° east of south	Semi-flexion	None	14"
BL-4	Due east	Full extension	None	15"
BL-5	Due south	Full extension	Sandstone "headrest", large shell gorget, two strands of disc shell beads	14"
BL-6	Due east	Semi-flexion	Worked fresh-water bivalve spoon, limestone elbo pipe	13" - 16"
BL-7	Due north-east	Semi-flexion	Two strands of eight tubular shell beads, notched shell spoon	12" - 14"

cation. The vertebral arches present (cervical and thoracic) showed no evidence of union at the apex. Length of the intact left tibia was 102 mm. These data, in addition to those derived from the dentition, (see below) provided the basis of age assessment at 12 months ± 2 months.

Pathology: Inspection of the tibiae by roentgenograms revealed new periosteal bone formation on the medial aspects of both tibiae (Plate XVIII, A). Gross inspection showed a mild swelling on the proximal-medial portion of the left tibia. This bilateral osteitis was probably caused by local trauma leading to hemorrhage beneath the periosteum and subsequent inflammation, although infection can not be excluded as a possible cause.

Dentition: Teeth present were one lower left first molar; two upper canines; one upper lateral incisor (left); and one lower left lateral incisor. The crown of the molar was fully developed with no root formation; the crowns of the upper cuspids were fully developed with only minimal root formation; the upper lateral incisor displayed a root about 50 percent complete, as did the lower lateral incisor.

Cause of Death: The condition of the lower legs was not sufficient of itself to be the probable cause of death. No other possible cause of death was discovered in excavation or in the skeleton.

SUMMARY

The excavation of the Blain Mound, an integral feature of the Blain Village Site, in Ross County, Ohio, has been described, and the probable structure of the mound has been considered. Archaeological data from the excavation have been systematically presented and are summarized in Table 17. Because of inadequate genetic investigation of most metrical and non–metrical variations in skeletal material, such data have not been systematically presented. However, all non–metrical variations noted, and the basic osteometrics suggested by Brothwell (1963) have been included. All physical anthropological data have been summarized in Table 16. No conclusions as to the genetic affinity of the Blain Mound population were possible because of the lack of applicable indicators for small populations and adequate comparative populations. The only population of possible genetic relationship to the Blain Mound series that has been systematically reported is that of the Madisonville Site (Hooton, 1920). No non–metrical variants present in the Blain Mound series were reported to be present in the Madisonville population. Major emphasis of this paper has been on demographic data derivable from small skeletal series, including a systematic presentation of the evidence on which conclusions were based.

XIII

The Blain Site Vertebrate Fauna
Paul W. Parmalee and Orrin C. Shane, III

This chapter is divided into three sections. The first consists of an analysis and interpretation of the remains recovered in 1966; this study was made by Dr. Paul W. Parmalee of the Illinois State Museum. The second section deals with the fauna from the 1968 excavations, analysed by Shane. The final section is an attempt at interpreting the combined data of the 1966 and 1968 field seasons. Although this manner of presentation and analysis was dictated by circumstances that arose from the unforeseen second field season, it proved to be of considerable interest, because the results of both analyses, done independently by different investigators, were essentially identical. In a methodological sense, as well as in terms of the postulated cultural homogeneity of Blain Village, this is of some significance.

As far as field procedures are concerned, it should be noted that all *in situ* bone material was saved. Features with substantial remains of fishes were flotated to ensure maximum recovery. Surface and plowzone material was discarded because of the precise provenience uncertainties involved. However, the faunal remains from the Blain Mound fill, which obviously constitute secondarily deposited material, are included in the analysis.

1966 SEASON (Parmalee)

The Blain Site (33 Ro-49) is a Fort Ancient Village of approximately twelve acres, and it is located on the west bank of the Scioto River south of Chillicothe near Renick Junction (Scioto Township). Preliminary survey work in the spring of 1966 produced large quantities of Baum Focus ceramics as well as stone artifacts and faunal remains (Prufer and McKenzie, 1967). More extensive excavation of several large units and numerous pits during the summer of 1966 by Dr. Olaf H. Prufer and students from the Department of Humanities and Social Studies, Case Institute of Technology, Cleveland, resulted in the recovery of a great number of stone and pottery artifacts, mollusk shells, and approximately 23,800 pieces of bone.

Of this total number of bones, 3,765 (15.8 percent) were determined to the genus or species level; of the 20,039 specifically unidentifiable fragments, 1,876 were fish, 1,852 were birds, and 16,311 were mammals. All classes of vertebrates were represented, with a minimum number of species in each class as follows: fishes, 10; amphibians, 3; reptiles (turtles), 7; birds, 15; mammals, 23. The identified species, provenience, total number of remains of each species, percent of total, and the minimum number of individuals represented are listed in Table 19.

Occupants of the Blain Site utilized several habitat types in their search for game, although it is apparent that primarily timbered areas and forest edge were hunted for their basic source of meat animals. The Scioto River provided a variety of fish and turtles, and although these aquatic species were important supplements for the diet of these people, in terms of actual pounds of edible meat, combined they would not have equalled one adult black bear, elk or white-tailed deer. Except for turkey and possibly passenger pigeon, little effort was devoted to hunting birds. Mammals, on the other hand, provided the primary source of meat in the total food economy of the Blain Site inhabitants, and the white-tailed deer was singly the most important species.

ACCOUNTS OF SPECIES

Fishes: at least ten species of fish, representing a minimum of forty-two individuals, were identified from the faunal sample and their remains accounted for approximately 10 percent of the total. Redhorse and other suckers were the fishes most often taken, although numerous elements of bass, small centrarchids and the freshwater drum attest to their general use as well by these people. Elements of both small and large individuals of most species were noted, although generally the majority of fish taken was small to medium-sized. The few exceptions included elements from large specimens of walleye, bass (probably largemouth, *Micropterus salmoides*), hog sucker, and redhorse (probably northern, *Moxostoma macrolepidotum*). The only evidence as to methods of catching fish was the recovery of one broken bone fish hook (Plate: XVI, I).

Amphibians: the presence of toad and frog bones in the midden debris is probably incidental to the human occupation of the site; the four individuals represented were small, and there is no evidence to suggest any use of these amphibians by the Indian. Recovery of a single humerus of an adult hellbender (a large aquatic salamander) in Feature 4b was of interest since this animal attains a size (about two feet in length) that might have made it a desirable food species, but on the basis of only one element, the reason for its presence in the pit and its possible use by the Indian is a matter of speculation.

Reptiles (turtles): remains of turtles were encountered commonly throughout the midden deposits, although judging from frequency of occurrence (in all excavation units except Feature 8) and number of remains, it was apparent that the terrestrial box turtle was taken and used with greater frequency than all of the aquatic species combined. As a group, turtle bone (primarily shell) amounted to approximately 15 percent of the total number of identified remains, with elements of *Terrapene* accounting for 10 percent.

In the summer of 1963, Dr. Prufer excavated a portion of the McGraw Site, a Hopewell village adjacent to the Blain Site (Prufer, 1965). Turtle remains were also numerous in the McGraw Site middens, but it is of interest to note that, compared with the Blain Site material, box turtle comprised only 18 percent of the turtle at McGraw while it accounted for 66 percent at Blain. The occupants of the earlier Hopewell site (McGraw) made more extensive use of the aquatic species, especially the snapping turtle, than did the inhabitants of Blain. Nearly 28 percent of all identified remains from the McGraw Site were turtles as compared with 15 percent from the Blain Site.

Eight carapaces of the box turtle—about one-half to nearly complete—were recovered that had been altered for use as cups or bowls. Modification of the shells was slight; the ribs and vertebrae had been broken away and partially smoothed down, and the edges (marginals) in at least four specimens had been slightly ground and smoothed. In all probability turtles were eaten although, based on the Blain Site faunal sample, the total quantity of meat realized from these animals would have been small. Box turtles may have been sought after as much, or more, for their carapace for use as a utensil than for food.

Birds: of the fifteen species of birds identified from the Blain Site, only the turkey can be considered significant as a food animal. Although at least twenty-two passenger pigeons were represented in the sample, they would have provided a very minor supplement in the total food economy of thess people; the amount of edible meat derived from one or two geese (or large turkeys) would surpass that of all the passenger pigeons represented. Inhabitants of the Blain village made little use of waterfowl (ducks, geese, swans) or upland game birds (bobwhite, prairie chicken), probably because they were never present in numbers large enough to warrant concentrated hunting activity.

Turkey bones accounted for nearly nine percent of the total identified elements (65% percent of the birds) from the Blain Site, and at least twenty-nine individuals were represented. An estimated 90 to 95 percent of the specifically unidentifiable bird bone fragments were those of large birds, in all probability turkey. Butchering cuts were noted on or near the distal and/or proximal ends of several humeri; these cuts resulted from the wing being severed from the sternum or "shoulder" (proximal end cuts), and from sectioning the wing at the point of articulation with the radius/ulna (distal cuts). The proximal end of one carpometacarpus had been cut as the tip of the wing was removed at the point of articulation with the distal ends of the radius/ulna. One coracoid was cut near the point of attachment to the sternum. Turkeys were apparently numerous in the wooded areas surrounding the village site, and these large birds provided a constant source of food to the inhabitants.

It is a matter of conjecture whether the hawks, owl, and the eagle were killed for food or whether they were used for ceremonial or other purposes. The use of wings and claws of raptorial birds by Mississippian and other late cultural groups for ceremony and as grave offerings has been discussed by Parmalee (1957, 1967) and others. An incomplete lower mandible of a raven found in the Blain Mound (Plate XVI, P) was part of a grave offering. Two bird bone beads were found in Feature 4b one a bead or "tube"—possibly cut from turkey radii) in Feature 1 (Plate XVI, K) and two in Unit III.

Mammals: sixty percent of the identifiable pieces of bone recovered at the Blain Site were mammals, and of this total nearly 47 percent were those of the white–tailed deer. A minimum of thirty–nine individual deer was represented; by using the method of calculating estimated pounds of edible meat of various food animals proposed by White (1953), these deer would have supplied approximately 3,900 pounds of usable meat. White (1953) estimated that a 200-pound deer, after being dressed out (removal of entrails, hide, bone), would provide about one–half the live weight or 100 pounds of edible meat. Such estimates are highly variable, of course, since some of the organs (heart, liver, kidneys, plus the brain) were probably utilized—and fawns and yearling animals would weigh considerably less than the average estimated weight of adults—but the size of a deer and its availability throughout the year made it the single most valuable animal in the food economy of these people.

Obviously, although the deer provided the basic meat staple in the Indians' diet, a variety of the smaller species of animals and/or those taken only infrequently, contributed significantly to the total subsistence pattern of these people. However, six of the small mammals identified from this sample (shrew, mole, deer mouse, chipmunk, vole, rice rat) probably occurred at this site naturally and were incidental to the human occupation. About one half of the cottontail remains were those of two juveniles recovered in Features 2 and 8, and probably these individuals had died there and were not part of the faunal debris discarded by the Indians. Several other small mammals—opossum, striped skunk, woodchuck, squirrels (*Sciurus* spp.), and muskrat—were taken occasionally, but the few individuals represented suggest that these mammals were either uncommon in the vicinity of the village or the Indian expended more time and effort to the hunting of other preferred species.

The beaver would have provided an excellent source of meat (large adults, 70–80 lbs.) and hides for these people, but the few remains found in the midden debris suggest that this rodent was locally uncommon. Butchering cuts were noted at the distal end of one tibia (removal of the hind foot), and chop marks on the ilium near the acetabulum (an attempt to sever the hind limb from the pelvis); an altered, ventrally grooved section of incisor (Plate XVI, M) had been worked and used probably as a chisel. Remains of the raccoon were fairly common and occurred in most units and pits; the wooded banks and flood–plain areas along the Scioto River would have provided good habitat for this animal. Occupants of the Blain Site utilized the raccoon somewhat more extensively than other aquatic or semi-aquatic species (muskrat, beaver), all probably in direct proportion to abundance and availability. The following raccoon elements possessed cut marks: one astragalus (removal of hind foot), one pelvis section (iliosacral joint—separating the hind limb from the pelvis), the inferior border of the neck of a scapula (severing the forelimb at the shoulder); two lower jaws exhibited skinning cuts on the lateral surfaces near the ventral margin that were inflicted as the pelt was removed from the head. Two, or possibly three, raccoon bacula had been shortened and the distal ends sharpened, possibly for use as awls.

Judging by the number of elements recovered and individuals represented, the larger carnivores—bears, bobcats, wolves—were not numerous in the region and/or were seldom taken by the Indians. Remains of only one gray wolf, comprising several skull sections of a large adult, were found at the Blain Site. Three adult bobcats (number of individuals determined from skull parts in Feature 4b) and one kitten (Feature 15) were represented, and as evidenced by the skinning cuts on two lower jaws and two skull sections, the pelts were probably used and the flesh eaten. Four gray foxes were represented in the faunal sample, and of the five lower jaws recovered, three exhibited skinning cuts (removal of the pelt from the head) on the cheek side or along the ventral edge. Judging by the paucity of canid remains in the Blain faunal assemblage, dogs were not numerous in the village.

Bear ceremonialism was a well–established cultural trait among prehistoric Indian groups and, to a lesser extent, in the early historic tribes of the eastern United States. Although drilled bear canine teeth and worked skull and jaw ornaments are occasionally found with human burials (Parmalee, 1959, et al.), post–cranial elements are rarely encountered in midden desposits at prehistoric sites (Guilday, Parmalee, and Tanner, 1962). The bear represented something more than a food animal to these prehistoric groups, and if the animal was utilized for its meat and hide, the bones were disposed of in areas other than the garbage middens. This cultural trait was still evident at an early historic Fox site in Wisconsin (Parmalee, 1963), but at a later (1790-1810) Sauk–Fox village in northwestern Illinois (Parmalee, 1964), bear elements in the midden debris and lack of bear bone artifacts with the associated burials indicated the animal had lost its ceremonial significance and was being utilized as a food species. Swanton (1946), in discussing food animals of historic tribes in the southeastern United States, stated that "The bear was probably the next most useful animal [to the deer]. It was hunted for its flesh, but still more for its fat, which was preserved in skins."

The Blain Site inhabitants represent an interesting transition, since they were a prehistoric group (with no evidence of European contacts) that had apparently utilized the bear as a food animal. Except for two drilled canine teeth (Plate XVI, J), ornaments which are characteristic of both prehistoric and historic groups, no evidence was encountered to suggest ceremonial use of the animal. Although not numerous, unworked jaws, isolated teeth and post cranial elements were recovered in eleven excavation units. Butchering cuts were present on: the proximal end of one radius and one ulna (severing the forelimb at the "elbow"), an astragalus (removal of the hind foot), the neck of a femoral head (removal of the "thigh" or hind limb from the pelvis), and an axis (severing the head from the body).

Recovery of thirty-three elements (representing at least seven individuals) of the rice rat, *Oryzomys palustris,* is of interest since this rodent no longer occurs in Ohio, and because all previous prehistoric records of its presence in that state (summarized by Goslin, 1951) are associated primarily with villages of the Fort Ancient culture. Baker (1936), Guilday and Mayer-Oakes (1952), and others have discussed the former occurrence of the rice rat in other areas, based on remains from Indian sites. Although the Indian may have inadvertently extended the range of *Oryzomys* northward by accidentally transporting individuals in goods, stored food and the like, these areas (Illinois, Ohio, West Virginia, Pennsylvania) probably represented the northern limits of its range, and extirpation later possibly resulted from change in historic land use practices.

In all probability the Blain Site was a permanent village that was occupied throughout the year. Antler sections were still attached to seven frontal bones of white-tailed deer skulls, indicating the animals had been killed sometime between midsummer (July) and the end of December. Around the first of the year, the antlers are shed; therefore, the two individuals with only the antler base or pedicel in evidence were probably taken during the winter or spring months. Evidence based on the number of antlered vs. anterless skull remains is hardly sufficient to state with certainty that hunting was practiced throughout the year, but the presence of both conditions suggests continuous village occupation. Fishing could have been practiced during all seasons, although fresh-water mussel shells and remains of both aquatic and terrestrial turtles are indicative of hunting/ collecting activities carried out during the warmer months, April through October.

Complete and/or nearly complete lower jaws of the white-tailed deer were individually aged by following techniques developed by Severinghaus (1949) which were based on degree of tooth wear and eruption. The resulting data are listed in Table 18.

The sample of jaws sufficiently complete for aging was small, but assuming these elements represent a true picture of the age classes of deer killed by the inhabitants of Blain Village, one noteworthy fact becomes apparent. Approximately 52 percent of the jaws were from individuals less than two years old. All individuals in this category still retained the deciduous premolars—or the premolars had

Table 18.   Age distribution of deer (percentage of each
grouping)

Age	
Approximate Age in Years	Number of Individuals (Percentage)
0—6 months	2 (5.55)
6 months—1 year	6 (16.66)
1—2	11 (30.55)
2—3	2 (5.55)
3—4	5 (13.88)
4—5	5 (13.88)
5—6	2 (5.55)
6—7	1 (2.77)
7—8	2 (5.55)
	Total 36

recently been lost but the permanent molars had not yet erupted above the gum line—actually, these deer were less than eighteen months of age. Unlike the situation at the Graham Site, another Fort Ancient village in Hocking County, Ohio, where approximately 42 percent of the deer were in the two–to–three year age class (Cleland: in *Studies in Ohio Archaeology,* Prufer and McKenzie, 1967) at least half of the deer taken by the Blain Site people had not yet reached their prime. These young animals—and old individuals— would be the most likely to fall prey to the Indian hunters.

Skinning and butchering marks on deer elements: procedures employed by prehistoric Indians in butchering large herbivores such as elk and deer have proved to be basically similar for most cultural groups. Detailed descriptions of these techniques have been presented by Guilday, Parmalee and Tanner (1962), Parmalee (1965), and others. Deep or pronounced cut marks, all apparently inflicted while attempting to disarticulate carcasses, were observed on the following deer elements:
scapula (9)—the inferior border of the neck, and the proximal end of the humerus (1): separation of the forelimb at the shoulder; atlas (2) and axis (2)—severing the head immediately behind the base of the skull; hyoid (1)—probably cut during removal of the tongue; radius, proximal end (2) and humerus, distal end (13)—severing the fore-

limb at the "elbow"; metacarpal, proximal end (6)—separating the lower leg (cannon bone) of the forelimb from the point of articulation with the distal ends of the radius/ulna; astragalus (11), fourth tarsal (18), tibia, distal end (19), and calcaneum (6)—removal of the lower hind limb at the hock; tibia, proximal end (5)—severing the hind limb at the knee.

Several limb bone fragments, probably those of deer, possessed cut marks that may have resulted during removal of the flesh since they were not inflicted at points of articulation ("joints"). The blades of three scapulae had been scored, probably as a result of defleshing of the shoulder. Knife marks were noted, parallel to the tooth row, on two maxillae and one lower jaw; these were made as the pelt was removed from the head.

The only butchering cuts observed on any of the elk bones occurred on the distal ends (malleoli) of two tibiae; these resulted as the lower hind limb was severed at the hock.

Bone Artifacts: with few exceptions, the majority of bone utensils and tools found at the Blain Site had been fashioned from large mammal bones, most of which were deer. Turtle shell bowls, the few bird bone beads (and "tubes"?), and the one section of worked beaver incisor recovered in the village midden and mound have been described. In addition to the two bear canines with holes drilled near the root base, two smaller canine teeth (raccoon?; Plate XVI, H) which were drilled in similar fashion occurred in Unit II and Feature 6. These teeth were probably worn as pendants or strung as a necklace. The baculum of a large mustelid, found in Feature 9, had been shortened and the distal end sharpened for probable use as an awl or punch (XVI, E). An unusual thin, flat, cut section of bone, drilled along one edge (Plate XVI, L) was recovered from Feature 1; the arifact was incomplete and its original function problematical, but it may have been part of a suspended ornament.

Eighteen deer antler tines showed some evidence, in the form of cut and scrape marks and/or artificially worn tips, of having been used as tools—probably flakers (Plate XVI, G). Nine antler tines, hollowed out in the center and ground or cut to a point at the tip (one with a hole drilled near the base; Plate XVI, F), were probably used as arrowheads. At least four cut sections of antler were recovered that varied considerably in size and shape, and the use to which they were put is questionable (Plate XVI, B). Several worked (awl?) fragments were found in addition to six awls that had been fashioned from large mammal (deer) done splinters (Plate XVI, C). Proximal ends of two deer ulnae appeared to have been worked and were possibly used as awls (both distal ends were missing). At least three large mammal bone awls (Plate XVI, D) had been fashioned from the same element (scapulae of the deer?), but the bone had been altered by cutting and scraping so that identification of the animal and bone was uncertain.

Beamers (Plate XVI, A), tools thought to be used for scraping excess fat and tissue from hides, were fashioned from the metatarsals (cannon bone of the hind limbs) of deer. Except for one nearly complete beamer (Plate XVI, R from Feature 4b) all others were fragmentary (sixteen pieces or sections). The specimen from Feature 4b is especially interesting; the proximal end had been broken off, and the main shaft of the beamer (but not the broken end pieces) were later burned. Also, an attempt had been made to re-fashion or alter the broken end of the shaft and the other fragments by grinding down the bevelled edge of one side of the original beamer tool.

Four phalanges of the deer (Plate XVI, N) and one in the elk (Plate XVI, O) had been modified by drilling a hole in the distal end and cutting off the proximal end. The function of these toe bones as part of the cup–and–pin gaming device has been adequately explained and illustrated by Guilday (1963).

SUMMARY

The nearly 24,000 pieces of bone recovered in the Blain Site village in 1966 provided a sample of animal remains that can be considered as probably indicative of the vertebrate species utilized by these people of the Fort Ancient culture. It was possible to determine approximately 3,800 elements to the genus or species level, and at least 57 species were represented. Sixty percent of the identified elements were those of mammals. Remains of the white–tailed deer accounted for nearly half of all identifiable bone, and as a source of meat and bone for the manufacture of tools and implements, this animal was singly the most valuable to the occupants of Blain Village.

Table 19. Vertebrate remains identified from the Blain Site, Ohio—1966.

S P E C I E S	I	III	1	2	3	4a	4b	5	6	7	8	9	10	11	14	15	16	44	Total	%	Minimum No. of Individuals
FISHES																			388	10.30	43
Lake Sturgeon, Acipenser fulvescens			2																2	.05	1
Gar, Lepisosteus sp.		1	1													2			4	.11	1
Pike, Esox sp.			1																1	.03	1
Suckers: Catostomidae	3	19	47	4	3	3	2			1		5	1	1	8	3	16		116	3.08	—
Redhorse, Moxostoma spp.		18	41	2	3	1	4								15		20		107	2.84	18
Hog Sucker, Hypentelium nigricans			2	2															4	.11	3
Sunfish, Bass: Centrarchidae			21									4					12		37	.98	3
Walleye, Stizostedium cf. vitreum			6													2	3		11	.29	3
Fresh-water Drum, Aplodinotus grunniens		7	20		1	3	1					2	1		2	1			43	1.14	5
Bass, Micropterus sp.			18												2	2	11		37	.98	4
Catfish, Ictalurus sp.	3	3	13																25	.66	3
Madtom, Noturus sp.		1																	1	.03	1
AMPHIBIANS																			11	.29	5
Toad, Bufo sp.			2																3	.08	2
Frog, Rana sp.			6					1											7	.18	2
Hellbender, Cryptobranchus allegan.						1									1				1	.03	1
TURTLES																			578	15.34	25
Turtle, spp.	52	34		2		2	2			1			2			4	4		100	2.65	—
Snapping Turtle, Chelydra serpentina	1	1																	1	.03	1
Musk Turtle, Sternothaerus odoratus		8	8		1										3		18		32	.85	5
Box Turtle, Terrapene cf. carolina	15	181	68	11	5	16	14	10	6	1		2	3	2	18	19	10	1	382	10.15	12
Painted Turtle, Chrysemis picta	2	2	1												1	1			4	.11	1
Pond Terrapin, Pseudemys scripta												1		1					1	.03	1
Map Turtle, Graptemys cf. geographica	1	1	2									1		1					6	.16	2
Turtle: Graptemys, Pseudemys group	1	5	5																10	.26	—
Softshell Turtle, Trionyx sp.	5	7			1	3	4		3	1				13	2	2	3		42	1.11	3

Table 19. (Continued)

S P E C I E S	I	III	1	2	3	4a	4b	5	6	7	8	9	10	11	14	15	16	44	Total	%	Minimum No. of Individuals
BIRDS																			517	13.75	66
Least Bittern, Ixobrycus exilis			1																1	.03	1
Canada ? Goose, Branta canadensis			1																1	.03	1
Snow/Blue Goose, Chen sp.			2																2	.05	1
Merganser, Mergus sp.			1																1	.03	1
Sharp-shinned ? Hawk, Accipiter striatus						1													1	.03	1
Cooper's Hawk, Accipiter cooperi						1?													1	.03	1
Golden Eagle, Aquila chrysaetus									1										1	.03	1
Prairie Chicken, Tympanuchus cupido			6			1?	1?			1?									9	.24	1
Bobwhite, Colinus virginianus	1														1		2		4	.11	1
Turkey, Meleagris gallopavo	7	66	112	1		20	33	2	6	1	1	6	1	7	44	7	23		337	8.95	29
Sandhill Crane, Grus canadensis																	2		2	.05	1
Passenger Pigeon, Ectopistes migratorius	4		89		34			2				2			1	4	6		142	3.71	22
Barred Owl, Strix varia	2		2									2					2	1	9	.24	1
Raven, Corvus corax			1																1	.03	1
Crow, Corvus brachyrhynchos			2															1	3	.08	2
Passerines			2																2	.05	1

Table 19. (*Continued*)

S P E C I E S	I	III	1	2	3	4a	4b	5	6	7	8	9	10	11	14	15	16	44	Total	%	Minimum No.of Individuals
MAMMALS																			2271	60.31	114
Opossum, Didelphis marsupialis		7	1													2			10	.26	2
Eastern Mole, Scalopus aquaticus		9																	9	.24	2
Short-tailed Shrew, Blarina brevicauda		2																	2	.05	1
Black Bear, Ursus americanus	3	8	5			2	3		1	1	1				4				28	.74	3
Raccoon, Procyon lotor	20	22		2		2	3	1	1	1	1				4	5	2		64	1.70	11
Striped Skunk, Mephitis mephitis		2					1												3	.08	1
Gray Fox, Urocyon cinereoargenteus		8				1	1	1							2		2		15	.40	4
Gray Wolf, Canis lupus	1																		1	.03	1
Dog, Canis familiaris		2				1													3	.08	2
Canid, Canis sp.	1																		1	.03	1
Bobcat, Lynx rufus		2				1	10								1	1	1	1	17	.45	4
Woodchuck, Marmota monax	6	7			2	1				1					5	2	1		25	.66	4
Eastern Chipmunk, Tamias striatus	4	1					1					1			1		2		10	.26	3
Gray? Squirrel, Sciurus carolinensis	8	6			1	1		3						1	1		4		25	.66	2
Fox? Squirrel, Sciurus niger		5			2	2	4								4	1	8		26	.69	4
Squirrel, Sciurus spp.	3	31				1	11								8	4	6		64	1.70	5
Beaver, Castor canadensis	4	8				1	1			1					2		6		23	.61	3
Deer Mouse, Peromyscus sp.	1																		1	.03	1
Rice Rat, Oryzomys palustris	1	11				3				1					1	10	6		33	.88	7
Vole, Microtus sp.		1																	1	.03	1
Small Rodents spp.		6													1		1		8	.21	3
Muskrat, Ondatra zibethica		3													1				4	.11	1
Cottontail, Sylvilagus floridanus	2	10		12		6	3	1	1	1					10		2		48	1.27	4
Elk, Cervus canadensis	3	22	25								14				10	7			81	2.15	5
White-tailed Deer, Odocoileus virginianus	86	490	506	32	43	67	111	18	60	5	8	5	14	4	107	91	111	11	1769	46.99	39
GRAND TOTAL:	131	960	1186	72	99	137	223	44	86	14	27	29	23	18	252	176	272	16	3765		253

Fish were an important supplement in the diet of these people, as was the turkey and several species of smaller mammals such as raccoon, gray fox, bobcat, squirrels and beaver. A black bear or elk would have provided a large quantity of edible meat, but the small number of individuals represented in the sample suggests that, like most of the species, these animals were killed only occasionally. In all probability most game and preferred food animals were hunted in direct proportion to their availability and abundance.

1968 SEASON (Shane)

The 1968 excavations at the Blain Village Site produced 9,449 pieces of bone. Of these, 2,159 were identified to the genus or species level; of the 7,290 specifically unidentifiable fragments, 482 were fish, 87 birds, and 6,635 mammals. The identified species, provenience, total number of the remains of each species, the percentage of the total, and the minimum number of individuals represented are listed in Table 20.

A comparison of this sample with the collection of 1966 analyzed by Parmalee, both in terms of the species present and percentage of the total, shows the two samples to be remarkably similar. Furthermore, an analysis of butchering cuts on deer, raccoon, fox, and turkey remains shows butchering techniques identical to those observed by Parmalee.

One species not present in the 1966 material, but found in 1968, is the mountain lion, eight elements of which occurred in Feature 21. Of these, two metatarsals were altered by cutting and grinding, apparently representing a stage in a tool-manufacturing process (see pages 135–36).

ACCOUNTS OF SPECIES

Fishes: at least eight species of fish, representing a minimum of thirty-three individuals, were identified. As was the case in the 1966 sample, redhorse and other suckers were the fishes most commonly taken, although catfish and freshwater drum appear to have been important. The majority of specimens was of medium size. The remains of fishes occurred in several features, but the bulk of the 1968 collec-

Table 20. Vertebrate remains identified from the Blain Site, Ohio—1968.

S P E C I E S	17	18	19a	19b	20	21	22	23	25	26	27	28	29	30	31	33	34	35	36	37	Unit IV	Total	%	Minimum Number of Individuals
FISHES																						233	10.75	33
Gar, _Lepisosteus_ sp.						2																2	0.09	1
Pike, _Esox_ sp.														3		7	1			1		11	0.51	2
Suckers, _Catostomidae_		11	4			1		11			2			1		19	1	2	2	2		52	2.41	9
Redhorse, _Moxostoma_ sp.	9	4														48				20		86	3.98	8
Walleye, _Stizostedium_ cf. _vitreum_			1	1																		1	0.05	1
Fresh-water Drum, _Aplodinotus grunniens_	1	5	2					11						5		23	2	4				43	1.99	6
Catfish, _Ictalurus_ sp.	17	2														18						32	1.48	4
Bass, _Micropterus_ sp.		4														2						6	0.28	2
TURTLES																						393	18.20	30
Musk Turtle, _Sternothaerus odoratus_	1	24	25			16								16		3				74		6	0.28	1
Box Turtle, _Terrapene_ cf. _carolina_								61			7			6			19		8	4		263	12.18	18
Painted Turtle, _Chrysemis picta_		1						4						1						1		4	0.19	2
Map Turtle, _Graptemys_ cf. _geographica_		2				4		6						2								7	0.32	2
Softshell Turtle, _Trionyx_ sp.	17					4		16						8		14				21		52	2.41	4
Turtle, spp.	1					4														18		61	2.83	3
BIRDS																						294	13.62	22
Turkey, _Maleagris gallopavo_	19	15	19	2	8	9		6			32		2	26	3	14	14	26	1	99		281	13.02	18
Passenger Pigeon, _Ectopistes migratorius_	5	5	1					1			1			1				1				9	0.42	2
Bobwhite, _Colinus virginianus_																						1	0.05	1
Barred Owl, _Strix varia_											3											3	0.14	1

Table 20. (Continued)

S P E C I E S	17	18	19a	19b	20	21	22	23	25	26	27	28	29	30	31	33	34	35	36	37	Unit IV	Total	%	Minimum Number of Individuals
MAMMALS																						1240	57.43	67
White-tailed Deer, *Odocoileus virginianus*	17	34	44	7	3	71	11	36	1	6	159	2	44	64	46	6	96	87	17	248	1	1000	46.32	22
Elk, *Cervus canadensis*		1			3	2		1			1		2	3		1	1	1		3		19	0.88	2
Raccoon, *Procyon lotor*	4		1			4	2	2			2		1	3		5	5	4		8	1	35	1.62	7
Bear, *Ursus americanus*		1											1				1					3	0.14	3
Mountain Lion, *Felis concolor*						8																8	0.37	1
Grey Fox, *Urocyon cinereoargenteus*	1	1				3				1	3			1						2		11	0.51	2
Fox, *Urocyon* ?	1					1					2											6	0.28	1
Beaver, *Castor canadensis*	3																			3	2	7	0.32	1
Muskrat, *Ondatra zibethica*		2						2														4	0.19	1
Opossum, *Didelphis marsupialis*										1	1		1				1			2		9	0.42	2
Striped Skunk, *Mephitis mephitis*		4								2				1								3	0.14	2
Dog, *Canis familiaris*																				5		5	0.23	2
Bobcat, *Lynx rufus*	2														1		1			1		3	0.28	1
Woodchuck, *Marmota monax*	2	1													1					1		5	0.23	2
Grey Squirrel, *Sciurus carolinensis*		1				1				6					1		1	1		1		12	0.56	2
Fox Squirrel, *Sciurus niger*	1					1								2				2				7	0.32	2
Squirrel, *Sciurus* spp.	2	2	1			1		2			11			2			11			3		31	1.44	3
Cottontail, *Sylvilagus floridanus*	1	1				1					3			1	3		1	1				13	0.60	1
Eastern Chipmunk, *Tamias striatus*	2	1				3										5	6					10	0.46	1
Eastern Vole, *Microtus pennsylvanicus*				1													1					6	0.28	2
Short-tailed Shrew, *Blarina brevicauda*										1	1						6					2	0.09	1
Deer Mouse, *Peromyscus* sp.	1	1				1											2					2	0.09	1
Rice Rat, *Oryzomys palustris*														10		1	12	2	6			29	1.34	4
Rodent, Rodentia																7						7	0.32	1
GRAND TOTAL:	82	119	104	12	14	132	12	165	1	9	236	2	51	150	60	139	177	146	28	517	4	2160	100.00	152

tion was obtained from Feature 33, a refuse pit containing a large basal deposit of fish remains, representing at least ten individuals. This feature produced very few bones of other vertebrate classes, suggesting direct association of the refuse pit with some activity involving procurement and/or preparation of fish.

Reptiles (turtles): remains of turtles were recovered from all refuse pits and most other features. In agreement with Parmalee's findings, the terrestrial box turtle was taken and utilized to a greater degree than other forms. Two carapaces of box turtle were altered for use as cups or bowls.

Birds: four species of birds were identified in the 1968 sample, as compared with 15 species in the 1966 collection. Turkey clearly dominates the avifaunal remains, with at least 27 individuals scattered throughout 15 features. Passenger pigeon is the next most abundant species.

Many of the turkey bones exhibited butchering cuts, particularly the humerus (for wing removal) and the tarsometatarsus (removal and/or modification of the lower leg). Tarsometatarsi showed scoring at the proximal end of the shafts and around some spurs.

Mammals: Fifty-seven percent of the identified bones were mammals, and of these 80 percent were white-tailed deer. Other species of importance, listed in order of their occurrence, are squirrels, raccoon, elk, cottontail, grey fox, bobcat, and beaver. These animals provided the bulk of meat and manufacturing raw materials (bone and skins) utilized by the villagers.

In addition to the fauna listed in Table 20, the remains of one human infant were recovered from Feature 17. Included were the following intact bones: both illia, both femora, left humerus, left radius, right pubis, and right ischium. The incomplete remains include proximal fragments of right and left ulna, distal right radius, proximal left humerus, fragmentary right scapula, and left squamasol part of the skull. No epiphyses were recovered. All indications are that this infant was of approximately new-born age. The femoral necks are undifferentiated and undeveloped. The pelvic bones are at a stage of development characteristic of new-born age.

Maximum length of the femora are 73 mm, of the left radius 51 mm, of the left humerus 62 mm. No pathological conditions were noted. No teeth, mandible, ribs, or other skull fragments were found in the feature, suggesting either a massively disturbed casual burial or a secondary burial.

Interpretive Statement 1966 and 1968. An estimate of the population of the Blain village can be derived from an analysis of the food remains. Although any such estimate must be based upon assumptions that are difficult to test for validity, I (Shane) feel that certain limits can be placed on population size with this kind of analysis. The method to be used here is as follows:

1. Calculate the total weight of food available to any population given the food remains from the site.
2. Assume some amount of food needed for maintainence of normal activity. Here we assume one half pound of meat and one half pound of vegetal food.
3. Given these food requirements, a relationship of population to time (P/t) emerges. For any given time, a population figure exists.
4. Assuming a margin for error in recovery of data, preservation, some limits can be set.
5. The estimate can be further refined by breaking a population down into age groups with assigned food needs.

Weight of food (animal) obtained from excavation:

Mammal	10,055 lbs.
Birds	560 lbs.
Fish	150 lbs.
Molluscs	500 lbs.
Total	11,265 lbs.

11,265 lbs. in 29 refuse pits = 388 lbs./pit

If there were 29 pits in 6,175 square feet, and the site covers approximately 360,000 square feet, then one might expect by calculation 1,690 refuse pits. This figure is too high because the mound and plaza area appear to be devoid of pits. Therefore, a figure of 1,500 pits is assumed to approximate the actual number present. If the average poundage of meat/pit is 388 lbs., then the total poundage in the site would be 388 x 1,500 = 582,000 lbs. or 1,164,000 ½lbs. of meat. Assuming this figure to be too low by 100 percent due to off–site butchering and/or disposal, a figure of 2,328,000 ½lbs. of meat is obtained. To convert to years divide by 365, obtaining a figure indicating that one person could be maintained for 6,378 years, or 100 people for 63.78 years, or 200 people for 31.89 years, or 400 for 16 years.

Table 21.   Percent of meat represented by faunal mammalian remains.

SPECIES	NO. OF BONES	APPROX. NO. OF INDIVIDS.	TOTAL LBS. USABLE MEAT	% OF TOTAL MEAT
Deer	2729	61	6100.0	60.67
Elk	100	7	2450.0	24.27
Bear	30	3	630.0	6.27
Raccoon	99	18	315.0	3.13
Beaver	29	4	126.0	1.25
Bobcat	23	5	125.0	1.24
Mountain Lion	8	1	120.0	1.19
Dog	8	3	45.0	0.45
Woodchuck	20	5	28.0	0.28
Grey Fox	25	6	27.0	0.27
Grey Wolf	1	1	25.0	0.25
Opossum	17	2	17.0	0.17
Cottontail	64	7	14.7	0.15
Squirrels (all)	153	21	21.0	0.21
Striped Skunk	6	2	5.0	0.05
Muskrat	6	1	2.1	0.02
Fox (?)	6	1	4.5	0.04
Rice Rat	50	11	-	-
Eastern Chipmunk	20	5	-	-
Eastern Vole	9	2	-	-
Short-tailed Shrew	4	2	-	-
Deer Mouse	3	1	-	-
Vole	1	1	-	-
Small Rodents	8	3	-	-
Totals:	3419	173	10,055.3	100.00

Population size can also be estimated by assuming a figure for family size per house and calculating the number of houses on the site. The Blain structures are assumed to be houses. One house unit (including surrounding area for refuse pits and open area) may cover 2,500 square feet. Given the area of the site, 100 houses may have existed at any time. Assuming a nuclear family of 5 persons per house, and this is reasonable given the size of houses, a population figure of 500 persons is obtained. Because of the mound and plaza area where there were no houses, this figure is too high; a figure of 400 persons may be more accurate. A comparison of this figure with the population estimate obtained from food data shows no considerable disperity, and a population estimate of from 100 to 400 persons for Blain village seems reasonable. These data further suggest that the village was occupied for a relatively brief interval (1–4 generations), which is not inconsistant with other data (ceramics).

As Cleland (1966; 1967) has shown, the age frequency distribution of deer can provide useful information about the hunting patterns and economic bases of prehistoric populations. A total of 58 dentitions, each representing a single individual, were analyzed. The age distribution is essentially similar to the distribution of deer from Chesser Cave (Prufer, 1967). There, Cleland has argued that "Theoretically we can expect to find a bimodal age curve where stalking is the primary hunting technique. When this hunting technique is employed, the hunter is likely most easily to approach and kill young, inexperienced deer or infirm deer of advanced age." (1967 :46–47). Stalking is assumed to have been practiced by the Blain villagers. Furthermore, this distribution suggests that the villagers were not dependent upon deer as a main source of food. This is not surprising, given the evidence for a horticultural base to their economy.

Table 22. Distribution of common mammalian species.

SPECIES	RANK	HABITAT ZONE
Deer	1	Forest Edge, Second Growth, Oak Prairie
Squirrels	2	Mature Deciduous Forest
Raccoon	3	Mature Deciduous Forest
Elk	4	Forest Edge, Second Growth, Oak Prairie
Cottontail	4	Forest Edge, Second Growth, Oak Prairie
Grey Fox	5	Forest Edge, Second Growth, Oak Prairie
Bobcat	6	Forest Edge, Second Growth, Oak Prairie
Woodchuck	6	Forest Edge, Second Growth, Oak Prairie
Beaver	7	Sreams with wooded banks
Bear	8	Mature Deciduous Forest
Striped Skunk	9	Forest Edge, Second Growth, Oak Prairie
Opossum	9	Forest Edge, Second Growth, Oak Prairie

The mammals from Blain Village show that the inhabitants were primarily utilizing the Prairie environment around the site and the Forest Edge between the Scioto Valley floor and the climax deciduous forest of the upland areas. Table 22 is a listing of mammalian species, ranked by frequency of occurrence, and showing preferred habitat zones. Clearly, there is selection for species preferring Forest Edge, Second Growth, or Oak Prairie zones. Mature Deciduous Forest species are relatively rare, although squirrels and raccoon are common, suggesting forays into the forests for these species.

XIV

The Molluscan Fauna

James L. Murphy

The molluscan remains from the Blain Site consisted of 17,169 identifiable naiad valves, representing a miminum number of 8,975 individuals of 26 species. In addition there were 1,741 identifiable terrestrial, and 143 aquatic gastropods, representing 24 and 5 species respectively. All specimens were derived from the excavations beneath the plowzone. The figures given above are somewhat misleading. In the case of the naiads it is estimated that the identifiable remains represent only about one third of the total number of specimens discovered during the excavations. The remainder was too poorly preserved for purposes of identification. The gastropod sample is even less representative. Here, in addition to large numbers of badly broken specimens, many of the very small specimens escaped attention unless they adhered to the naiads or were preserved in the process of flotation of certain features. It is estimated that the identified sample constitutes only one quarter of the total remains from the excavation untis.

GASTROPODS

As noted, the gastropod sample recovered is uneven because of recovery conditions at the site. Especially extremely small specimens, such as *Hawaiia* and *Gastrocopta* must have been involved, because their recovery at Blain proved to be a function of flotation and of the fact that most of the extant specimens accidentally adhered to the mussels which were cleaned and sorted after the field season in the laboratory. Since flotation did not take place in all features, and since only some features proved to be rich in naiads which were recovered *en masse* without cleaning, it can safely be postulated that the occurrence of these tiny gastropods in precisely these specially handled features, could probably have been duplicated in other excavation units as well.

Of the terrestrial gastropods it should be noted that *Helicodiscus parallelus*, *Mesodon clausus*, *M. mitchellianus*, *Stenotrema fraternum*, *Triodopsis albolabris*, *Gastrocopta contracta*, *G. pentodon*, *Succinea ovalis*, *Mesomphix inornatus*, *Ventridens ligera*, and *Zonitoides arboreus* have not previously been reported from Ross County. The following notes on individual species are in order:

Anguispira alternata: the most abundant species, all specimens represent Pilsbry's form *angulata*. The usual variation in color markings and relative height are shown; bases range from completely plain to tiger–striped. Some specimens, except for lacking the reddish–brown shell coloration, cannot be distinguished from *A. alternata jessicae* (Kutchka). H/D ratio: .55 to .67.

Anguispira kochi: whorls two to four possess mottled pink ornamentation. Banding is present on all specimens. Maximum height and diameter: 20, 21.8 mm. H/D ratio: .71 to .74.

Helicodiscus parallelus: maximum height and diameter: 1.7, 4.5 mm, unusually large for this species, though otherwise typical.

Mesodon clausus: some specimens appear intermediate between *M. clausus* and *M. pennsylvanicus*, possessing the rudimentary tooth and inflected aperture of the latter, but the unclosed umbilicus of the former.

Mesodon inflectus: distance between lip teeth average to widely spaced. One specimen represents the variety *edentatus* (Sampson), not previously reported from Ross County.

Table 23. Feature distribution of gastropods.

S P E C I E S	1	III	1	2	3	4a	4b	5	8	10	11	14	15	16	18	19a	19b	21	23	27	29	30	31	34	35	36	37	44	TOTAL
TERRESTRIAL																													1741
Anguispira alternata (Say)	5	120	28	14	107	298	25	2	1	5		8	36	3	16	6	23	69	10	9	7	1		3	4	1	4	2	807
A. kochi (Pfeiffer)	2	56	20	18	10	28	8	3		3			17	1	5	2	2	31	2	3			2	1	1			4	219
Helicodiscus parallelus (Say)		26			2								15																43
Haplotrema concavum (Say)																													7
Allogona profunda (Say)																													4
Mesodon clausus (Say)	2		14																										48
M. inflectus (Say)			23																										84
M. mitchellianus (Lea)																													6
M. pennsylvanicus (Green)			11																										38
M. thyroidus (Say)																													2
M. elevatus (Say)																													1
M. zaletus (Binney)																									1				2
Stenotrema fraternum (Say)																													1
S. hirsutum (Say)																													8
Triodopsis fraudulenta (Pilsbry)																													2
T. albolabris (Say)																													17
Gastrocopta armifera (Say)																													10
G. contracta (Say)																													1
G. pentodon (Say)																													30
Succinea ovalis (Say)			71																										79
Hawaiia minuscula (Binney)																													51
Mesomphix inornatus (Say)			16																										22
Ventridens ligera (Say)			219										27															1	258
Zonitoides arboreus (Say)																													1
AQUATIC																													143
Goniobasis livescens (Menke)	2	21	38	6	3	8	8					16	2	1		7			6						1			15	134
Pleurocera acuta (Raf.)		3																										1	6
Helisoma antrosa (Conrad)																													1
Gyraulus parvus (Say)																													1
Physella Sp.																													1
T O T A L	11	233	493	66	155	389	53	21	18	18	2	31	114	11	25	17	26	108	34	12	7	1	2	4	20	1	4	23	1884

Mesodon pennsylvanicus: marginal tooth variable in prominence. Umbilicus not generally closed, a slight cleft remaining open, shells resembling *M. clausus* in this respect but differing in the presence of a marginal tooth and the irregular apertural outline.

Mesodon thyroidus: one specimen with parietal tooth wanting.

Triodopsis albolabris: two specimens, both representing the mutation *dentata* (Binney).

Succinea ovalis: shells are generally narrower than typical of this species, and with a shorter aperture. As Pilsbry notes, however, the species is quite variable. Average measurements of ten specimens: height: 15.2 mm; width: 8.3 mm; apertural length: 10.4 mm; and apertural width: 7.6 mm.

Goniobasis livescens: specimens resemble *G. livescens* s.s. more than the usual stream variety *correcta.* Measurements of largest specimen: height: 15.8 mm; width: 7 mm; apertural length: 6mm; apertural width: 3.8 mm.

Pleurocera acuta: typical representatives of the stream variety *tracta* (Anthony). Measurements of largest specimen: height: 22 mm; width: 9.6 mm.

Unfortunately, when the differences due to more careful recovery at Blain are taken into consideration, there remain no particularly significant differences between the gastropods from Blain and those found at previously excavated sites in Ross County. None of the species represented are out of place on a wooded flood plain or river terrace.

It is tempting to contrast the relative abundance of *Anguispira alternata* and *A. kochi* from site to site, the latter being the more abundant at Morrison Village (Prufer and Andors, 1967) and McGraw (Stansbery, 1965), but the converse being the case at Blain Village. Goodrich's comment that *Anguispira kochi* is " . . . one of the typical mollusks of the older forests, and seldom found even in thick second growth timber." (1932 : 35) suggests that there may exist a useful ecological differential between the two species. *Anguispira alternata*, on the other hand, is so cosmopolitan as to be nearly ubiquitous.

The aquatic gastropods are equally cosmopolitan in habitat, though all represent river or creek forms. The small amount of aquatic shells present suggests shallow water with considerable vegetation. The presence of all four aquatic species within refuse pits negates the possibility that the shells had been carried into the features by flood waters. It is more probable that they were incidentally brought to the site clinging to river cobbles, naiads, or aquatic plants.

It is doubtful whether any of the gastropods were economically used at the site. Their size and distribution within the features, often occurring on the capping deposits of refuse pits as if they died in the process of scavenging, suggest that they are incidental to the occupation of the settlement.

PELECYPODS

Initially it was hoped that a detailed tabulation of all individuals by species and excavation units might result in revealing significant distributional differences—primarily temporal but indirectly cultural in character as well. With this thought in mind, the shells from each of the 31 units and features were tabulated separately, as shown in Table 24. Because of the large number of shells involved in the study, both halves of an individual could not usually be matched. It was thought best, therefore, to express the number of each species present by a minimum number of individuals; that is by the number of either left or right valves, whichever number was the higher. In Table 24 the total number of shells is expressed as a ratio of left valves to right valves. The minimum number of individuals present was obtained by adding the extra valves in the right column for each species to the total of the left column.

After tabulation of the minimum number of each species present in the features, these statistics were converted to percentages for both, the most abundant species and for each of the three families represented in the collection. The same had been done for the McGraw Site sample (Stansbery, 1965), which is important because it was taken from a nearby portion of the Scioto River, and because it is several hundred years older than the Blain material.

Table 24. Feature distribution of pelecypods.

S P E C I E S	I	III	1	2	3	4a	4b	5	6	9	10	11	14	15	16	18	19a	19b	21
UNIONINAE (Swainson) Ortmann, 1910																			
Fusconaia flava (Raf.)		7:12	3:2											1:0					
Fusconaia subrotunda (Lea)		0:2												2:1					
Amblema costata (Raf.)	3:1		38:36	1:0	0:3	3:3	0:2	1:0	0:2		1:1	0:1	3:1	113:114	2:1	2:1	1:0		3:1
Quadrula cylindrica (Say)			2:3					0:2		1:0				6:5			1:1		
Tritogonia verrucosa (Raf.)			17:31			1:0	0:1		0:1					4:2					
Cyclonaias tuberculata (Raf.)	1:0	3:2		2:1	2:1	1:1	1:1			1:0			0:2	29:33	1:0	1:1	0:1		
Pleurobema cordatum coccineum (Conrad)	2:2	6:8	74:75			1:1	1:1		1:1	1:0			1:0	165:152	3:3	0:3	2:3		2:5
Pleurobema clava (Lamarck)			45:38				1:1		2:2				1:0	97:116	3:3		2:1		
Elliptio dilatatus (Raf.)		29:36	1068:1018	4:1	4:1	30:28	14:13	4:1			1:1		8:8	263:255	22:29	15:14	13:5	4:2	14:15
Elliptio crassidens (Lamarck)	2:0	1:1	10:11			2:1						0:1	0:1	5:6	2:1	0:2	0:1		2:1
ANODONTINAE (Swainson) Ortmann, 1910																			
Lasmigona costata (Raf.)	1:1	1:1	30:38	2:0	1:0	0:2	2:0			1:0	1:0		2:1	36:38	1:0	3:1			3:1
Lasmigona complanata (Barnes)			1:1										1:1	4:1					
Anodonta grandis (Say)														0:1					
Anodonta ferrussacianus (Lea)																			
Alasmidonta marginata (Say)			27:27				1:2					0:1		8:12		1:0			
Strophitus undulatus (Say)			49:57											1:1					
LAMPSILINAE (von Ihring) Ortmann, 1910																			
Ptychobranchus fasciolaris (Raf.)	6:4	52:50	1367:1359	5:6	10:10	17:15	52:46	4:8	1:3	1:0	2:1	3:1	15:18	553:540	25:36	16:17	7:9	0:2	14:17
Cyprogenia irrorata (Lea)			0:1											0:1	0:1				
Obovaria subrotunda (Raf.)			3:2	1:0		0:1					0:1		1:2	37:53	0:1	1:0	0:1	0:1	2:0
Actinonaias carinata (Barnes)			5:6											10:11					
Truncilla truncata (Raf.)			9:5	1:3	1:0	3:1	0:1		1:0				0:1	1:2	1:0				
Ligumia recta (Lamarck)			8:9	5:4	4:1	6:6	6:6	1:0		1:0	1:0		6:5	44:40	4:5			1:0	1:0
Lampsilis ovata (Say)	2:2	11:14	50:41			1:2			1:2	1:0	1:0		5:2	17:35	3:0	3:4	3:4	1:0	5:6
Lampsilis radiata siliquoidea (Barnes)		4:1	176:159	2:4	6:8	16:10	30:31	3:4		1:0	1:0		2:3	339:336		4:2			1:0
Dysnomia torulosa rangiana (Lea)		25:29	2577:2579								2:1				36:25	12:9	4:8	4:0	3:8
Dysnomia triquetra (Raf.)			14:11									3:1			0:1				
TOTAL	16:9	143:163	5574:5510	17:17	29:24	81:71	110:110	13:15	6:11	8:1	9:5	6:5	45:45	1735:1754	103:106	58:54	33:34	9:5	50:54
Minimum No. of Individuals	16	170	5612	22	34	85	119	20	12	8	10	9	54	1804	125	65	44	12	63

Table 24. (*Continued*)

SPECIES	23	27	28	29	30	31	33	34	35	36	37	44	TOTAL	% of Total Based on Minimum Nos.	% Within Families Based on Minimum Nos.
UNIONINAE (Swainson) Ortmann, 1910													2389:2326	27.9	
Fusconaia flava (Raf.)	1:0									0:1			4:2		
Fusconaia subrotunda (Lea)	1:2	1:2	0:1							1:1	1:1		3:2		
Amblema costata (Raf.)	3:3				2:1			2:1	2:0		0:1	1:0	189:188	2.3	8.2
Quadrula cylindrica (Say)	1:0				0:1			1:1					14:16		
Tritogonia verrucosa (Raf.)								1:0		0:1	1:0		5:4		
Cyclonaias tuberculata (Raf.)	4:1	1:0	1:2	2:1			0:1			0:2			62:81		
Pleurobema cordatum coccineum (Conrad)	9:6								0:1	1:0	3:2		274:265	3.2	11.4
Pleurobema clava (Lamarck)	13:11	0:1		1:4	0:1			0:1	4:5	1:0		2:1	174:187	2.2	7.9
Elliptio dilatatus (Raf.)	76:59	7:10			6:3	2:2		4:4	29:27		11:8	0:1	1635:1552	18.5	66.0
Elliptio crassidens (Lamarck)	2:2				1:2				3:0		1:0	6:5	29:29		
ANODONTINAE (Swainson) Ortmann, 1910													203:210	2.7	
Lasmigona costata (Raf.)	8:5	0:1		1:1				0:1	1:0				93:90		
Lasmigona complanata (Barnes)							1:0				2:0		8:3		
Anodonta grandis (Say)						2:0							0:1		
Anodonta ferrussacianus (Lea)													8:11		
Alasmidonta marginata (Say)	5:9								0:1	1:0	1:0		44:47		
Strophitus undulatus (Say)	4:5								1:0				50:58		
LAMPSILINAE (von Ihring) Ortmann, 1910													6063:6005	69.4	
Ptychobranchus fasciolaris (Raf.)	39:46	15:10	1:2	1:6	10:4	2:2	11:8	4:8	18:24	0:4	21:12	9:5	2281:2274	26.0	37.5
Cyprogenia irrorata (Lea)													0:1		
Obovaria subrotunda (Raf.)	3:3	1:0	1:0										3:4		
Actinonaias carinata (Barnes)									0:2	0:1			53:72		
Truncilla truncata (Raf.)											1:1		19:17		
Ligumia recta (Lamarck)	1:1								1:0		1:0		23:20		
Lampsilis ovata (Say)	16:14	5:1	1:0	4:3	2:1	1:1	1:1	2:1	7:0	0:1	7:7	0:1	200:170	2.3	3.3
Lampsilis radiata siliquoidea (Barnes)	28:23		0:2					1:0	1:3	2:2	2:2	0:2	250:235	3.0	4.4
Dysnomia torulosa rangiana (Lea)	101:93	11:10		3:1	4:2	1:0	2:0	2:3	8:16	0:1	12:9	10:4	3220:3199	35.3	52.3
Dysnomia triquetra (Raf.)												0:1	14:13		
TOTAL	315:283	41:35	4:7	12:16	25:15	8:5	15:10	17:20	75:79	6:14	64:43	28:20	8655:8541		
Minimum No. of Individuals	328	47	9	20	28	8	16	24	96	17	65	33	8975		

Unfortunately, the only available list of species currently inhabiting the river (Stansbery, 1965: 121–22) cannot be considered entirely reliable, for the list is based upon dead shells collected along the banks of the Scioto.

Notable differences between the Blain and McGraw samples are few. This is especially noticeable when the breakdown by family is considered (Table 25). From this it transpires that it is highly unlikely

Table 25. Percentage distribution of pelecypod families for selected features at Blain, compared with Morrison Village and McGraw.

PROVENIENCE	UNIONINAE	ANODONTINAE	LAMPSILINAE
Unit-III	38.8%	0.6%	60.0%
Feature-1	22.7%	2.2%	75.1%
Feature-3	26.5%	2.9%	70.6%
Feature-4a	44.7%	2.4%	52.9%
Feature-15	39.3%	3.1%	57.6%
Feature-23	33.8%	6.7%	59.5%
Blain Total	28.0%	2.7%	69.3%
McGraw	21.7%	2.3%	76.0%
Morrison	33.3%	--	66.7%

that any significant changes in the composition of the river fauna took place between Hopewellian and late prehistoric times. When the Morrison Village fauna is considered (Prufer and Andors, 1967), it is tempting to postulate a gradual increase in the Unioninae at the expense of the other two families, but the Morrison sample is too meager (48 specimens) to support generalizations on faunal changes. This is especially true when one considers that differences in samples collected from different stations may owe their specific composition to ecological differences rather than to changes in the overall riverine population. Only more collecting from additional single–component sites could substantiate such a hypothesis.

When individual species at Blain and McGraw are considered, the only conspicuous differences between the sites consist of a relatively greater proportion of *Lampsilis ovata, Actinonaias carinata,* and *Amblema costata* at McGraw, coupled with a significantly smaller percentage of *Dysnomia torulosa* and *Elliptio dilatatus* at that site. Because all of these species either prefer the same environment—

riffles with fine to coarse gravel bottoms and a swift stream flow—or, in the case of *Elliptio dilatatus*, are practically ubiquitous, it is difficult to ascribe these differences to specific ecological variants, especially so because the precise ecology of the stations at the time the shells were originally collected must remain unknown. The most plausible explanation is the apparent selectivity based upon shell size at McGraw. Stansbery (1965:122) assumes that the inhabitants of the McGraw Site preferred larger specimens; such a preference, natural though it may be, does not seem to have been displayed at the Blain locality, for two of the three most common species (*Elliptio dilatatus* and *Dysnomia torulosa*) are abundantly represented by very small specimens.

Table 26. Percentage distribution of selected pelecypod species from seven Blain features.

SPECIES	III	F-1	F-3	F-4a	F-15	F-23	F-44
Amblema costata	7.0	.7	8.8	3.5	6.3	.6	3.0
Cyclonaias tuberculata	1.8	.6	---	1.2	1.8	1.2	---
Pleurobema cordatum coccineum	4.7	1.3	5.9	1.2	9.2	2.7	6.1
P. clava	2.3	.8	---	1.2	6.4	3.9	3.0
Elliptio dilatatus	21.2	18.8	11.8	47.0	14.6	23.1	18.2
E. crassidens	.6	.2	---	2.3	.3	.6	---
Lasmigona costata	.6	.7	2.9	---	2.1	2.3	---
Strophitus undulatus	---	1.0	---	---	---	---	---
Ptychobranchus fasciolaris	30.6	24.4	29.4	20.0	30.7	14.0	27.3
Actinonaias carinata	.6	.1	---	1.2	2.9	.9	---
Lampsilis ovata	8.2	.9	11.8	7.1	2.4	4.5	3.0
L. radiata siliquoidea	2.4	3.1	2.9	2.3	1.9	8.5	6.1
Dysnomia torulosa rangiana	17.0	46.0	23.5	18.8	18.8	30.7	30.3

To determine how much variation might be expected from one archaeological component to another, collections were made at three sites in the West Virginia panhandle. The Childers, Globe Hill, and East Steubenville shell heaps have never been thoroughly excavated, and there is some debate as to their precise chronological position. The Carnegie Museum of Pittsburgh excavation at Globe Hill (Mayer-Oakes, 1955) indicates that they are all Archaic and roughly contemporaneous. More recent excavations by amateurs at the Childers and Globe Hill sites have revealed evidence for additional, considerably more recent occupations during Early and Middle Woodland times, but no evidence was found to suggest that the major occupations were other than Middle or Late Archaic. All three sites are similarly located on high terraces overlooking the Ohio River, at the confluence of small tributaries with that stream. The exact nature of the Ohio River at these localities during the prehistoric occupation period, when the shellfish were gathered, cannot be determined.

Statistics for the shell populations at the three sites are given in Table 27. Remarkable are the small numbers of species restricted to a single site (four), and the considerable amount of variation in the numbers of each species from site to site—over 10 percent in several instances. The overall uniformity of the sample is emphasized by the fact that the three most common genera—*Pleurobema, Elliptio,* and *Ptychobranchus*—occur in that order of abundance at all three sites. In short, there is so little significant variation between the sites that, although an unknown sample from one of them might be assigned to the correct locality, it is equally possible that it might not. And there is even less chance, should a fourth Panhandle Archaic shell heap be discovered, that its molluscan fauna could be used to correlate specifically with one of the other three. It might further be noted that there is no essential difference between the fauna as represented in the three Archaic shell heaps and that collected from the Ohio River during the first part of this century (Ortmann, 1919), suggesting that whatever faunal changes have occurred in the river population, are either too slight or too gradual to be of help to the archaeologist.

The same conclusions apply to the Blain Site. The imponderable variables already mentioned, make it highly improbable that site to site comparisons of molluscan faunas, even when the sites are in close proximity, will ever be of use in distinguishing such localities temporally.

Comparison between individual excavation units and features within the Blain sample is likewise beset with difficulties. Specimens from most features are so few in number that the ratio of the number of any one species in a given pit, to the total number of shells from the same pit, is of doubtful significance. Conversely, the more productive features, such as Feature 1 and Feature 15, though containing large enough samples, may well represent several

Table 27.   Species distribution of pelecypods from three Archaic shell heaps in the
Upper Ohio Valley (Murphy collection).

SPECIES	CHILDERS		GLOBE HILL		E.STEUBENVILLE	
Fusconaia flava	---		---		1:0	(.5%)
Amblema costata	0:1	(.6%)	1:0	(.5%)	---	
Quadrula cylindrica	0:1	(.6%)	1:1	(.5%)	4:3	(2.2%)
Q. metanevra	8:4	(5.0%)	14:5	(7.9%)	3:8	(4.4%)
Q. pustolosa	---		---		1:0	(.6%)
Cyclonaias tuberculata	7:12	(7.5%)	8:8	(4.5%)	6:3	(3.3%)
Plethobasus cooperianus	---		2:0	(1.1%)	0:3	(1.6%)
Pleurobema cordatum catillus	55:44	(34.4%)	61:67	(37.8%)	47:41	(25.7%)
P. cordatum pyramidatum	0:1	(.6%)	0:2	(1.1%)	2:1	(1.1%)
P. clava	---		0:1	(.5%)	---	
Elliptio dilatatus	11:8	(6.9%)	22:16	(12.4%)	31:28	(16.9%)
E. crassidens	36:21	(22.5%)	26:33	(18.6%)	28:32	(17.5%)
Alasmidonta marginata	---		---		0:1	(.5%)
Ptychobranchus fasciolaris	14:17	(10.6%)	9:9	(5.1%)	13:6	(7.1%)
Cyprogenia irrorota	1:2	(1.2%)	6:3	(3.4%)	5:4	(2.7%)
Obovaria subrotunda	4:1	(2.5%)	1:1	(.5%)	1:1	(.5%)
Actinonaias carinata	6:1	(3.8%)	3:3	(1.6%)	3:5	(2.7%)
Ligumia recta	1:1	(.6%)	0:2	(1.1%)	1:6	(3.3%)
Lampsilis ovata	2:1	(1.2%)	1:0	(.5%)	7:4	(3.8%)
L. radiata siliquoidea	3:1	(1.9%)	1:0	(.5%)	1:5	(2.7%)
Dysnomia torulosa	---		1:3	(1.6%)	5:0	(2.7%)
Total	148:117		157:154		159:151	
Minimum number of specimens	160		177		183	

collections, and are likely to contain shells from more than one collecting area. Thus, although in theory it might be possible to seriate
excavation units in a manner similar to pottery seriation, in practice
the effort is fruitless—at least as far as Blain Village is concerned.
When the data for the two largest units, Feature 1 and Feature 15,
are examined, there seem to be considerable differences between the
proportion of species in each unit. However, attempts to correlate the
refuse pits with one or the other of these two features failed to reveal
any consistent differences that could be used to determine the relative
ages of the several units. The difficulty of arranging the units in any
significant order can be seen by considering Table 26, where a percentage breakdown by species is given for seven of the more important excavation units and features at Blain. The fact that *Elliptio
dilatatus*, *Ptychobranchus fasciolaris*, and *Dysnomia torulosa* are
the three most common species in every feature, although the three
species differ in order of abundance from feature to feature, suggests
just how uniform the fauna is throughout the site. One can correlate

some of the units on the basis of the relative abundance of these three species. Thus, Feature 1 and Feature 44 yielded the largest percentage of *Dysnomia,* followed by *Ptychobranchus* and then *Elliptio.* In Feature 3 and Feature 15, *Ptychobranchus* was the most abundant, followed by *Dysnomia* and then *Elliptio.* In Unit III, *Ptychobranchus* is also the most abundant, but the positions of *Dysnomia* and *Elliptio* are reversed. In Feature 23 *Dysnomia* is most common, followed by *Elliptio* and *Ptychobranchus.* Feature 4a is unique in having an extremely high percentage of *Elliptio,* with *Ptychobranchus* in second, and *Dysnomia* in third place. Such correlations, however, are not supported by the distribution of the less common species in the units and, if they mean anything at all, simply suggest that the units involved were contemporaneous. There is no way of estimating whether a given unit is older or younger than another. It is highly improbable that any single–component site—even one inhabited for a relatively long period of time—at which the molluscs were obtained from a single source, would yield features datable solely by molluscan content. Even relative dating of multiple components, separated in time by as much as several hundreds of years, seems to be out of the question, at least until much more is known about whatever gradual changes may have taken place in the river fauna.

XV

Maize from the Blain Site*

Walton C. Galinat

If there was maize in Ohio which pre-dated the eight-rowed race, *Maíz de Ocho*, in this area, it would probably be of the race *Chapalote*, an older race indigenous to Mexico and the Southwest (Galinat, 1965). The identity of the Blain Site maize as *Maíz de Ocho* will be documented and the significance of its date at A.D. 1040 will be discussed in this paper.

The remains of maize from the Blain Site were completely carbonized as a result of burning and severely mutilated. Dissection of some fused masses of charcoal which escaped complete incineration yielded cross-section portions of two ears and nine long sections of rachis. The screening of a quart of largely pulverized material separated it out into numerous very small rachis fragments (largely isolated cupules) and several hundred kernels many of which were sufficiently intact to permit their identification by certain taxonomic key characters. While the embryo from many of the kernels was burned away, the carbonized endosperm usually remained in a crescent shape which perserved the essential dimensions of the original kernel.

The two races of maize under question, *Chapalote* and *Maíz de Ocho*, are compared on the basis of the taxonomic key characters usually available in the archaeological remains of such specimens (Figure 21, 1–10).

*This investigation was aided in part by a grant from the National Science Foundation (GB-6715).

The ear of *Chapalote* (Figure 21, 1-5) averages twelve rows of small flinty kernels which are deeper than wide (w/d < 1). Though constant in shape, the kernels from the tip (Figure 21, 2), the mid-region (Figure 21, 3) and the basal position (Figure 21, 4) along the ear differ in size. The internode length (i) in these races corresponds in dimension to the height of the cupule (and kernel thickness) (Figure 21, 5) but is equal to or less than the width of the cupule (w/i ≤ 1).

The ear of *Maíz de Ocho* has eight rows of kernels (Figure 21, 6). These are large and constant in shape regardless of their position on the ear (Figure 21, 7-9). However, being wider than deep, they give a w/d ratio of greater than unity, unlike the kernels of *Chapalote*. Similarly the width of the cupules progressively decreases from the base of the ear to the tip while the internode length is more or less constant. Thus, while the w/i ratio is always more than one, a feature in contrast with the cupules of *Chapalote*, the ratio itself varies from two to one at the base to a little over one to one at the tip of the ear.

In referring to the various planes of dimensions of the kernels, the term *depth* (d) is used here to mean the same as that referred as *length* (l) in some of the previous studies (Wellhausen et al., 1952; Mangelsdorf and Camara-Hernandez, 1967). In both cases, the plane of kernel is the one which lies parallel with the axis of the embryo. The term *depth* is preferred to *length* for greater accuracy and specificity. Both in the applied terminology of corn breeders and in the descriptions of early taxonomic treatments (Burtt Davy, 1914),

Figure 21 (*opposite this page*). Archaeotaxonomy of Chapalote and *Maíz de Ocho*. (1-5) Chapalote: (1) Cross Section of an ear showing narrow deep cupules, long glumes, and 12 rows of small kernels that are deeper than wide. (2-4) Samples of some individual kernels from the tip, mid and basal positions on the ear showing constance in shape despite differences in size. (5) A single cupule, front view parallel to rachis, with a pair of spikelet bases attached. Note that the intermode length (height of cupule) is equal to or greater than the width of cupule. (6-10) *Maíz de Ocho:* (6) Cross section of an ear showing wide shallow cupules and 8 rows of large kernels that are wider than deep. (7-9) Samples of some individual kernels from the tip, mid and basal positions on the ear showing constancy in shape despite differences in size. (10) A single cupule, front view parallel to rachis, with a pair of spikelet bases attached. Note that the width of the cupule is greater than the internode length. (Symbols: (c = cupule, d = depth, g = glume, i = internode, k = kernel, w = width).

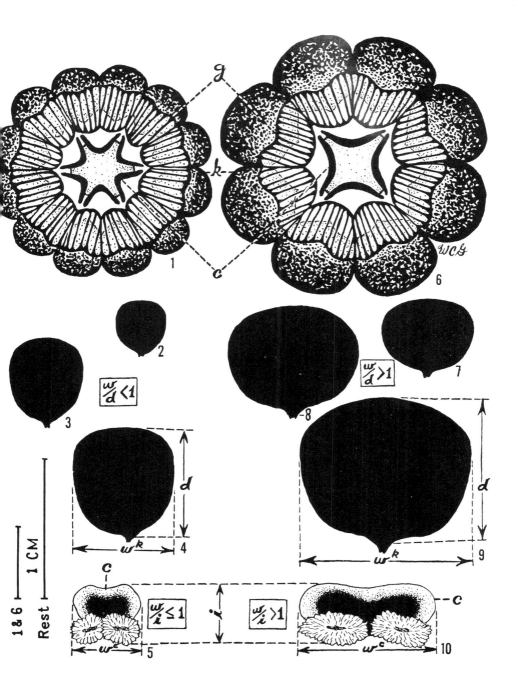

$\dfrac{w}{d} < 1$

$\dfrac{w}{d} > 1$

$\dfrac{w}{i} \leq 1$

$\dfrac{w}{i} > 1$

1 CM

1&6
Rest

the term *kernel depth* has precedence, and the term "length" is defined as the "longest or longer dimension of any object, in distinction from breadth or width" (Webster's Dictionary). To be consistent with these, the kernels of *Maíz de Ocho* when described as *wider than deep* convey a more accurate meaning rather than when described semantically as *wider than long*!

A random sample of 240 of the prehistoric kernels from the Blain Site (Plate XXVI, A) illustrates not only the variation in kernel size but also the relatively high frequency of small kernels. Many of the smaller kernels (upper five rows in this photographed sample) are of the same size as mature kernels of the race *Chapalote*. However, when the shape of these prehistoric kernels is compared in the enlarged view (Plate XXVI, B) to that of their counterparts from a single ear of *Maíz de Ocho*, variety Hidatsa flour, placed at the right end of each horizontal row and to a typical kernel of *Chapalote* (right end of the scale), their identity with *Maíz de Ocho* is clear. The reduction in size of kernels borne near the tip of an ear of *Maíz de Ocho* is apparent in the right specimen of (Plate XXVI, C). These smaller "tip-kernels" maintain a constant width/depth ratio of greater than one (Figure 21, 7–9), although their thickness (internode length) may become proportionately greater.

The width and depth measurements on 281 of the Blain Site kernels are summarized in Table 28. The data show that the kernel width is consistently greater than the depth, a key characteristic distinguishing *Maíz de Ocho* from *Chapalote*.

The higher proportion (*ca.* 25 percent of small, *Maíz de Ocho*–shaped kernels then coming from near the tip of a mature ear (*ca.* 10 percent) as well as the fact that many of the small kernels were not rounded or relatively thick in the manner of tip-kernels (Plate XXVI, C) indicates that some factor in addition to position on the ear is involved. It is suggested that the excess of small *Maíz de Ocho* kernels resulted from either stunting produced by a poor growing season and/or poor adaptability to a short growing season of a race then recently arrived from the South or Southwest. The early date of A.D. 1040 at this location indicates that the factor of adaptability could be at least partially involved. I (1967) consider that the transformation of *Harinoso de Ocho* from the Southwest to the

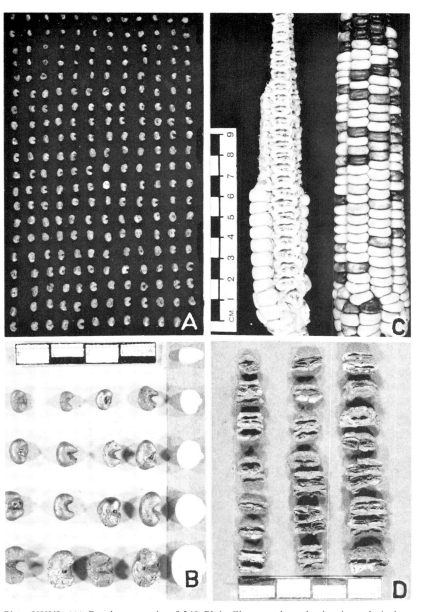

Plate XXVI. (A) Random sample of 240 Blain Site corn kernels showing relatively high frequency of small kernels. (B) Comparison of the prehistoric kernels with their counterparts in size from an ear of Maíz de Ocho (right end) and with a typical kernel of Chapalote (end of scale). (C) Two ears of *Maíz de Ocho*. The dissected ear (left) shows reduction in cupule size toward the tip while its intact counterpart (right) shows a similar reduction in kernel size. (D) Sample of the carbonized cupules which were screened from the pulverized portion of the remains. The small cupules have the same shape as the large cupules.

northern flints of New England would have required several hundred years. The early fall frosts associated with shorter growing seasons may very well have cut short the maturation of some of the ears and, thereby, resulted in some smaller kernels and smaller cupules. While it is difficult to ascertain from carbonized corn such as this, it is not felt that some of the corn was small just because it was picked "green" before it was ripe. Green corn is generally consumed immediately and not put in storage as was the Blain Site maize.

A reduction in cupule width normally parallels the reduction in kernel size along an ear as is illustrated by the dissected ear of *Maíz de Ocho* (on left) in (XXVI, C). The prehistoric material also contained some small isolated cupules among the fragmented cob material. The small cupules were present in about the same frequency as the small carbonized kernels (25 percent) (Plate XXVI, D). Although the width of the smallest cupules (5 mm) approximates that of *Chapalote* cupules (Figure 21, 5), the shape of these cupules is definitely that of *Maíz de Ocho* (figure 21, 10) as represented by a w/i ratio of greater than one.

Perhaps the most convincing evidence of the identity of the Blain Site maize as *Maíz de Ocho* comes from two cross–sections of ears and nine rachis fragments which were dissected from the fused masses of charcoal. The ear cross–sections and the nine rachis fragments (Plate XXVII, A–B) are typical of *Maíz de Ocho*. One section of rachis shown in the lower left corner (Plate XXVII, B) was ten–rowed at the base (reflected in twisted cupules) and then changed to the eight–rowed condition as is occasionally found with ears of *Maíz de Ocho*. The remaining rachis sections are eight–rowed and typical in every way of *Maíz de Ocho*.

Data mapping the prehistoric spread of the eight–rowed race of maize, *Maíz de Ocho*, are still meager. This race left the Southwest after A.D. 700 on a course across the Transition Life Zone toward New England (Galinat and Gunnerson, 1963) where it probably arrived later than A.D. 1000 (Brown and Anderson, 1947). The date of A.D. 1040 for the *Maiz de Ocho* from the Blain Site reported here represents the earliest collection of this race yet known from Ohio.

Plate XXVII. (a) Cross-section portions of two *Maíz de Ocho* ears which were dissected from a fused mass of charcoal from the Blain Site. (B) Nine sections of radius, also typical of *Maíz de Ocho*, which were isolated from the Blain Site charcoal. One specimen (lower left) is ten-rowed at the base. The others are eight-rowed.

Table 28.   Frequency (percent of corn kernels having various widths and depths in a total of 281 from the Blain Site.

		Kernel depth in mm			
		5	6	7	8
Kernel width in mm	6	1.4	—	—	—
	7	7.1	1.8	—	—
	8	7.8	10.0	4.3	—
	9	5.0	13.9	10.7	1.4
	10	0.7	8.9	9.6	2.5
	11	—	3.2	4.6	5.0
	12	—	—	2.1	—

If the Blain Site maize is descended from the *Maíz de Ocho* which spread from the Southwest through southeastern Colorado, older remains of it than the A.D. 1135 date reported by Galinat and Campbell (1968) should be discovered in corridors to the Southwest. The possibility of multiple connections between the Plains and the Southwest is supported by early dates for this race from Tamaulipas, Mexico at A.D. 200–850 (Mangelsdorf *et al.,* 1967) and from the Davis Site in Texas at A.D. 800–1000 (Jones, 1949). In any case, the approach of this date of A.D. 900 for eight–rowed maize from Ohio to the earliest data of *ca.* A.D. 1000 from New York and the complete absence of such early dates for it in the Southeast, traces the northern flints of the Northeast back to the Plains area.

XVI

Plant Remains from the Blain Site

Lawrence Kaplan*

About 5000 grams of charred plant materials exclusive of maize were available for study. This material had previously been separated from non–plant remains by flotation or screen washing and was further separated manually and by sieving in the laboratory. A summary of the remains is presented in Tables 29 and 30.

The seed remains are autumnal. Abundant seeds of *Rhus glabra*, smooth sumach, might have been derived from a few heads—perhaps one quarter pound of the dried heads in late summer or fall. The heads can be stored and have been widely used as a source of malic acid flavoring for fresh drinks and sauces (Fernald and Kinsey, 1958). The presence of pawpaw seeds could be taken to indicate deposit of the plant materials of Feature 4b, Feature 14, and Unit III in the autumn after the first frost. Pawpaw fruit is said to be improved by exposure to frost.

The occurrence, the earliest in eastern North America, of eight–rowed corn (Galinat, this volume, chapter XV), pumpkin (Cutler and Whitaker, 1961) and beans (Kaplan, 1965 a),a at the Blain site may be interpreted as the simultaneous introduction of these cultigens as a single complex from the Southwest.

Although remains of the vegetative parts of bean plants are not present, it is probable that the seeds are derived from vining rather than erect or bush type plants and that the vines were interplanted

*The assistance of Miss Carolyn Levi is acknowledged with thanks.

Table 29.   Feature distribution of identified seeds and nuts from Blain.

Seed Remains	Feature 1	Feature 3	Feature 4a	Feature 4b	Unit III
Rhus glabra I. Smooth sumach	1			4,700	3
Juglans nigra L. Black walnut	1	1		150 estimated	3
Carya ovata (Mill.) Koch. Hickory nut	1	1		35	3
Quercus sp. Acorn				8	
Prunus serotina Ehrh. Wild black cherry				3	
Vitis riparia Michx. Frost grape				13	
Ipomoea sp. Wild morning glory				5	
Asimina triloba (L.) Dun. Pawpaw				26	
Cucurbita pepe L. Pumpkin—cultivated				16	
Phaseolus vulgaris L. Common bean—cultivated	2			5	

with corn since this is the common horticultural combination in aboriginal eastern North America. Such vining beans were grown at Mesa Verde, Wetherill Mesa (Kaplan, 1965 b) and elsewhere in the Southwest where humid conditions prevailed locally or where irriga-

Table 30.   Feature distribution of identified wood remains from Blain.

Wood Remains	Feature 4b	Unit III
Betula sp. Birch	3.5 gm	1.0 gm
Gleditsia triacanthos L. Honey locust	1.0 gm	
Prunus sp. Cherry	1.0 gm	1.0 gm
Quercus, sp. Oak		1.0 gm
Quercus sp. (decayed) Oak	26.5 gm.	
Juglans nigra L. Black walnut	1.0 gm	1.0 gm
Pinus sp. Pine	.3 gm	

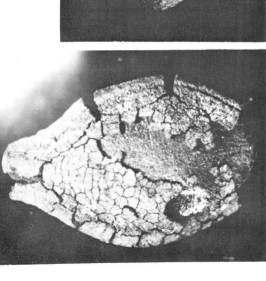

A   B   C

Plate XXVIII. Seeds from Blain Village, Feature 4b, circa 10x natural size. (A) *Cucurbita pepo*; (B) *Ipomoea* sp.: (C) *Vitis riparia*

tion was practiced. Southwestern common bean varieties can be grown successfully under growing season, and photoperiod conditions prevailing in most of the Midwest and Northeast. Beans adapted to lower latitudes cannot mature under the short growing season and long–short night conditions of the Midwest and Northeast. It is likely then that the beans of southern Ohio derived from the Southwest; it is possible that this introduction took place as a single step.

Because the remains derived from this site do not reflect a random sample of plant dietary components it is not possible to form conclusions concerning the degree to which subsistence was based on cultivated as opposed to wild plants. However, there seems to be no particular evidence of storage of wild plant foods that would not be best described as minor supplements in any rural economy in southern Ohio.

The most abundant single class of material present consists of masses of amorphous materials layered with a harder substance. Identification was problematic because, as it became apparent, the characteristics that would enable identification had been largely obliterated by decay. This material proved to be charred remains of fungus decayed oak wood interleafed with layers of bark. This determination was assured by the presence of charred fungal hyphae and basidia that were observed under high magnification (900 X). This wood was put into the pit thoroughly rotted by a basidiomycete fungus but presumably dry at this point and must have smoldered long and hotly. Such thoroughly rotted wood could have had no use as a structural component of the pit (note that it occurs only in Feature 4b) and could only have been used for bulk or for its special punky burning properties. Although a total of only 23.5 grams of this material is shown in the chart, the actual amount is much greater but has been reduced to dustlike form that could not economically be separated from the soil and other fragmented materials.

That Feature 4b was indeed intended for burning when it was filled is suggested by the presence and condition of the black walnuts and hickory nuts. The nut kernels have not been extracted, and the shells show no abrasions that might have resulted from cracking and burning; nor are there signs of rodent gnawing that might be expected had the nuts been stored for any length of time, cracked or not, prior to burning. A reasonable conclusion might be that these thick-shelled nuts were placed in the pit as fuel to ensure a very hot, steady fire. The shells burn with a hot flame and the oil of the kernels contributes greatly to the same result.

Against these observations, one should note that as far as plant materials are concerned, there appear no striking differences between Feature 4b and other pits. The larger quantities of materials from it could merely be a reflection of the larger total mass excavated.

XVII

Radiocarbon Dates and Fort Ancient Chronology

Five radiocarbon assays are available for establishing the absolute chronology of Blain Village. They have given the following values:

Table 31. Radiocarbon dates for Blain Village.

Lab. No.	Feature	Material	Value	Normalized Value
M–1910	6	Charcoal	490 ± 100 (A.D.1460)	A.D. 1440
M–1911	1	Charcoal	760 ± 100 (A.D.1190)	A.D. 1225
OWU–247a	4a	Corn	405 ± 150 (A.D.1545)	A.D. 1303*
OWU–247b	4b	Charcoal	970 ± 220 (A.D.980)	A.D. 1040
OWU–248	2	Charcoal	1035 ± 155 (A.D.915)	A.D. 970

These dates require comment. First, we consider the assays M–1911, OWU–247b, and OWU–248 to be approximations of the true age of the site. They are in line with the internal chronological evidence, and they compare favorably with the date obtained for Graham Village in the Hocking Valley (OWU–183: A.D. 1180 ± 45, normalized to A.D. 1210). They are also in agreement with general estimates for the temporal position of the Baum Focus. In connection with these assays, it should be pointed out that OWU–248 dates the pit which yielded the curious Woodland vessel (Plate X, A) that strikes such an odd note in the overall Blain ceramic assemblage. As stated elsewhere, this vessel closely resembles the cordmarked type of the Middle Woodland McGraw series. OWU–247b dates the ceremonial

*Normalized for fractionation only.

232

pit which contained a massive deposit of charred vegetable matter and what is assumed to have been a ceremonial bundle, while M-1911 dates the most productive large pit which was characterized by a very considerable amount of pottery, numerous bone and stone tools, and great quantities of mollusc shells.

Now as to the aberrant dates. M-1910 is clearly too young. It was run on a charcoal sample derived from one of the charred logs of Feature 6. These logs are thought to represent the burnt remains of a house structure. Inasmuch as they were directly associated with quantities of typical *Baum Cordmarked Incised, var. Blain* pottery there is no apparent reason why this date should be so far off any reasonable estimate. The only possibility is that this sample was contaminated because of its proximity to the surface. It was removed from the six–inch level beneath the plowzone. There was evidence of considerable root growth in this soil zone.

Finally, there remains OWU-247a. This was a corn sample from the same feature as OWU–247b and should have yielded approximately the same value as the latter. The value obtained is obviously out of line. The explanation appears to be fractionation, a phenomenon that has frequently been observed in dates run on corn samples (Hall, 1967). This date was normalized for C^{14} enrichment and for initial C–14 activity to A.D. 1303. Although this value is better than the original date it is still somewhat too low.

From these dates it follows that the acceptable temporal range for Blain Village is from A.D. 970 to A.D. 1225, i.e. on the evidence of radiocarbon dates the site spans an occupational period of approximately two hundred and fifty years. Actually this range, on the evidence of the total absence of observable change in the ceramics and other artifacts, appears far too great. Because of the lack of any discernible change in the material culture from the site, and in the light of the proven precise contemporaneity of some of the pits, it is believed that the total time span of Blain Village, as reflected by the excavated areas, was probably no greater than one hundred years.

We are inclined to consider the earlier dates OWU-247b and OWU–248 to be closer to the true date of the site than M–1911. This is based on a number of considerations:

(1) If it is correct—and we assume it is—that in Fort Ancient shell-tempered pottery increases, as a rule, through time, Blain with 3.3 percent shell temper, and Graham Village with 2.7 percent rank lowest and therefore presumably earliest on the shell temper scale. The available radiocarbon dates do not contradict this conclusion. To this may be added the Brush Creek locality in Adams County, Ohio, where shell temper proved to be absent (Griffin, 1943:63). At the classic Baum and Gartner sites shell–tempered pottery accounts for approximately 20 percent (Griffin, 1943: 45, 53), and at Baldwin for less than 10 percent (Griffin, 1943:55). It is apparent from the above data that within Griffin's Baum Focus, Blain, Graham, and Brush Creek should be the oldest localities, followed by Baldwin and finally by Baum and Gartner.

(2) The second consideration derives from the Voss Mound and Village site in Franklin County, Ohio. Thus far, only the mound has been published (Baby, Potter, and Mays, 1966), but we have had occasion to examine the ceramics from the village site. Voss is located in central Ohio near the northernmost margin of the Fort Ancient culture area. Only two other Fort Ancient sites, in Griffin's sense of the definition, are known from roughly the same latitude. One of these is a Madisonville site near Troy, in west–central Ohio, the other is Honey Run on the Walhonding River in Coshocton County (data on file at Kent State University). The latter is of relevance since it is culturally and chronologically affiliated with the Graham Village site in the Hocking Valley (McKenzie, 1967). Baby, Potter, and Mays, (1966) have interpreted the Voss site as Late Woodland. For the following reasons we believe this interpretation to be erroneous. As far as the unpublished village material is concerned, suffice it to say that, based upon our cursory examination of the ceramics, they exhibit to a very large extent stylistic and morphological characteristics of undoubtedly early Fort Ancient affiliation. In fact, they reflect ceramic elements identical with those from both the Scioto Valley Baum sites and the Hocking Valley localities such as Graham Village and Baldwin. As to the mound, the rather extensive sherd collection from the fill and mound floor reflects strong Fort Ancient similarities. Rim appendages and incised guil-

loche designs were noted. On the whole, the similarities here are closest with Graham Village in the Hocking Valley. Shell–tempered sherds are extremely rare. The content of the mound shows other striking parallels to early Fort Ancient, specifically as far as the Blain Mound is concerned. The limestone elbow pipes from Voss are very closely related to the pipe found with one of the Blain Mound burials; at each site a burial was associated with a bird beak deliberately deposited with the body; the striking large triangular bifacial blade found in the hand of one of the Blain burials can be precisely duplicated at Voss both as far as typology and manner of disposition with the body are concerned. Finally, the large polished bone pin from Voss, while not duplicated at the Blain Mound, is a typical Fort Ancient trait (Griffin, 1943: 208), although there is much variation in the treatment of the proximal end of such pins. A somewhat similar pin was found at Graham Village (McKenzie, 1967). All things considered, there is nothing at the Voss Mound that does not fit into early Fort Ancient. The Woodland flavor of some of the pottery is certainly present in the ceramic complex of the Hocking Valley sites as well. At Voss it might also be a function of that site's marginality to the classic Fort Ancient territory. To these typological comparisons should be added the date obtained for the Voss Mound. It has a value of A.D. 966 ± 79 (OWU–92A). Normalization for the Suess Effect gives a corrected value of 970 A.D. which is identical, to the year, with the date for Feature 2 at Blain.

Thus, the close similarities between Voss and Blain in terms of certain typological and stylistic elements, in terms of the scarcity of shell–tempered sherds, and in terms of the radiocarbon chronology, suggest not only a close relationship between these sites, but also support the very early temporal position of Blain.

At this stage in the discussion it becomes necessary to consider the regional variations within Fort Ancient in Ohio (Figure 22). At the time of Griffin's classic study such differentiations were but poorly understood. Clearly, the existence of such local variants at any given time level has important overall chronological implications. On the basis of the discussion so far, the sequence in the Scioto drainage area would seem to begin with Blain Village, to be followed by Baum and Gartner at a somewhat later date. In the Hocking valley the earliest site of Baum affiliation in the sense of Griffin's terminology should be Graham Village, followed by Baldwin.

To the west the situation is not clear. This is because the Feurt Focus and its variants, which in the eastern part of the state seem to follow immediately upon the heels of Baum, appear to be absent west of the Scioto River. In that area, Griffin's Anderson Focus would seem to be the dominant Fort Ancient manifestation prior to the demonstrably late Madisonville Focus. On comparative grounds the Anderson Focus is obviously related to Griffin's Baum Focus. At this time in the discussion, and in the light of the striking differences between Baum in the Scioto drainage and in the Hocking Valley, it may be wise to refrain from an assessment of the closeness in formal similarities between the two foci as defined by Griffin. Suffice it to say that, in terms of the classic 1943 scheme, Anderson is certainly more closely related to Baum than to either Feurt or Madisonville.

If we now turn to absolute chronology, it should be noted that the Anderson dates presently available indicate a later temporal position for this complex than Baum. The two dated sites are Erp in Miami County, Ohio, with a value of 1435 A.D. (M–1086) and the Incinerator site in Montgomery County, Ohio, with a value of A.D. 1310 ± 100 (M–1965).

Inasmuch as there is internal archaeological as well as radiocarbon evidence for the temporal position of Feurt as a direct successor to Baum in southeastern and south–central Ohio (M–1757 with a value of A.D. 1320 ± 100 for the McCune site in Athens County, and OWU–253 with a value of A.D. 1525 ± 155, normalized to A. D. 1450 for the Gabriel Site also in Athens County), we must stress the fact that the Anderson Focus dates in the west correspond in time with the age of the Feurt Focus as presently known. From this it follows (a) that there is no evidence for the early part of the Fort Ancient sequence in southwestern Ohio, and (b) that Anderson is a temporal equivalent of Feurt.

To return now to the relationship between Anderson and Baum. It is difficult to avoid the conclusion that Anderson, on formal grounds, seems closely linked to Baum in the Scioto drainage. How

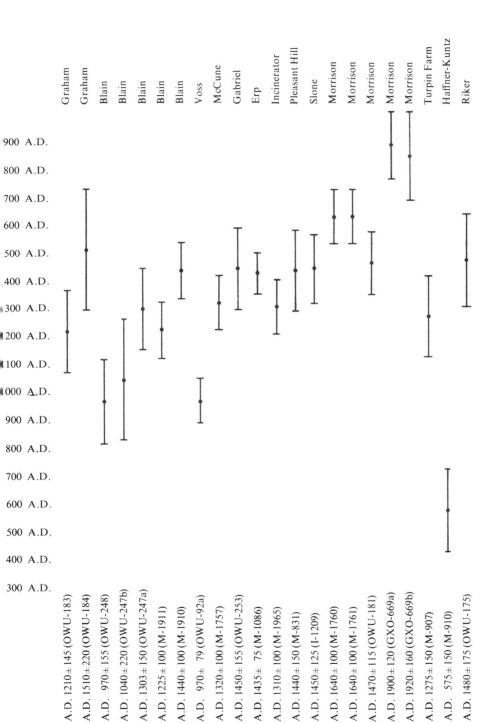

Figure 22. Radiocarbon dates for Fort Ancient and related localities.

can this be resolved? In his classic study Griffin (1943) included in the Baum Focus the Brush Creek Component at Serpent Mound, in Adams County, Ohio. This site is located west of the Scioto drainage. A formal examination undertaken by Shane in 1966 at the Peabody Museum of Harvard University, indicates that as far as decorative motifs and technical modes are concerned, the Brush Creek ceramics are characterized in the main by rectilinear guilloches, etc., typical of Anderson material, and by the virtual absence of shell–tempered sherds. Although Griffin (1943:62–63) was not explicit about this, he too appears to have been struck by the similarities between this material and the Anderson ceramics. In the light of the evidence, and with all due caution, we here suggest that the Brush Creek component in fact constitutes the predecessor of the Anderson Focus. It should be a temporal equivalent of Baum. We further suggest that in the last analysis Baum and Anderson are "genetically" related in the sense that both derive from the same ultimate source.

In this connection, it is worth quoting Griffin from his discussion of the Brush Creek ceramics. He notes that "By the surface finish and tempering alone it would be difficult to distinguish this group of body sherds from Woodland pottery." (1943:62–63). Further he notes that "The Brush Creek Component pottery is also a somewhat less complex, rich, or well developed Baum Cord-marked type." (1943:69). Turning now briefly to the East, it is illuminating to cite Griffin on the ceramics from Baldwin in the Hocking Valley, a site which is, as will be remembered, virtually identical to Graham Village. Griffin states that "There is a definite resemblance to Woodland pottery, and were it not for certain Fort Ancient cultural attributes, primarily in the rim and decorative treatment, it would be difficult to separate this pottery from that of the Woodland pattern." (1943:55).

We conclude from these data that some of the roots of early Fort Ancient are to be sought for in local Late Woodland cultures. From this it follows that those assemblages which exhibit the greatest resemblance to Late Woodland materials are probably the earliest in the Fort Ancient sequence. By this token—and taking into consideration possible cultural lag in local areas—Graham, Baldwin and Brush Creek ought to be the oldest Fort Ancient sites in southern

Ohio. Voss Mound and Village would be the local early equivalent in central Ohio. Blain with its scarcity of shell–tempered pottery on the one hand, but with its well–developed Fort Ancient rim and decorative treatment should be contemporary with, or very slightly later than these sites. Baum and Gartner with relatively high frequencies of shell–tempered sherds should be at the tail end of the Baum Focus as originally defined by Griffin. It is at this point in time that the sequence becomes substantially altered. In southeastern and south–central Ohio the Feurt Focus is the successor to Baum, whereas in the south–western part of the state, the Anderson Focus evolves out of the Brush Creek Component.

It seems to us, in the light of the evidence that has accrued since the publication of Griffin's study, that the old four–focus scheme of classification is no longer adequate to understand the dynamics of Fort Ancient. Neither in a cultural sense nor in terms of the chronological picture does this scheme do justice to reality as presently understood. A theoretical revision is therefore suggested along the following lines.

In consonance with our recent work on the Woodland cultures of Ohio (Prufer, 1965, 1967a; Prufer and McKenzie, 1966), we have applied to Fort Ancient a modified version of Willey and Phillip's scheme (1958) which conceptualizes archaeological units in terms of *Traditions* and *Phases*. In our view, a prehistoric Tradition is a cultural pattern, traceable through time within determinable geographic boundaries, notwithstanding sub–regional and temporal variations due to internal change or external influences. In a Tradition the component units in space and time are always more closely related to each other than they are to other, neighbouring Traditions or their component units. Although in an archaeological context the term Tradition can only apply to the material data recovered from the ground, the concept is obviously inclusive of non–material culture elements which can only be inferred from the often scanty and ambiguous material evidence. The sub–units of a Tradition are Phases. They are characterized by internal homogeneity through space and time, but the range of variation remains within the framework of the overall Tradition to which they belong.

Whatever the socio–cultural reality of these theoretical constructs may have been, must, of course, remain a matter of educated speculation. We venture the guess that they corresponded to some sort of *effectively interacting* socio–cultural units of varying degrees of magnitude. Such units, whether on the Tradition or Phase level, presumably had some sense of in–group identity. Furthermore, and to the extent to which we are obviously dealing with material culture only, the specific material manifestations of these units may also reflect more or less specific environmental adaptations. Also, we venture to guess, that it may in the future prove to be easier to isolate environmental–ecological factors on the phase level, rather than on the tradition level, because there are at least some indications that Phases correspond to specific limited environments, whereas Traditions tend to cut across numerous, more or less easily definable, environmental boundaries.

Accordingly we view Fort Ancient as a *Tradition* of the *Mississippian Horizon*. At present we can distinguish on the earliest time level of the *Fort Ancient Tradition* three regional phases which appear to be tied to specific geographic areas. They are from east to west:

1. The *Baldwin Phase* in the Hocking Valley, presently represented by three sites: Baldwin (Griffin, 1943:54–56), Graham Village (McKenzie, 1967), and Gabriel (Murphy, n.d.).
2. The *Baum Phase* in the Scioto drainage area, presently represented by five sites: Baum (Mills, 1906), Gartner (Mills, 1904), Blain (Prufer and Shane, in this volume), McGraw's Garden Site (data on file at Kent State University), and Kramer A (data on file at Kent State University).
3. The *Brush Creek Phase* of southwestern Ohio, presently known only from the Brush Creek locality (Griffin, 1943:56–64).

These three phases are roughly contemporaneous. Their individual distinctiveness is primarily based upon ceramics and secondarily upon other traits such as settlement pattern and the composition of diverse tool categories. In terms of absolute chronology the temporal range of these phases should be from *circa* 950 to 1250 A.D. This is based upon some reliable radiocarbon dates for Graham Village and

Blain, the date for the Voss Mound (Baby, Potter, and Mays, 1966), and upon the ratios of shell– and grit–tempered sherds at the relevant localities. It should be noted, that in all probability additional early phases of the *Fort Ancient Tradition* exist in central Ohio. At present their representatives would be the Voss Site and Honey Run.

The upper temporal limits for the three phases here defined are set by the radiocarbon dates for Griffin's Feurt and Anderson Foci, combined with the evidence from the ceramics, notably but not exclusively in terms of temper ratios. Based upon the evidence we suggest a temporal range from 1250 to 1400 A.D. for these units which are here defined as the *Feurt* and *Anderson Phases* of the *Fort Ancient Tradition*. Two comments are in order at this point. First, it should be noted that, based upon current evidence, by the beginning of the fourteenth century at the latest, only two instead of three phases can be distinguished in southern Ohio. In the eastern part of the state the *Feurt Phase* is dominant, whereas west of the Scioto drainage the area is characterized by the *Anderson Phase*. Second, it seems reasonably clear that the *Anderson Phase* grew out of the *Brush Creek Phase* and that the *Feurt Phase* is a continuation of the *Baum Phase*. In this connection it should further be noted that the shell–tempered sherds of the *Baum Phase*, at first only minimally present, can well be interpreted as being ancestral to the characteristic shell–tempered *Feurt Incised* type (Griffin, 1943:343). Just as some shell–tempered pottery reminiscent of Feurt pottery begins to appear in Baum times, so does *Baum Cordmarked Incised, var. Blain* ware continue in decreasing quantities into the *Feurt Phase*.

Anderson pottery, with its typically angular incised designs, can be derived without difficulty from the conspicuous angular designs already present on Brush Creek ceramics. In view of the fact that *Feurt Incised* pottery is also characterized by angular patterns, it is well possible that during this middle period of the Fort Ancient Tradition certain ties existed between the two component phases. We would further argue that the *Feurt Phase* represents, as far as the Hocking Valley is concerned, an intrusive element from the Scioto area. In other words we do not see, on the evidence of the ceramics from the *Baldwin Phase*, how the Feurt ceramic complex could have grown out of the earlier pottery. The primary arguments here are rim form and decoration. *Baldwin Phase* rims are much less ornate (more reminiscent of Woodland rims) than either *Baum Cordmarked Incised, var. Blain* or *Feurt Incised* rims. On Baldwin ceramics, decorations are minimally represented (at Graham only 2.8 percent of the sherds bore incised designs) whereas at Baum and Feurt sites the incidence of decorated sherds is to the order of nearly 10 percent.

Finally, to complete the picture, there remains to be discussed very briefly the terminal phase of the *Fort Ancient Tradition*. At this time, and subject to modifications once some of the numerous known late Fort Ancient sites will be published, it seems to us that after 1450 A.D. or 1500 A.D., Griffin's Madisonville Focus, here styled *Madisonville Phase*, encompassed the entire area of the Ohio River drainage in Ohio, Kentucky and West Virginia. The *Madisonville Phase* clearly reaches up to proto–historic and historic times (Griffin, 1943:189; Prufer and Andors, 1967). In Ohio its sites occur all along the Ohio River; they are present in the Miami Valley right up to the vicinity of Piqua, Ohio. In the central part of the state Madisonville elements have been noted at the Morrison site in Ross County (Prufer and Andors, 1967) and at Seip, in the Paint Creek Valley, again in Ross County (Griffin, 1943:214–215). In western Ohio the distribution of Madisonville sites is not well documented. Some Madisonville material appears to have been recovered from the vicinity of Marietta (Griffin, 1957). None has been reported thus far from the Hocking Valley (Shane and Murphy, 1967); and the Muskingum Valley is, archaeologically speaking, virtually unknown. However, at the very extensive Riker site in Tuscarawas County on the Tuscarawas River, one of the headwater streams of the Muskingum, *Madisonville Cordmarked* occurs as a minor ceramic trait. If nothing else, this implies that Madisonville influences travelled as far northeast as this area (data on file at Kent State University). The Riker site yielded a radiocarbon data of A.D. 1560 ± 170 (OWU-175) which was normalized to A.D. 1480. This date is in line with other Madisonville dates and with independent archaeological estimates for this phase. Reliable radiocarbon dates for the *Madisonville*

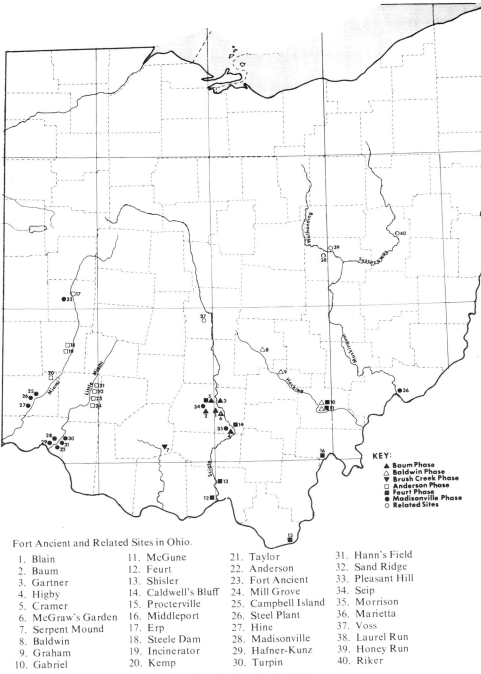

KEY:
▲ Baum Phase
△ Baldwin Phase
▼ Brush Creek Phase
□ Anderson Phase
■ Feurt Phase
● Madisonville Phase
○ Related Sites

Fort Ancient and Related Sites in Ohio.

1. Blain	11. McGune	21. Taylor	31. Hann's Field
2. Baum	12. Feurt	22. Anderson	32. Sand Ridge
3. Gartner	13. Shisler	23. Fort Ancient	33. Pleasant Hill
4. Higby	14. Caldwell's Bluff	24. Mill Grove	34. Seip
5. Cramer	15. Procterville	25. Campbell Island	35. Morrison
6. McGraw's Garden	16. Middleport	26. Steel Plant	36. Marietta
7. Serpent Mound	17. Erp	27. Hine	37. Voss
8. Graham	18. Steele Dam	28. Madisonville	38. Laurel Run
9. Graham	19. Incinerator	29. Hafner-Kunz	39. Honey Run
10. Gabriel	20. Kemp	30. Turpin	40. Riker

Figure 23.   Distribution map of major Fort Ancient sites in Ohio.

Phase have given values of A.D. 1485 ± 125 (I–1209) normalized to A.D. 1450 for the Slone Site in Kentucky (Hanson, 1966), A.D. 1480 ± 150 (M–831) normalized to A.D. 1450 for the Pleasant Hill site in Miami County, Ohio (Crane and Griffin, 1962:188), and for the Morrison Site in Ross County, Ohio, where five dates ranging from A.D. 1550 to A.D. 1920 averaged out to a mean date of A.D. 1744 (Prufer and Andors, 1967). After normalization these dates range from A.D. 1470 to A.D. 1900, with a mean date of A.D. 1718. Since it is believed that the Morrison Site is identical with a historically known settlement known in 1751 A.D. as Hurricane Tom's Town, an early to middle eighteenth century dating is entirely in order. From these *Madisonville Phase* dates it is apparent that the range for the later period of the *Fort Ancient Tradition* should be from about 1400 A.D. to the first half of the eighteenth century. Historic trade items at the Madisonville Site near Cincinnati further confirm the very late position of this phase (Griffin, 1943:189). As far as the origins of the *Madisonville Phase* are concerned, little can be said at this time. The phase is complex and, in the main, poorly known. Clearly, many new elements make their appearance here, a point that should especially be stressed in relation to the ceramics which are typologically quite diversified. Nonetheless it seems clear that many earlier Fort Ancient elements are well represented as well. The dominant pottery type, shell–tempered *Madisonville Cordmarked* (Griffin, 1943:346–347) incorporates decorative and morphological elements that have their obvious antecedents and relatives in *Baum Cordmarked Incised, var. Blain, Feurt Incised, and Anderson Cordmarked*. It should be noted, however, that no convincing link can be established between *Madisonville Cordmarked* and the ceramics from the Hocking Valley sites of the *Baldwin Phase*. In the light of this, it is interesting to note that the *Madisonville Phase* sites, at present at least, appear to be considerably less common in the southeastern sections of Ohio than in areas further west.

To return now to the early phases of the *Fort Ancient Tradition:* using the basic hypothesis that the increase of shell-tempered ceramics is a reasonably reliable chronological indicator, it is possible to construct a relative chronology for sites within the framework of the early *Fort Ancient Tradition.* The following table illustrates this point:

Table 32.   Shell-temper distribution in the early *Fort Ancient Tradition.*

Percentage of Shell Temper	Baum Phase	Baldwin Phase	Brush Creek Phase
20%	Baum, Gartner	?	?
>9%	?	Baldwin	?
0–4%	Blain	Graham	Brush Creek

There is nothing in the reliable absolute chronology thus far available which contradicts this scheme.

XVIII

Interpretations

ARCHAEOLOGICAL SUMMARY

The Blain Site proved to be a large village belonging into the *Baum Phase* of the *Fort Ancient Tradition.* On the basis of radiocarbon dates and comparative archaeology, it must have flourished sometime between A.D. 970 and A.D. 1225, probably in the earlier part of this time span. Internal archaeological evidence points to the conclusion that the site is entirely homogeneous, and that the village was relatively short–lived within the *Baum Phase.* The excavations uncovered forty-seven features, including a central burial mound, a plaza, three house patterns, a ceremonial pit, and numerous refuse pits and small sheet middens. There is evidence that some of the houses were destroyed by fire. The ceremonial pit appears to have been involved in Green Corn ceremonialism.

The overall layout of the village suggests that single–family dwelling areas were present surrounding a plaza–like open space in which the burial mound was located. There is no evidence of a stockade or earthwork. Agriculture is indicated by the presence of corn, beans, and squash. The abundant vertebrate and invertebrate faunal remains suggest considerable reliance on hunting and fishing, involving a diversified and wide range of species. In addition, a variety of wild plant foods was gathered.

The mound yielded seven burials, all of which appear to have been interred at the same time. In structure it was a simple affair, and neither the orientation of the skeletons, nor their sex, age, and burial associations permit significant interpretive statements.

Abundant cultural refuse occurred in all excavation units and features. The following is the quantitative distribution of all classes of artifacts:

Table 33.

Potsherds	13,317	(60.81%)
Chipped flint	7,738	(35.33%)
Stone artifacts	184	(.84%)
Pipes	4	(.02%)
Bone artifacts	257	(1.16%)
Shell artifacts	392	(1.79%)
Other	10	(.05%)
	21,902	(100.00%)

This list does not include lumps of ochre, sandstone débitage, and fire-cracked rocks.

Except for the obviously significant association of burial goods with the human remains, and the evidence from the ceremonial pit (Feature 4b), the distribution of the remainder of the assemblage revealed no particular pattern. There is no clustering that might be of significance as far as processual interpretations are concerned.

Based upon the size of the site, the probable time span of its existence as a "living" village, and extrapolations from the statistical analysis of faunal remains and possible numbers of houses, we suggest that the population of the settlement, at any given time, consisted of approximately one hundred to four hundred individuals.

Detailed discussions and interpretations of Blain Village and its position in Fort Ancient archaeology will be presented in the following sections of this chapter.

ECONOMIC ORGANIZATION

The extensive cultural, faunal, and floral remains recovered at Blain Village permit a summary of the economic organization of this prehistoric community and comparison with other contemporary communities in southern Ohio. If we view this economy as a system ". . . in which resources, technology, and work are combined to satisfy the material requirements of human beings and of social groups . . ." (Bohannan, 1963:211), relevant variables are population, settlement pattern, resources, resource utilization, land use, hunting patterns and technology, farming patterns and technology, trade and travel, and work.

Inasmuch as population estimates for the village range between one hundred and four hundred persons, the size of task groups engaged in farming, hunting, collecting, and other economic activities could not have been large, even for co–operative ventures. The number of adults available for work ranges between fifty and two hundred, of which one–half were males and one–half females. Excluding from this number the old and infirm, one arrives at a maximum work force of some one hundred and fifty persons.

The settlement pattern of the Blain Village appears to have been one of relatively closely–spaced houses bordering a plaza containing a burial mound, the whole forming a nucleated community surrounded by farmland, open grassland, and second growth cover. Survey data from this portion of the Scioto Valley indicate no outlying camps or hamlets, and no *Baum Phase* sites of possible Blain affiliation have been found in the hills above the village. Indeed, at those hinterland sites that have been excavated (Prufer and McKenzie, 1966; Prufer, n.d.; Shane, n.d.), *Baum Phase* materials have been conspicuous by their absence. One has the impression of a community whose activities are largely confined to the floor of the Scioto Valley and its immediate environs.

Resources available to the Blain people include various earths and minerals, wild flora and fauna, and a complex of cultigens (corn, beans, and squash). Although no attempt has been made to determine the exact origin of clays used in the pottery manufacture, local sources are assumed. Minerals used for pottery temper and raw materials for the Blain stone industries can be found in nearby gravel deposits and rock outcrops. Wild plant foods which were used include various woods, nuts, seeds, fruits, and berries, particularly oak, black walnuts, hickory nuts, and sumac berries. Deer, elk, bear, squirrel, raccoon, and cottontail contributed the majority of meats eaten, while birds, fishes, and molluscs were utilized as supplementary foods.

Although farming was practiced by the Blain villagers, it is not clear to what extent cultivated vegetal foods contributed to their diet. For later Fort Ancient communities the evidence for intensive food production involving a developed corn-beans-squash complex is overwhelming. Further, the long history of corn in the Scioto Valley prior to the *Baum Phase* and the occurrence of large quantities of maize at the Baum and Gartner sites suggests that a pattern of well-developed horticulture was present during early Fort Ancient as well. However, cultigens cannot be considered widespread in the refuse deposits at Blain, and corn kernels, the most commonly found items, were concentrated in a few refuse pits, while the other features yielded no cultigens at all. Moreover, corn cobs were recovered from a single feature only. Even recognizing that vegetal remains are highly perishable, and that refuse pits open at times when cultigens were not being harvested and processed would lack such remains, the total absence of corn or other cultigens in storage pits such as were found at Baum and Gartner is significant. Notwithstanding the fact that maize and cucurbits have a long history in the Scioto Valley and Ohio, and that intensive food production is clearly in evidence in later Fort Ancient times, it may well be that the corn–beans–squash complex at Blain is in an early stage of development.

If, as Galinat has indicated (page 224, this volume), the *Maíz de Ocho* from Blain was recently introduced into southern Ohio from the south and west, it is reasonable to assume that this variety of maize was not fully adapted to its new environment, and therefore, was less productive than corn grown by later Fort Ancient groups. A similar argument might be raised for beans which appear in Ohio for the first time during the *Baum Phase*, although the history of *Phaseolus* in the eastern United States is not clear. (The argument here for reduced productivity of Blain *Maíz de Ocho* is based primarily upon the history of the spread of this variety rather than the immature state of the specimens analyzed by Galinat from Feature 4b. If indeed the condition of these specimens is due to less than perfect environmental adaptation, then the case for low productivity of Blain corn farming is strengthened. However, a question arises due to the context of the specimens studied. Feature 4b is an unusual refuse pit showing considerable evidence indicating association with activities possibly related to Green Corn ceremonialism (see Chapter 4). If this *Maíz de Ocho* had been picked while still in an immature state, as for use in some form of Green Corn ceremony, its condition might not be due solely to poor environmental adaptation.)

The mere presence of components of the corn–beans–squash complex at the major *Baum Phase* sites does not prove that this complex was fully developed or that Blain villagers derived any quantity of food from farming activities. Although the maize from Baum and Gartner has not been recently studied, because these sites must be included with Blain in the early Fort Ancient *Baum Phase*, it is reasonable to assume that this corn is *Maíz de Ocho*. Therefore, even if the large "caches" of corn reported from these sites reflect considerable horticultural activity, corn farming need not have been productive or efficient, given the suggested low yield of the newly introduced eight row variety of maize. Food production in general may have been less extensive in early Fort Ancient times than in later phases of the *Fort Ancient Tradition*. Furthermore, it might be added that some evidence, notably the very low percentage of shell–tempered pottery at Blain, could be used to argue that this village existed somewhat earlier in time than Baum and Gartner. If this were indeed so, and if *Maíz de Ocho* is to be derived from regions south and west of Ohio as Galinat (1967; Galinat and Campbell, 1967) and Galinat and Gunnerson (1963) have argued, then it is not unreasonable to view the horticulture practiced by the Blain villagers as an incipient stage of a new and rapidly developing food production system in the Ohio Valley. The implication from this is that a novel economic pattern, based upon the cultivation of eight-row maize supplanted the earlier incipient food production systems of Woodland cultures. The rapid expansion of Mississippian cultures in the Ohio Valley may be due to the introduction of the potentially highly productive *Maíz de Ocho* which allowed a "prehistoric population explosion" similar to that which followed the introduction of this variety of maize into the Southwest at the beginning of the Pueblo II period (Galinat, 1965:355).

Resource utilization beyond subsistence involved the use of wood for fires and house construction, black walnuts for fires with high heat intensity, and possibly sumac berries for a beverage. Deer, raccoon, and fox were taken for skins and pelts as indicated by skinning cuts on certain bones of these animals, and numerous mammalian species provided bone for beamers, awls, pins, fishhooks, and other bone tools. Deer provided much of the raw material for an elaborate bone and antler industry. Mollusc shells were modified for use as spoons and "shell hoes", and the carapace of turtles was used for cups. Teeth of several mammals, usually the larger canids and felids, were apparently perforated for stringing.

Land use involved cultivated land for farming, as well as lands covered by a variety of floral communities. It seems safe to assume that farming was practiced on the fertile alluvial soils of the bottom-land and lower terraces of the valley which immediately surround the village. Low–lying land subject to annual flooding may have been utilized for flood–plain horticulture, while the higher terraces could have been farmed by slash and burn techniques. That one of the many forms of slash and burn farming was practiced by the villagers is supported by two pieces of circumstantial evidence: (1) While some animals preferring a Mature Deciduous–Forest habitat zone were hunted, the majority of species taken prefer Forest Edge, Second Growth, or Prairie habitat zones. Such zones develop in areas that have been burned over to clear land for farming. (2) Historic records indicate that Prairie conditions prevailed in the immediate site locality when the area was opened for White settlement in the late eighteenth century (see Chapter 3).

If slash and burn farming was practiced, Forest Edge, Second Growth, and Prairie conditions may have been interspersed with cultivated areas surrounding the village. Whatever the precise situation may be, it is clear that land use was concentrated in the floor of the Scioto Valley, further emphasizing the terrace–riverine adaptation of Blain culture.

The hunting activities of the villagers, as inferred from the analysis of certain species, are extremely interesting. The high frequency of deer and elk indicates a preference for these large species which provided the majority of meat consumed. As has been pointed out by Cleland (1966; 1967), such a hunting pattern may be a variable in an economic system which is not focused entirely upon hunting, but rather is based upon some other more permanent food source such as stored cultigens. Furthermore, an age frequency distribution analysis of the deer from Blain is in fundamental agreement with the findings of Cleland at Chesser Cave (Cleland, 1967), although the Blain analysis shows less selectivity in hunting than was witnessed at Chesser. Such a distribution might be expected for a people who subsisted on cultigens for part of the year, but were forced to revert to subsistence hunting after stores of crops were depleted.

Cleland (1967) has argued that age frequency distributions such as those for Chesser and Blain show selectivity which reflects stalking as a hunting technique. It follows from this that Blain hunters stalked deer individually or in small groups, and did not often use techniques whereby animals were taken in large numbers at once. The implication is that task groups involved in this activity were small and often did not include large numbers of the village males at any one time. This was primarily a fall and winter activity.

The occurrence of very large numbers of molluscs in single features (5500+ in Feature 1; 1800+ in Feature 15), randomly selected with respect to size and maturity, suggests that this resource was at times collected *en masse* by task groups including several individuals using some mass collection technique such as raking or seining. This was probably a warm–weather activity practiced from late spring to early fall in near–by stretches of the Paint Creek or the Scioto River.

Fishing, which was a limited activity, appears to have been practiced by individuals using hook and line. The high frequency of bottom–feeders appears to indicate purposeful selection of these species, possibly reflecting a procurement pattern involving set lines, spearing, or bow–and–arrow fishing. Because these species prefer deeper waters in streams such as the Scioto, a system of set line fishing may have been practiced. It should also be pointed out that fishes often become land–locked in shallow depressions after the flooding of the streams near the village. In the spring of 1968 large numbers of fishes were observed in ponded waters on the site and in the bottom–land immediately to the southwest. These could have been collected by hand with relative ease.

There is every indication that the Blain villagers did not often travel great distances from their homes. The majority of economic activities appears to have been conducted in the Scioto Valley proper, within a few hundred yards of the village, although some hunting trips into the forested hills were obviously made. The occurrence of ornaments of conch shell, probably derived from the Gulf Coast, is clear evidence of external contacts. However, these items may well have been obtained by trade rather than by long treks through the potentially hostile country to the south.

Many aspects of the economic organization of the Blain villagers suggest a strong orientation toward the floor of the Scioto Valley. The evidence indicates a definite terrace–riverine adaptation of such intensive specialization that one is tempted to look for non–economic (possibly political) causes for this localism. As a matter of specula-tion one might envisage a larger settlement pattern for the Scioto Valley in which older and possibly hostile Woodland peoples occupy the hilly uplands, while Fort Ancient activities are restricted to the lowland areas. This hypothesis is supported to a certain extent by the cultural differences to be seen between upland sites such as Chesser Cave (Prufer, 1967a), and Rais Rock Shelter (Shane, n.d.), and the evidence from the Blain Mound.

SOCIAL ORGANIZATION

The evidence for social organization is somewhat meager. It rests upon the content of the mound, and upon the nature of the house structures. In a broader sense these unimpressive data can be com-bined with evidence from such closely related sites as Baum and Gartner. The combined data permit some modest inferences as to the social reality that underlay the archaeological remains at Blain Village.

The mound proved to have been a rather simple, low structure, containing seven burials, all of which appear to have been interred at the same time. Furthermore, the mound was erected in an open area, here interpreted as a plaza which, in turn, was delineated by the settlement proper.

Mound building is not a very characteristic Fort Ancient trait. Certainly, wherever adequate data are available, the modal burial practices did not involve interments in mounds to any great extent. At *Baum Phase* sites burials normally occur in clusters at one side of the house structures (Mills, 1906:56). There are no cemeteries distinct and separate from the villages proper. Mounds always seem to have been the exception rather than the norm. From this we conclude that the individuals buried under mounds were special people, presumably reflecting specific status differences within the society. Inasmuch as the Blain Mound was also placed in what appears to have been an open plaza, relatively central in the village, this would seem to add further strength to the argument that the individuals involved had occupied a privileged position in life. Whatever these status differences signify in terms of actual social organization cannot be determined from the evidence.

Within the mound, the disposition of the skeletons does not give evidence of particular status differences. There is no central burial, nor does the burial furniture suggest any particular status differentials. Even the fact that two of the burials had no grave goods whatsoever, does not seem to be of significance, because the grave goods in general are rather meager in quantity as far as any given burial is concerned. Thus, on the whole, we consider the seven individuals in the Blain Mound to have been of roughly equal status, possibly reflecting a single family group or, at least, a number of related individuals from a single social unit. In view of the fact that children, adolescents, adults, males and females were involved, we suggest that this unit must have been some sort of kin group.

Although no other burials were found, there is some evidence that the burial pattern noted at Baum was also present at Blain. In the vicinity of the houses (Features 5 and 42) human remains occurred on the surface in the area south of the structures. In agreement with the situation at Baum, these presumed burials—probably destroyed by the plow—were located on that side of the house which is opposite to the one characterized by refuse pits. Just as at Baum, testing in the presumed burial area revealed no refuse pits whatsoever.

If the evidence from the Baum Site can be taken to apply to Blain as well, it would seem that the people interred near the houses were their inhabitants. If this pattern holds true for the *Baum Phase* as a whole—and there are strong indications that at the Gartner Site the situation was similar—it would imply that the social unit inhabiting a house, or a cluster of houses, kept its dead literally attached to the dwellings they formerly inhabited. Inasmuch as it must be assumed that the social unit inhabiting a dwelling was some kind of kin group, it follows that in terms of the site as a whole, the characteristic kin groups, however constituted, were distinctive indeed: the residential pattern in life was perpetuated in death.

By the same token, individuals from ranking kin groups (clans? lineages?) were interred in a special manner at a special location.

If burial goods *per se* were an indication of wealth and/or status, one would expect some kind of differentiation in the quantitative and qualitative distribution of such items. However, in sites of the *Baum Phase* this is not the case. The evidence from Baum and Gartner, both sites with mound burials and regular interments, shows no differential distribution of burial goods. From this we conclude that in the *Baum Phase* burial goods are not indicators of wealth or status. In other words, the crucial social differences are to be sought for in the manner of burial rather than in the offerings that accompany the dead. Wealth does not seem to have been a defining factor as far as status and position were concerned.

There remains to be discussed the evidence from the houses. The shape and dimensions of these structures at Blain and Baum appear to have been roughly the same. They were oval in plan, measuring approximately 23-by-18 feet in maximum dimensions. The size of a house structure is obviously a rough index of the number of people it could contain. The dimensions of the Blain and Baum houses suggest that these dwellings could not have been inhabited by more than a nuclear family. From this residential pattern it would seem to follow that the basic residential unit on *Baum Phase* sites was the nuclear family, composed of five to seven individuals.

Any further extrapolation from the data is a matter of pure speculation. Keeping this in mind, we want to suggest here, with all due caution, that the evidence such as it is, permits the conclusion that the inhabitants of Blain Village and other related sites may have been organized in a unilinear descent system with ranked clans and lineages. Certainly, the available evidence does not contradict such a conclusion.

RELIGION AND CEREMONIALISM

This is the subject least well documented at Blain Village. To the extent to which burial practices reflect religious beliefs and ceremonies, the Blain Mound provides practically no useful data. Neither in orientation of the bodies, nor in the manner of placement in the mound, is there anything that permits inferences regarding religious ceremonialism. Only certain items among the burial goods suggest that they may have been of significance. They include the curious sandstone headrest from Burial 5, the composite object consisting of a Raven's beak and two small shell gorgets, from Burial 1, and possibly the elbow pipe from Burial 6. These data do not permit a meaningful interpretive statement. In fact, that the *Baum Phase* funeral ceremonialism was somewhat more complex than the evidence from Blain would suggest, is indicated by the data from Baum and Gartner. This is especially true of the former site, where, in addition to the burials associated with dwellings, the stratified platform mound gave evidence of fairly sophisticated funeral practices (Thomas, 1894).

As far as the village is concerned, the only direct evidence for ceremonialism derives from Feature 4b, where the configuration of the charred vegetable remains, combined with the find of a cluster of artifacts suggesting a medicine bundle, may be indicative of Green Corn Ceremonialism. The only other finds with possible ceremonial implications are the ubiquitous yellow and red ochre fragments, and the two discoidals or chunkey stones. The latter, a characteristic Mississippian trait, are of interest because the Chunkey game, as described by early historic observers, definitely had ceremonial connotations (Adair, 1775:401).

This exhausts the data from Blain Village that might be of significance to a discussion of religious and ceremonial activities. Although the evidence from other *Baum Phase* sites does add to the factual information, there is little point in pursuing this topic, because these additional data do not permit further interpretive statements. On the whole, our impression of the *Baum Phase* is that compared to the succeeding middle and late Fort Ancient phases, its ceremonialism is relatively poorly developed.

ORIGINS, RELATIONSHIPS AND CHRONOLOGICAL POSITION

The substantive evidence for these considerations has been presented in Chapter 17. As will be remembered, meaningful conclusions regarding the position of Blain Village within the overall Fort Ancient framework necessitated a re–evaluation of the original definition of this culture complex (Griffin, 1943). As a result of this, we have abandoned the concept of Griffin's *Fort Ancient Aspect* with its four component *Foci* in favor of conceptualizing Fort Ancient as a *Tradition* consisting of a number of regional–temporal *Phases*. The data used for this are partly those also used by Griffin, and partly a wealth of new material that has been unearthed since the classic formulation was published in 1943.

In a chronological sense it proved feasible to divide the *Fort Ancient Tradition* into three periods, here styled *Early*, *Middle*, and *Late*. These temporal subdivisions also coincide with certain chronological phase boundaries. In a regional sense it could be shown that the phases through time vary in number. On the basis of current evidence, it would appear that in Early Fort Ancient times, three distinct phases can be distinguished: the *Baldwin Phase* in the Hocking Valley of southeastern Ohio, the *Baum Phase* in the Scioto–Paint Creek drainage area, and the *Brush Creek Phase* west of the Scioto Valley. By Middle Fort Ancient times, present evidence permits the definition of two phases, *Feurt* in southeastern and south-central Ohio, and *Anderson* in the southwestern parts of the State. The boundary between these two phases seems to have been the Scioto River. Finally, in Late Fort Ancient times, we have been able to distinguish only one unit, the *Madisonville Phase*, which encompasses geographically all of southern Ohio.

Whether or not this quantitative reduction in regional phases through time corresponds to reality, can only be determined if and when new data on Middle and Late Fort Ancient sites become available. Also, there are indications that additional Fort Ancient phases may have to be defined in the poorly known areas of central Ohio. We anticipate that in the vicinity of Columbus, Ohio, it may soon be possible to determine a Voss Phase belonging to the early *Fort Ancient Tradition*.

The chronological boundaries of the three periods are relatively well established on the basis of radiocarbon dates (Figure 22), and, for the late period, also on the basis of historical evidence. The chronological sequence at present looks as follows:

Early Fort Ancient:	950—1250 A.D.
Middle Fort Ancient:	1250—1450 A.D.
Late Fort Ancient:	1450—1750 A.D.

In the context of this study, the phases of the early *Fort Ancient Tradition* are of primary concern, because Blain Village, on the basis of radiocarbon dates and comparative archaeology, was a settlement of the early *Baum Phase*. It is clear that in every sense the three component phases of this period are related. The regional differences are based on differing pottery styles, settlement patterns and size, and certain considerations pertaining to the utilization of the environment.

In any discussion of early Fort Ancient, a consideration of Fort Ancient origins cannot be avoided. At first glance, the differences between Fort Ancient as a whole (including the early phases), and the preceding Late Woodland phases of the *Scioto Tradition* (Prufer, 1967a; Prufer and McKenzie, 1966; Shane, n.d.) appear to be radical indeed. Especially as far as the obvious differences in material culture are concerned, the sharp break between the two traditions seems obvious indeed. In an impressionistic sense, it is as if Fort Ancient appears full–blown, without obvious antecedents, on the prehistoric scene of southern Ohio. From this, it follows that it would be difficult to explain Fort Ancient as a gradual modification of the Late Woodland cultural pattern. The appearance of Fort Ancient is too abrupt to permit this latter interpretation. From this it would further follow that Fort Ancient cannot be explained in terms of slow acculturation as a result of gradual direct diffusion or stimulus diffusion of new traits and ideas from outside sources. The alternative to this would be the postulation of an actual invasion of southern Ohio by Mississippians, resulting in the physical and/or cultural annihilation of the older Woodland cultures. There is some evidence in support of this theory. It can be shown, reasonably conclusively, that by the time early Fort Ancient settlements occupy exclusively the broad and fertile valleys of southern Ohio, Late Woodland occupations linger on in the hilly hinterland (Prufer, 1967a, n.d.; Shane, n.d.). The evidence here rests on comparative radiocarbon dates, and on the occurrence of occasional shell–tempered sherds in otherwise pure Late Woodland contexts. The implications of this evidence, on an interpretive level, are that local Woodland groups were displaced into the hilly hinterland, as a result of the arrival of strong Mississippian population units in the major valleys. As a matter of fact, the scarcity of Fort Ancient remains in the many excavated caves of southern Ohio would seem to indicate that the Late Woodland cultures survived in these remote and inaccessible areas until the very end of the prehistoric sequence (Prufer and Andors, 1967). The reason why the Fort Ancient people avoided the dissected hilly areas is fairly obvious. The Fort Ancient folk were strongly agricultural in orientation. Consequently, they were primarily tied to the fertile bottom lands of the great river systems. The mountainous sections of the area were not sufficiently suitable for agricultural activities. This, in fact, is still true today, so that one may almost speak of a transcultural pattern in this area: the hills are, and have always been, characterized by cultural lag.

Although this general explanation of cultural dynamics in southern Ohio is enticing, and can actually be documented to some extent, it may well be overly simplistic as far as Fort Ancient origins are concerned. We do not doubt that some sort of population intrusion into the area actually did take place. The massive and sudden appearance of too many new traits around 950 A.D. argues in favor of this supposition. On the other hand, there are regional differences in the degree of Mississippification of the various phases.

As far as present evidence goes, the *Baum Phase* in the Scioto Valley represents the most "Mississippified" early Fort Ancient unit in all of southern Ohio. The Scioto Valley happens to be the most fertile and centrally located avenue into Ohio. It is probably not accidental that even in pre–Fort Ancient times, this valley and its tributaries were *the* classic, nay climactic, areas of the Ohio prehistoric scene: this is the most attractive region of southern Ohio, certainly for agricultural populations.

Both the *Brush Creek* and *Baldwin Phases* seem to represent less "Mississippified" aspects of early Fort Ancient. Also, the configuration of these units seems to be structurally much simpler than that of the *Baum Phase*. Griffin (1943) has noted that both the Brush Creek locality and the Baldwin Site are curiously Woodland in many respects. This has also been observed by McKenzie (1967) in relation to the Graham Village Site of the *Baldwin Phase*. Finally, if the Voss Site in central Ohio be considered a marginal Fort Ancient phenomenon, the same observation holds true here as well. This, incidentally, also explains why Baby, Potter, and Mays (1966) conceived of Voss as a unit of their Late Woodland *Cole Complex*. These sites do indeed exhibit Woodland characteristics.

Thus, the picture that emerges indicates that in some areas early Fort Ancient phases show greater affinities with Late Woodland than in other areas. Moreover, the degree of these similarities is a function of geographic and environmental considerations. The farther such phases are removed from the centrally located Scioto Valley, the less completely "Mississippified" they are. As far as Blain Village is concerned, Woodland elements are restricted to a few sherds of *Peters Cordmarked* and *Peters Plain* pottery, the curious vessel from Feature 2, the occurrence of some Woodland projectile points, and perhaps the burial mound concept—a trait that may or may not have Woodland origins in this context. On the other hand, in all other respects, the Blain material inventory, and the lay–out of the village, are in no sense related to Late Woodland.

By contrast, the material assemblages from the Hocking Valley localities and from Brush Creek, especially as far as ceramics are concerned, suggest strong Woodland affinities. Also the internal settlement pattern, which at all major *Baum Phase* sites suggests Mississippian connections, does not show any Mississippian characteristics in the *Brush Creek* and *Baldwin Phases*. Here there are no centrally located burial mounds as at Blain and Gartner, no plaza as at Blain, and certainly no platform mound as at Baum. All of this implies that the *Brush Creek* and *Baldwin Phases* represent acculturational situations. Only in the case of the *Baum Phase* is there evidence of a direct incursion of outsiders largely displacing the local Woodland cultures.

If we now return to the question of cultural lag in the hinterland, the available evidence does not contradict the original interpretation presented earlier in this chapter. As indicated, the key to the situation is the high degree of agricultural adaptation of Fort Ancient on the one hand, and the unsuitability of the hilly hinterland for agriculture on the other hand, resulting in a situation characterized by cultural lag in the uplands. Viewed in other terms, the situation represents differential environmental adaptations. That this in fact was so, cannot be doubted. The problem to be resolved is that of determining to what extent, by Fort Ancient times, the "hinter-landers" were displaced valley dwellers.

The best way to approach this problem is by a consideration of the archaeological evidence from rockshelters in the uplands. These sites vary in size and content. Our own first hand experience is based upon the excavation of five shelter systems. In addition we are personally familiar with the remains from a number of other such sites ex-cavated in recent years by various amateurs, and finally, there are the published data from caves excavated in the past by the Ohio Histor-ical Society. From all available evidence it transpires that the Ap-palachian highlands had certainly and continuously been occupied since Archaic times. In other words, regardless of what took place in the broad valleys, some people were living in the dissected hills as well. It is interesting to note that during the two climactic Hope-wellian and Fort Ancient periods, there is but a minimal reflection of the valley cultures in the cave deposits. Instead we find in the cor-responding levels evidence of generalized Woodland occupations. In the case of early Fort Ancient times, these material remains belong to the various Late Woodland phases of the *Scioto Tradition*. They do not differ to any extent from the local Late Woodland remains that ante–date the Mississippification of southern Ohio.

From this it can be concluded that, regardless of possible popula-tion displacements in, say, the Scioto Valley, where the evidence for such a movement is best, Late Woodland peoples were already living in the hills and continued to do so after the Mississippification as well. In other words, as far as Late Woodland groups are concerned, there is good evidence that some had always inhabited the cave country. Others may have moved into that area in the wake of the Mississippian intrusion, especially in the Scioto Valley area, where the *Baum Phase* of the *Fort Ancient Tradition* shows the least amount of evidence for acculturation, and where the break between Late Woodland and Fort Ancient appears to have been most abrupt. As far as the *Baldwin* and *Brush Creek Phases* are concerned, there is evidence of amalgamation. Here we find significant numbers of more or less modified Woodland traits persisting into early Fort Ancient. This is particularly obvious in the case of the *Baldwin Phase* which, as of this date, is better known than the *Brush Creek Phase*.

The same seems to be true of the Voss Site in central Ohio. All this indicates that in the areas outside of the southerly Scioto Valley, the *Baum Phase* may represent an actual intrusion of newcomers. If this interpretation has merit, we would further suggest that the acculturation process of the other phases originated from the Scioto Valley, i.e. from the *Baum Phase*. Such dates as are presently available, support this hypothesis.

ETHNIC IDENTIFICATION

This subject is, obviously, a matter of speculation. Whatever can be said about it, hinges largely on (a) the arguments presented in the preceding section and in Chapter 17, and (b) on earlier considerations of Fort Ancient ethnic identifications (Griffin, 1943; Hanson, 1966; Olafson, 1960; Prufer and Andors, 1967).

That the apparent overall unity of the *Fort Ancient Tradition* need not represent a single ethnic unit, however conceived, is obvious. On the other hand, this very unity, which has led to the definition of Fort Ancient as a distinctive entity, does suggest that beyond mere material culture similarities, there must be some sociocultural and/ or linguistic unity as well. The crux of the matter is the nature of this unity. On a lower level, the component phases of the *Fort Ancient Tradition* pose the same problem of identification. To what extent, then, is it possible to isolate actual ethnic units ("tribes", "cultures", "societies", or whatever) on the basis of the prehistoric entities that have been determined?

Already, twenty-five years ago and much in line with our present reasoning, Griffin concluded that "The Fort Ancient Aspect then represents a Middle Mississippian offshoot which merged culturally with a basic Woodland group . . ." (1943:308). As far as early Late Woodland is concerned, we have presented arguments to the effect that this merger was, in fact, quite differentiated. It seems that the *Baum Phase* largely represents an actual phase–unit intrusion, whereas the *Baldwin Phase* for certain, and the *Brush Creek Phase* in all probability, represent local Woodland groups acculturated to early Fort Ancient, specifically the *Baum Phase*. The latter situation would also seem to apply to the Voss Site in Franklin County, Ohio.

From this it follows that in early Fort Ancient times the situation was already complex, and that presumably more than one or two distinctive socio–cultural groups were involved.

During the middle period of the *Fort Ancient Tradition* the picture is clear only insofar as we can, at this time, distinguish two regionally defined phases, *Feurt* and *Anderson*, which appear to be lineal descendents of the *Baum* and *Brush Creek Phases*. The apparent obliteration of the *Baldwin Phase* in the Hocking Valley, may again represent an acculturational situation caused by the massive spread of *Feurt Phase* elements into the southeastern sections of the State. Whether this did or did not involve population displacements from the Scioto Valley is open to argument. Certainly, in the *Feurt Phase* a number of new elements, apparently of southeastern derivation (most marked at the Schisler Site in Scioto County, Ohio; see Diamond, 1957), indicate that in addition to its presumed local derivation from the *Baum Phase*, Feurt also has far–flung and complex outside connections. As far as the *Anderson Phase* is concerned, the derivation from the *Brush Creek Phase* is very obvious, and the component sites show the least number of extraneously derived traits, and thus the greatest degree of continuity from the preceding phase.

The Late *Madisonville Phase*, in turn, would seem to represent an amalgamation of Feurt and Anderson traits, to which should be added various elements of outside origin. The precise dynamics of the *Madisonville Phase* expansion throughout southern Ohio and adjacent areas are not known. For that matter, it is our belief that this phase, more so than Feurt and Anderson, may well have to be further subdivided as more data become available; it certainly is the most complex and diversified Fort Ancient unit. Be that as it may, at present it appears that late in the sequence distinctive Madisonville elements massively dominated the entire Fort Ancient area, thus obliterating the clearly defineable and regionally homogeneous phases of the middle and early periods.

Whatever all of this may ultimately mean, it clearly seems to indicate that through time and space the Fort Ancient population was not homogeneous, but that its composition involved numerous, probably quite distinctive, tribal groups. On the basis of settlement pattern and material culture differences, we would further suggest that these groups considerably differed in social organization and ecological adaptation.

Already in 1943, after a thorough analysis of extant historical sources, Griffin came to the conclusion that precise ethnic identification, even of his proto–historic *Madisonville Focus*, was not possible. Nonetheless, if we correctly interpret the trend of his thought, he felt that the Shawnee are the best candidates, at least for the latest phase of the *Fort Ancient Tradition*. This argument has recently been strengthened in a closely reasoned paper by Olafson (1960), who argues that the present Buffalo Site on the Kanawha River in West Virginia was a Shawnee village seen by Gabriell Arthur during his Indian captivity in 1674. Hanson (1966) concurs with this view, noting that Gabriell Arthur's visit took place only one year after Marquette and Joliet had noted the presence of thirty-eight Shawnee villages along the banks of the Ohio. The account of Arthur's adventures, however, refers to the inhabitants of the village he visited not as Shawnee but as Monytons. The implications are that the latter were either a subdivision of the Shawnee, or else the term *Monyton* is synonymous with Shawnee. It is not clear whether, and if so which, other tribes were present in southern Ohio and adjacent areas during the latter half of the seventeenth century.

The eighteenth century has usually been excluded from considerations of Fort Ancient ethnic affiliations, because it was assumed that Fort Ancient did not survive past the third quarter of the seventeenth century. This assumption is based on the absence of positive archaeological data for the eighteenth century, and on the cultural disruptions and population movements subsequent to 1675. However, since the discovery and excavation of the Morrison Village Site in Ross County, Ohio (Prufer and Andors, 1967), and because of its identification with a historically documented Delaware settlement of the first half of the eighteenth century, there is no longer any reason for disregarding this later period. This settlement was known to Christopher Gist in 1751 as Hurricane Tom's Town, and it appears in the precise location of the Morrison Site on the Lewis Evans Map of 1755. Although the site yielded obvious *Madisonville Phase* ceramics, the features also produced abundant evidence for strong

Woodland connections. To the authors of the site report this suggested a re–emergence of Late Woodland *Scioto Tradition* trends at a time when the Fort Ancient culture had already largely disintegrated as a result of the catastrophic events heralding the European settlement of the area.

One may well pause at this point to take a brief look at such information as is available regarding the population of eighteenth–century aboriginal southern Ohio. The data derive from various early accounts and maps of the area. By this time the Shawnee had returned, the Delaware had appeared from the east, and the Miami from the northwest. As far as the Scioto Valley is concerned, we find that various Indian settlements, attributed to either the Shawnee or the Delaware, are now dotting the banks of the river right down to its confluence with the Ohio. The maps and vague descriptive references indicate that there is no particular territorial integrity as far as the distribution of these tribal units is concerned. Within close proximity, and alternating as one moves down the Scioto Valley, there are Shawnee and Delaware towns. We submit that this pattern, lacking all territorial cohesion, is highly abnormal and that it probably reflects a pattern of aboriginal disruption caused by the recent population movements, and by the European presence in the areas east and southeast of what is now Ohio.

As far as Morrison Village is concerned, the problem is that of reconciling the presence of the (recently arrived) Delaware in this settlement with the archaeological evidence of *Madisonville Phase* material. This can be looked at in a number of ways: (1) Christopher Gist was mistaken in his ethnic identification of the village. We reject this, because in all other respects Gist has proved to be a remarkably precise and accurate source. (2) Given the mélange of Shawnee and Delaware in southern Ohio during the crucial period, both peoples were present; thus, one could attribute the *Madisonville Phase* ceramics to the Shawnee and the other remains to the Delaware. (3) Local Delaware Indians had adopted a number of *Madisonville Phase*, i.e. Shawnee, traits into their material culture system. Of these propositions (2) and (3) are about equally acceptable.

It is, however, enticing to consider proposition (2) in some detail. If, indeed, both Shawnee and Delaware resided in this village, the question arises as to what the basis of this joint residence might have been. On the simplest level it need imply no more than that distinct and separate kin groups of both tribes lived side by side in the same settlement. Although somewhat unusual, it could probably be explained as a function of the chaotic conditions of the times, conditions which are also reflected in the curious interspersed settlement pattern throughout the Scioto Valley. Closer consideration, however, permits another interpretation. The village may in fact have been integrated in the sense that Shawnee and Delaware were inter-marrying, at least, to some extent. Thus, women being the potters, the Shawnee females made Madisonville ceramics, while the Delaware women were responsible for the other pottery types. Inasmuch as Morrison Village yielded relatively few sherds of Madisonville ceramics as opposed to considerable amounts of other pottery, this supposition lends support to Christopher Gist's credibility: this was indeed a Delaware town, into which some Shawnee women were introduced by way of marriage.

Be all that as it may, in terms of the ethnic identification of the Blain Village people, the affiliation of the *Madisonville Phase* is of no great help. Even granted that this phase reflects the historic Shawnee, there is no proof whatever that the preceding *Feurt* and/or *Anderson Phases* were, in terms of ethnic identification, ancestral to the Shawnee. Apart from all other considerations, this is so because no conclusive *nexus* can as yet be established between the Middle and Late Fort Ancient phases. The implications of this for early Fort Ancient are obvious. We happen to believe, although this cannot be proved, that the *Madisonville Phase*, via one or both of the middle period phases, is a linear descendent of the *Baum Phase*. In this connection it should be noted that in C. C. Trowbridge's account of the "Shawanese Traditions", written about 1825 on the basis of information from two Shawnee informants, there is a statement that the Shawnee used stone ". . . in making tombs for the reception of their dead, which was done by laying a long flat stone in the bottom of the grave, two others of equal dimensions at the sides and another on the top." (Kinietz and Voegelin, 1939). This statement is of interest since burial practices in the *Madisonville Phase* to some extent, and in the preceding *Anderson Phase* to a large extent involved stone cists similar to those described by Trowbridge. This might suggest that the Shawnee link beyond the time of the *Madisonville Phase* was through the *Anderson Phase*. Unfortunately no data whatever are available for the *Brush Creek Phase*. It should, however, be noted that some of the burials at Baum were covered with stone slabs; thus, a related trait is present in early Fort Ancient as well.

Admittedly, as far as Blain Village and the *Baum Phase* in general are concerned, the above data and speculations are somewhat less than satisfactory. All we can say is that, in our opinion, there is a possibility that at least some of the pre–Madisonville phases may have been ancestral Shawnee.

XIX

Bibliography

Adair, J. (1775) *The History of the American Indian.* London.

Anderson, J. E. (1968) "Skeletal Anomalies as Genetic Indicators." In: Brothwell, D.A. (Ed.), *The Skeletal Biology of Earlier Human Populations:* 135–148. Pergamon Press. London.

Baby, R. S., M. A. Potter, and A. Mays, Mr. (1966) "Exploration of the O. C. Voss Mound, Big Darby Reservoir Area, Franklin County, Ohio," *The Ohio Historical Society, Papers in Archaeology, 3.*

Baker, F. C. (1936) "Remains of Animal Life from the Kingston Kitchen Midden Site Near Peoria, Illinois." *Illinois State Academy of Science, Transactions, 29:* 243–246.

Bardeen, C. R. (1905) "Studies of the Development of the Human Skeleton." *American Journal of Anatomy, 4:* 265–302.

Bell, R. E. (1958) "Guide to the Identification of Certain Indian Projectile Points." *Oklahoma Anthropological Society, Special Bulletins,* 1.

Benfer, R. A. and T. W. McKern. (1966) "The Correlation of Bone Robusticity with the Perforation of the Coronoid–olecranon Septum in the Humerus of Man." *American Journal of Physical Anthropology,* 24: 247–252.

―――― and N. C. Tappen. (1968) "The Occurrence of the Septal Perforation of the Humerus in Three Non–human Primate Species." *American Journal of Physical Anthropology, 29:* 19–28.

Berry, R. J. (1968) "The Biology of Non–metrical Variation in Mice and Men." In: Brothwell, D.A. (Ed.), *The Skeletal Biology of Earlier Human Populations:* 103–134. Pergamon Press. London.

Bohannan, P. (1963) *Social Anthropology.* Holt, Rinehart and Winston. New York.

Brothwell, D. A. (1963) *Digging Up Bones.* British Museum of Natural History. London.

―――― and R. Powers. (1968) "Congenital Malformations of the Skeleton of Earlier Man." In: Brothwell, D.A. (Ed.), *The Skeletal Biology of Earlier Human Populations*: 173–204. Pergamon Press. London.

Brown, W. L. and E. Anderson. (1947) "The Northern Flint Corns." *Missouri Botanical Garden, Annals, 34:* 1–22.

Burtt-Davy, J. (1914) *Maize, Its Cultivation, Handling and Uses.* Longmans, Green and Co. New York.

Chapman, A. G. (1944) "Original Forests." In: Diller, O. O., "Ohio's Forest Resources." *Ohio Agricultural Experiment Station, Forestry Publications, 76:* 73–84.

Cleland, C. E. (1966) "The Prehistoric Animal Ecology and Ethnozoology of the Upper Great Lakes Region." *University of Michigan, Museum of Anthropology, Anthropological Papers,* 29.

———— (1967) "The Vertebrate Fauna of the Chesser Cave Site, Athens County, Ohio." In: Prufer, O. H. and D. H. McKenzie (Eds.), *Studies in Ohio Archaeology:* 43–48. The Press of Western Reserve University. Cleveland.

Coe, J. L. (1964) "Formative Cultures of the Carolina Piedmont." *American Philosophical Society, Transactions,* 54(5).

Converse, R. N. (1963) "Ohio Flint Types." *Ohio Archaeologist, 13:* 77–120.

————. (1966) "Ohio Stone Tools." *Ohio Archaeologist,* 16: 99–137.

Cross, W. P. (1946) "Floods in Ohio: Magnitude and Frequency." *Ohio Water Resources Board, Bulletin, 7.*

Cutler, H. C. and T. W. Whitaker. (1961) "History and Distribution of the Cultivated Curcurbits in the Americas." *American Antiquity, 26:* 469–485.

De Beer, G. R. (1937) *The Development of the Vertebrate Skull.* Oxford University Press. London.

Diamond, W. V. (1957) "An Ancient Ohio Engraving." *Ohio Archaeologist, 7:* 142–143.

Diller, O. O. and P. T. Lannan. (1944) "Present Forests." In: Diller, O. O., "Ohio's Forest Resources." *Ohio Agricultural Experiment Station, Forestry Publications, 76:* 85–106.

Dragoo, D. W. (1963) "Mounds for the Dead: An Analysis of the Adena Culture." *Carnegie Museum, Annals, 37.*

Fanno, J. T. (1967) *The Dentition of an American Indian Population from Ohio.* Unpublished Master's Thesis, Western Reserve University, School of Dentistry. Cleveland.

Fernald, M. L. and A. C. Kinsey. (1958) *Edible Wild Plants of Eastern North America,* revised by R. C. Collins. Harper and Brothers. New York.

Fitting, J. E. (1967) "The Camp of the Careful Indian: An Upper Great Lakes Chipping Station. *Michigan Academy of Science, Arts, and Letters, 52:* 237–242.

Fowler, M. K. (1957) "Rutherford Mound, Hardin County, Illinois." *Illinois State Museum, Scientific Papers, 7:* 2–43.

Galinat, W. C. (1965) "The Evolution of Corn and Culture in North America." *Economic Botany*, 19: 350–357.

———— (1967) "Plant Habit and the Adaptation of Corn." *Massachusetts Agricultural Experiment Station, Bulletins, 565:* 1–16.

———— and R. G. Campbell. (1967) "The Diffusion of Eight-rowed Maize from the Southwest to the Central Plains." *Massachusetts Agricultural Experiment Station, Monograph Series, 1.*

———— and J. H. Gunnerson. (1963) "Spread of Eight-rowed Maize from the Prehistoric Southwest." *Harvard University, Botanical Museum Leaflets, 20:* 117–160.

Gluckman, A. (1942) "The Role of Mechanical Stresses in Bone Formation in Vitro." *Journal of Anatomy, 76:* 231–239.

Goodman, K. and O. C. Shane. (n.d.) *The Archaeometer: An Instrument for Earth Resistivity Survey.* Manuscript on File at Kent State University.

Goodrich, C. (1932) "The Mollusca of Michigan." *University of Michigan, Michigan Handbook Series, 5.*

Goslin, R. M. (1951) "Evidence of the Occurrence of the Rice Rat in Prehistoric Indian Village Sites in Ohio." *Ohio Indian Relic Collectors Society, Bulletins, 26:* 19–22.

Griffin, J. B. (1943) *The Fort Ancient Aspect.* University of Michigan Press. Ann Arbor.

———— (1957) "The Late Prehistoric Cultures of the Ohio Valley." In: Webb, W. S., R. S. Baby, and J. B. Griffin, *Prehistoric Indians of the Ohio Valley:* 14–23. The Ohio Historical Society. Columbus.

———— (1967) Review of: Hanson, L. H., Jr., "The Hardin Village Site." *American Antiquity, 32:* 410–411.

Guilday, J. E. (1963) "The Cup and Pin Game." *Pennsylvania Archaeologist, 33:* 159–163.

———— and W. J. Mayer-Oakes. (1952) "An Occurrence of the Rice Rat (Oryzomys) in West Virginia." *Journal of Mammology, 33:* 253–255.

————, P. W. Parmalee, and D. P. Tanner. (1962) "Aboriginal Butchering Techniques at the Eschelman Site (36La–12), Lancaster County, Pennsylvania." *Pennsylvania Archaeologist, 32:* 59–83.

Hall, R. L. (1967) "Those Late Corn Dates: Isotopic Fractionation as a Source of Error in Carbon–14 Dates." *Michigan Archaeologist, 13:* 171–180.

Hanson, L. H., Jr. (1966) "The Hardin Village Site." *University of Kentucky, Studies in Anthropology, 4.*

Heiple, K. G. and O. C. Lovejoy. (1969) "The Antiquity of Tarsal Coalition." *Journal of Bone and Joint Surgery, 51–A(5):* 979–983.

Hiernaux, J. (1963) "Heredity and Environment: Their Influence on Human Morphology. A Comparison of Two Independent Lines of Study." *American Journal of Physical Anthropology, 21:* 575–589.

Hollinshead, W. H. (1960) *Functional Anatomy of the Limbs and Back.* W. B. Saunders and Co. Philadelphia.

Hooton, E. A. and C. C. Willoughby. (1920) "Indian Village Site and Cemetery Near Madisonville, Ohio." *Harvard University, Peabody Museum of American Archaeology and Ethnology, Papers, 8(1).*

Howard, J. H. (1968) "The Southeastern Ceremonial Complex and Its Interpretation." *Missouri Archaeological Society, Memoirs, 6.*

Hughes, D. R. (1968) "Skeletal Plasticity and Its Relevance in the Study of Earlier Populations." In: Brothwell, D.A. (Ed.), *The Skeletal Biology of Earlier Human Populations:* 31–56. Pergamon Press. London.

Jones, V. H. (1949) "Maize from the Davis Site; Its Nature and Interpretation." In: Newell, H. P. and A. D. Krieger, "The George C. Davis Site, Cherokee County, Texas." *Society for American Archaeology, Memoirs, 5:* 239–249.

Kaplan, B. A. (1954) "Environment and Human Plasticity." *American Anthropologist 56:* 780–800.

Kaplan, L. (1965a) "Archeology and Domestication in American *Phaseolus* (Beans)." *Economic Botany, 19:* 358–368.

———— (1965b.) "Beans of Wetherill Mesa." *American Antiquity, 31:* 153–155.

Keen, J. A. (1950) "A Study of the Differences Between Male and Female Skulls." *American Journal of Physical Anthropology, 8:* 65–79.

Kinietz, V. and E. W. Voegelin. (1939) "Shawanese Traditions: C. C. Trowbridge's Account." *University of Michigan, Museum of Anthropology, Occasional Contributions, 9.*

Laughlin, W. S. and J. B. Jorgensen. (1956) "Isolate Variation in Greenlandic Eskimo Crania." *Acta Genetica, 6:* 3–12.

Leslie V. (1954) "Stone Drills and Perforators." *Pennsylvania Archaeologist, 24:* 30–33.

McKenzie, D. H. (1967) "The Graham Village Site: A Fort Ancient Settlement in the Hocking Valley, Ohio." In: Prufer, O. H. and D. H. McKenzie, *Studies in Ohio Archaeology:* 63–97. The Press of Western Reserve University. Cleveland.

McKern, T. W. and T. D. Stewart. (1957) "Skeletal Age Changes in Young American Males." *Quartermaster Research and Development Command, Technical Reports, EP–45.*

Mangelsdorf, P. C., and J. Camara-Hernandez. (1967) "Maize from the Morrison Village Site." In: Prufer, O. H. and D. H. McKenzie, *Studies in Ohio Archaeology:* 209–212. The Press of Western Reserve University. Cleveland.

———— R. S. MacNeish, and W. C. Galinat. (1967) "Prehistoric Maize, Teosinte, and Tripsacum from Tamaulipas, Mexico." *Harvard University, Botanical Museum Leaflets, 22:* 33–63.

Massie, D. M. (1890) *Nathaniel Massie, A Pioneer of Ohio.* The Robert Clarke Co. Cincinnati.

Massler, I. and M. Schaur. (1944) *Atlas of the Mouth.* American Dental Association. Chicago.

Mayer-Oakes, W. J. (1955a.) "Prehistory of the Upper Ohio Valley," *Carnegie Museum, Annals, 34.*

———— (1955b.) "Excavations at the Globe Hill Shell Heap (46HK–34–1), Hancock County, West Virginia." *West Virginia Archaeological Society, Publication Series, 3.*

Miles, A. E. W. (1963) "Dentition in the Assessment of Individual Age in Skeletal Material." In: Brothwell, D.A. (Ed.), *Dental Anthropology:* 191–210. Pergamon Press. London.

Mills, W. C. (1904) "Explorations of the Gartner Mound and Village Site." *Ohio Archaeological and Historical Society, Publications, 13:* 129–189.

———— (1906) "Explorations of the Baum Prehistoric Village Site." *Ohio Archaeological and Historical Society, Publications,* 15:45–136.

Montagu, M. F. Ashley. (1933) "The Anthropological Significance of the Pterion in the Primates." *American Journal of Physical Anthropology, 18:* 159–236.

Murphy, J. L. (n.d.) "The Gabriel and McCune Sites: Two Fort Ancient Localities in the Hocking Valley, Ohio." Manuscript on File at Kent State University.

Murray, P. D. F. (1936) *Bones.* Cambridge University Press. London.

Olafson, S. (1960) "Gabriel Arthur and the Fort Ancient People." *West Virginia Archeologist, 12:* 32–42.

Ortmann, A. E. (1919) "A Monograph of the Naiades of Pennsylvania, Part III, Systematic Account of the Genera and Species." *Carnegie Museum, Memoirs 8(1).*

Parmalee, P. W. (1959.) "Use of Mammalian Skulls and Mandibles by Prehistoric Indians of Illinois." *Illinois State Academy of Science, Transactions, 52:* 85–95.

———— (1963) "Vertebrate Remains from the Dell Site, Winnebago County, Illinois." *Wisconsin Archeologist, 44:* 58–69.

———— (1964) "Vertebrate Remains from an Historic Archaeological Site in Rock Island County, Illinois." *Illinois State Academy of Science, Transactions, 57:* 167–174.

———— (1965) "The Food Economy of Archaic and Woodland Peoples at the Tick Island Cave Site, Wisconsin." *Missouri Archaeologist, 27:* 1–34.

Pearlman, H. S., R. E. Edkin, and R. F. Warren. (1964) "Familial Tarsal and Carpal Synostosis With Radial–Head Subluxation (Nievegelt's Syndrome)." *Journal of Bone and Joint Surgery, 46–A:* 585–592.

Pierce, L. T. (1959) "Climates of the States: Ohio." *U.S. Department of*

Commerce, Weather Bureau, Climatography of the United States, 60-33: 1–19.

Pi-Sunyer, O. (1965) "The Flint Industry." In: Prufer, O. H., "The McGraw Site: A Study in Hopewellian Dynamics." Cleveland Museum of Natural History, Scientific Publications, n.s. 4(1): 60–89.

Pratt, C. W. M. and R. A. McCance. (1958) "Histological Changes Occurring in the Long Bones of Chickens Dwarfed by Prolonged Undernutrition." Journal of Anatomy, 92: 655–664.

Prufer, O. H. (1963) "The McConnell Site: A Late Palaeo-Indian Workshop in Coshocton County, Ohio." Cleveland Museum of Natural History, Scientific Publications, n.s., 2(1).

_____ (1965) "The McGraw Site: A Study in Hopewellian Dynamics." Cleveland Museum of Natural History, Scientific Publications, n.s., 4(1).

_____ (1967a.) "Chesser Cave: A Late Woodland Phase in Southeastern Ohio." In: Prufer, O. H. and D. H. McKenzie, Studies in Ohio Prehistory: 1–62. The Press of Western Reserve University. Cleveland.

_____ (1967b.) "The Scioto Valley Archaeological Survey." In: Prufer, O. H. and D. H. McKenzie, Studies in Ohio Prehistory: 267–328. The Press of Western Reserve University. Cleveland.

_____ (1968) "Ohio Hopewell Ceramics: An Analysis of the Extant Collections." University of Michigan, Museum of Anthropology, Anthropological Papers, 33.

_____ (n.d.) "Stanhope Cave, Jackson County, Ohio: The Late Woodland Occupation." Manuscript on File at Kent State University.

_____ and E. Andors. (1967) "The Morrison Village Site (33Ro-3): A Terminal Prehistoric Site in Ross County, Ohio." In: Prufer, O. H. and D. H. McKenzie, Studies in Ohio Archaeology: 187–219. The Press of Western Reserve University. Cleveland.

_____ and D. H. McKenzie. (1966) "Peters Cave: Two Woodland Occupations in Ross County, Ohio." Ohio Journal of Science, 66: 233–253.

_____ and D. H. McKenzie. (1967) Studies in Ohio Archaeology. The Press of Western Reserve University. Cleveland.

Ritchie, W. A. (1961) "A Typology and Nomenclature for New York State Projectile Points." New York State Museum and Science Service, Bulletins, 384.

Scott, D. B. (1954.) "Dentition." In: Caldwell's Legal Medicine. C. V. Mosby and Co. St. Louis.

Sears, P. B. (1942) "History of Conservation in Ohio." In: "The History of the State of Ohio." Ohio State Archaeological and Historical Society, 6: 219–240.

Severinghaus, C. W. (1949) ' Tooth Development and Wear as Criteria of Age in White-tailed Deer." Journal of Wildlife Management, 13: 195–216.

Shane, O. C., III. (1967) "The Leimbach Site: An Early Woodland Village in Lorain County, Ohio." In: Prufer, O. H. and D. H. McKenzie, *Studies in Ohio Archaeology:* 98–120. The Press of Western Reserve University. Cleveland.

———— (n.d.) "Rais Rockshelter: A Stratified Site in Jackson County, Ohio." Manuscript on File at Kent State University.

———— and J. L. Murphy. (1967) "A Survey of the Hocking Valley, Ohio." In: Prufer, O. H. and D. H. McKenzie, *Studies in Ohio Archaeology:* 329–351. The Press of Western Reserve University. Cleveland.

Sheldon, J. M. Arms. (1925) *Pitted Stones.* Deerfield, Mass.

Squier, E. G. and E. H. Davis. (1848) "Ancient Monuments of the Mississippi Valley." *Smithsonian Institution, Contributions to Knowledge, 1.*

Stansbery, D. H. (1965) "The Molluscan Fauna." In: Prufer, O. H., "The McGraw Site: A Study in Hopewellian Dynamics." *Cleveland Museum of Natural History, Scientific Publications, n.s. 4(1):* 119–124.

Stewart T. D. (1950) Age Guidance of Neural Arch Defects in Alaskan Natives. *Journal of Bone and Joint Surgery,* 35–A: 937–958.

Swanton, J. R. (1956) "The Indians of the Southeastern United States." *Smithsonian Institution, Bureau of American Ethnology, Bulletins, 137.*

Thieme, F. P. (1950) "Lumbar Breakdown Caused by Erect Posture in Man." *University of Michigan, Museum of Anthropology, Anthropological Papers, 4.*

Thomas, C. (1894) "Report on the Mound Explorations of the Bureau of Ethnology." *Smithsonian Institution, Bureau of American Ethnology, 12th Annual Report.*

Trautman, M. B. (1957) *The Fishes of Ohio.* Ohio State University Press. Columbus.

Trotter, M. and P. F. Lanier. (1945) "Hiatus Canalis Sacralis in American Whites and Negroes." *Human Biology, 17:* 368–381.

Wellhausen, E. J., L. M. Roberts, and E. Hernandez X, in collaboration with P. C. Mangelsdorf. *Races of Maize in Mexico.* Harvard University, Bussey Institution. Cambridge.

White, T. E. (1953) "A Method of Calculating the Dietary Percentage of Various Food Animals Utilized by Aboriginal Peoples." *American Antiquity, 18:* 396–398.

Willey, G. R. and P. Phillips. (1958) *Method and Theory in American Archaeology.* University of Chicago Press. Chicago.

Wray, J. B. and C. H. Herndon. (1963) "Hereditary Transmission of Congenital Coalition of the Calcaneus to the Navicular." *Journal of Bone and Joint Surgery, 45–A:* 365–372.

Yarnell, R. A. (1964) "Aboriginal Relationships Between Culture and Plant Life in the Upper Great Lakes Region." *University of Michigan, Museum of Anthropology, Anthropological Papers, 23.*

Index

Part I

INDEX OF PROPER NAMES

Voegelin, E. W., 266

Warren, R. F., 177
Wellhausen, E. J., 220
Whitaker, T. W., 227

Willey, G. R., 239
Wray, J. B., 177

Yarnell, R. A., 28

Part II

INDEX OF PLACE NAMES

Note: All references to "Ohio" are omitted. All cities, towns, and countries, unless otherwise designated, are in Ohio.

Part III

INDEX OF ARCHAEOLOGICAL SITES

Note: All references to the Blain Site are omitted.

Part IV

SUBJECT INDEX